G000160680

BLACK BRITISH HISTOR

ABOUT THE EDITOR

Hakim Adi is Professor of the History of Africa and the African Diaspora at the University of Chichester. In January 2018, he launched the world's first online 'Master's by Research' programme on the History of Africa and the African Diaspora and he is the founder and consultant historian of the Young Historians Project: younghistoriansproject.org.

He is the author of *West Africans in Britain 1900–60: Nationalism, Pan-Africanism and Communism* (1998); *The 1945 Manchester Pan-African Congress Revisited* (with Marika Sherwood, 1995) and *Pan-African History: Political Figures from Africa and the Diaspora since 1787* (2003). His most recent books are *Pan-Africanism and Communism: The Communist International, Africa and the Diaspora, 1919–1939* (2013) and *Pan-Africanism: A History* (2018). He is currently writing a book on the history of African and Caribbean people in Britain to be published by Penguin.

Hakim has appeared in many documentary films, on TV and on radio, and has written widely on the history of Africa and the African diaspora, including three history books for children.

He has a website at www.hakimadi.org.

BLACK BRITISH HISTORY

NEW PERSPECTIVES

Edited by Hakim Adi

ZED

Black British History: New Perspectives was first published in 2019 by Zed Books Ltd, The Foundry, 17 Oval Way, London SE11 5RR, UK.

www.zedbooks.net

Editorial Copyright © Hakim Adi 2019
Copyright in this collection © Zed Books 2019

The right of Hakim Adi to be identified as the editor of this work has been asserted by him in accordance with the Copyright, Designs and Patents Act 1988.

Typeset in Plantin and Kievit by Swales & Willis Ltd, Exeter, Devon, UK
Index by Amelia Francis
Cover design by Alice Marwick
Cover images, from left to right:
© The Picture Art Collection / Alamy Stock Photo
© Chronicle / Alamy Stock Photo
© Homer Sykes Archive / Alamy Stock Photo

All rights reserved. No part of this publication may be reproduced, stored in a retrieval system or transmitted in any form or by any means, electronic, mechanical, photocopying or otherwise, without the prior permission of Zed Books Ltd.

A catalogue record for this book is available from the British Library

ISBN 978-1-78699-425-7 hb
ISBN 978-1-78699-426-4 pb
ISBN 978-1-78699-427-1 pdf
ISBN 978-1-78699-428-8 epub
ISBN 978-1-78699-429-5 mobi

MIX
Paper from
responsible sources
FSC
www.fsc.org   FSC® C013604

Printed and bound by CPI Group (UK) Ltd, Croydon, CR0 4YY

CONTENTS

ABOUT THE CONTRIBUTORS

Molly Corlett is a PhD student at King's College, London, where she researches eighteenth-century social relations. She is also working on a microstudy of a late eighteenth-century marital separation case, in which a naval captain's wife was accused of adultery with her black footman.

Kesewa John is a PhD student in History at the University of Chichester. Her doctoral research focuses on discursive collaborations between French- and English-speaking Caribbean activists from the 1920s to 1940; their articulations of freedom; and the place of Caribbean women in Caribbean historical narratives. She is interested in Caribbean people's intellectual and political histories and has taught for several years in the History and Anglophone Studies departments at the Université des Antilles.

W. Chris Johnson is an assistant professor in the Women and Gender Studies Institute and the Department of History at the University of Toronto. An interdisciplinary writer and historian of black diasporas, he has published essays on anti-colonialism, Pan-Africanism and Black Power movements in the Caribbean, the United Kingdom, and the United States. He is currently writing a transnational history of Black Power and the Third World. Anchored in the history of post-war Black Britain, the book traces the interwoven itineraries of migrant revolutionaries who struggled for solidarity around the Atlantic world.

Onyeka Nubia is a visiting research fellow at Huddersfield University and the Director of Studies and writer in residence at Narrative Eye. He is a pioneering and internationally known historian, writer and presenter committed to the study of comparative histories. For twenty-five years, Onyeka has consulted on, researched, taught and written about many aspects of history in the ancient, medieval, early modern and modern periods. He has discovered diversity in early modern England in *Blackamoores: Africans in Tudor England* (2016) and in the forthcoming *England's Other Countrymen* published by Zed Books (2019).

Kennetta Perry is Director of the Stephen Lawrence Research Centre at De Montfort University in Leicester. Her research interests include Black Britain, Europe and the African diaspora, transnational race politics and the relationship between the conditions of black citizenship and state power. She has published a book on Afro-Caribbean migration and race politics in post-war Britain, *London Is the Place for Me: Black Britons, Citizenship and the Politics of Race* (2016), and is currently developing a book project on histories of state-sanctioned racial violence in Britain during the twentieth century.

Carol Pierre is a freelance researcher, history workshop facilitator and youth worker. Her specialisms are twentieth-century London history and Black British History. After completing her MA at Goldsmiths University, Carol has presented her research on the New Cross Fire at the New Perspectives on Black British History conference and her findings on the contribution of the British West Indies Regiment to World War One at the CACOEU (Caribbean Communities in Europe) conference. Carol was a leading member of the Young Historians' Project, seeking to encourage and promote Black British History and encourage the development of young black historians.

Kevin Searle is a teacher and researcher based in London, who completed a PhD study of Yemeni migrants who came to work in the Sheffield steel industry after World War Two. His research interests centre on post-war migration. He has taught GCSE and A-level sociology at several schools and colleges in the city, including Hackney Community College, Lambeth College, and the College of North West London. He has also worked at the University of Birmingham on the Birmingham Stories project. It was the research for this project that inspired the chapter 'Before Notting Hill'.

John Siblon is a history teacher in London and is completing a PhD on hierarchy and the representations of black colonial servicemen post-World War One. He has campaigned for a more inclusive History curriculum and was a member of the Race, Equality and Ethnicity Working Group for the Royal Historical Society. He has published work on aspects of Black British History pre-1850 for the National Archives, on identity, and on the lack of monuments to Black Britons. His latest publication was 'Negotiating Hierarchy and Memory: African and Caribbean Troops from Former British Colonies in London's Imperial Spaces' in *The London Journal* (2016).

Esther Stanford-Xosei is completing her PhD at the University of Chichester on the history of the International Social Movement for Afrikan Reparations in Britain. She is a Jurisconsult, community advocate and internationally acclaimed reparationist who has charted new grounds as an interdisciplinary legal and history scholar-activist in the theory, research and praxis of Pan-Afrikan Reparations for Global Justice. Esther serves as the co-vice chair of the Pan-Afrikan Reparations Coalition in Europe, is co-founder of the Global Afrikan People's Parliament, spokesperson for the Afrikan Emancipation Day Reparations March Committee and co-initiator of the 'Stop the Maangamizi: We Charge Genocide/Ecocide!' campaign.

Claudius Adisa Steven is currently studying part-time towards a PhD in History at the University of Chichester. His thesis is entitled 'The Evolution of Ideas and Practices amongst African-centred Organisations in the UK 1975–2015'. The research is focused on the historical development of African-centred organisations in the UK (those which have precolonial African concepts and values as their cultural foundation). His passion is to help, inspire and nurture the minds of African and Caribbean students and communities.

Christopher Roy Zembe is a lecturer in History at De Montfort University. His research interests are the history of migration, colonial and postcolonial legacies and the African diaspora. His published work consists of a book entitled *Zimbabwean Communities in Britain: Imperial and Post-colonial Identities and Legacies* and an article in the *Journal of Migration History* entitled 'Migrating with Colonial and Post-colonial Memories: Dynamics of Racial Interactions within Zimbabwe's Minority Communities in Britain'. He was also involved in organising the 'History Matters' conference aimed at exploring why there are few history students of African or Caribbean heritage in British education institutions.

INTRODUCTION

Hakim Adi

The essays in this book originate in the work undertaken for the New Perspectives on Black British History conference, organised by History Matters and the University of Chichester and held at Goldsmiths University, London in October 2017.[1] The aim of the conference was to provide a showcase for young and emerging scholars, especially those of African and Caribbean heritage based in Britain, and to present new perspectives on what is often referred to as 'Black British History'. This aim is reflected in the contents of this volume, with contributions from eleven scholars, all but one currently based in Britain.

The term 'Black British History' might be considered a problematic one, although nobody contested it at the conference. Peter Fryer, writing in the 1980s, called his famous book *Staying Power: The History of Black People in Britain*. It included a historical account of people not only of African and Caribbean but also of South Asian heritage. The term 'black' was often used in this inclusive political sense at the time, although even then it was a contested term. In the twenty-first century, the term Black British has even been adopted by the Office of National Statistics, to refer to those of African and Caribbean heritage. The organisers of the New Perspectives on Black British History conference welcomed 'research papers focusing on historical periods before 1500; on women and gender history; on the history of continental African communities and organisations in Britain; and the historical relationships established by those of African and Caribbean heritage in Britain with the African continent and the wider African diaspora'. No further definitions of the term were given, nor requested by the participants at the conference. The organisers made clear that proposals 'covering all fields of Black British History are welcome'.

History Matters is an initiative that brings together academic historians, schoolteachers and students to address the fact that so few young people of African and Caribbean heritage engage with history as a subject, especially at university level. Among black students, only agriculture and veterinary science are more unpopular subjects. Consequently, and despite many history projects and great interest at community level, there are very few school history teachers of African and Caribbean heritage, and even fewer postgraduate research students and academic historians.

Unfortunately, the history of African and Caribbean people in Britain, which stretches back over two millennia, is still a hidden history to a large extent. This might appear a strange paradox. In 2017, the revelation that Cheddar Man was 'black' made the front pages of most British papers. During the same year, the broadcaster David Olusoga presented his acclaimed primetime television series *Black and British*, to be followed by a book of the same title.[2] A few years earlier, in 2014, the Black Cultural Archives, originally a community initiative that started in 1981 and 'the only national heritage centre dedicated to collecting, preserving and celebrating the histories of African and Caribbean people in Britain', opened a new purpose-built centre in Brixton, South London.

Olusoga's account of Black British History certainly gained significant media exposure. However, he was only one in a long line of 'black scholars', those of African and Caribbean heritage, who have addressed the fact that standard presentations of Britain's history have often neglected or excluded those of African and Caribbean heritage. One of the earliest scholars was a self-educated Jamaican, J. A. Rogers, who lived and worked in the United States. His research and publications were designed to combat Eurocentric and racist views of history. In several of his works he writes about the history of African and Caribbean people in Britain, although his focus is often on prominent individuals. A meticulous researcher, his most well-known works include *World's Great Men of Color* and *Nature Knows No Color-Line*, which were first published over seventy years ago.[3]

Another important scholar was Edward Scobie, a Dominican writer and publisher who produced one of the first surveys of the subject in *Black Britannia: A History of Blacks in Britain*, first published in 1972. During the 1970s, two pioneering books were published by the Nigerian historian Folarin Shyllon: *Black People in Britain, 1555–1833* and *Black Slaves in Britain*.[4] Ron Ramdin, a Trinidadian historian based in Britain, published another important survey, *The Making of the Black Working Class in Britain*, which first appeared in 1987.[5] Since that time there have been many other historical accounts by those of African and Caribbean heritage, including the work of Joan

Anim Addo, Delia Jarret Macauley, David Dabydeen, Cecily Jones, Gretchen Gerzina, Ray Costello, Gemma Romain and Hakim Adi.[6]

Yet despite these advances, such history is barely a feature of the National Curriculum in Britain's schools and very few university history departments teach it. There might be general recognition that the *Empire Windrush* docked at Tilbury in 1948, but beyond that people of African and Caribbean heritage are largely written out of Britain's history. In 2016, the *Daily Mail Online* was aghast at the prospect that a new GCSE history course and textbook might suggest to Britain's young people that Africans were in the British Isles before the ancestors of the English.[7] Historians still debate exactly who the ancestors of the English were, but clearly Africans were in Britain during Roman times and, it seems, quite probably long before that. It is unclear why such a possibility should be any more shocking than the revelation that Cheddar Man was black.

Clearly, for some, there is a necessity to continue to falsify history, to cling on to the notion that the history of Britain should only concern itself with white men of property, largely excluding women, those who work to produce that property and everyone else. However, today few want such a narrative, one that aims to create confusion not only about the past but also about the present, which has alienated so many and turned young people from the study and appreciation of history. What is new about the work of the scholars in this volume is that they approach the history of Britain not from a Eurocentric perspective but from the perspective of those wishing to enlighten others about the subject by including and focusing on those of African and Caribbean heritage. It might be added that what is also new is an edited volume in which most of the contributors are also of African or Caribbean heritage.

The evidence

The presence of Africans in Britain during the Roman period has been established for many years. It is therefore correct to say that Africans were present before the settlement, centuries later, of Angles, Saxons and Jutes.[8] The latest DNA evidence also suggests that the Angles and Saxons played a less important part in the ancestry of the English and that African migrants had reached Britain perhaps a thousand years before the Romans. Much of the evidence for an early African presence comes from archaeological sources, such as tooth enamel oxygen isotope evidence, which can be used to determine the geographical source of water drunk by an individual in childhood, but such evidence needs to be considered with caution.[9] However, when used with other archaeological evidence, this presents interesting questions regarding an early African presence in Britain.

An even more interesting development is the recent revelation, in February 2018, that those who might be considered some of the first Britons – that is, the first to provide genes that can be found among some of the modern inhabitants of Britain – had 'dark to black' skin as well as dark hair and blue eyes. Indeed, one newspaper headline boldly proclaimed that, according to the latest DNA study, 'the first Britons were black'.[10] The research analysed the skeletal remains of Cheddar Man, first discovered in a cave in Somerset in 1903, who is thought to have lived in England some 10,000 years ago among a population of only 12,000. That study showed that migrants who originated in Africa and came to Britain via western Asia and Europe maintained darker skin pigmentation for much longer periods than was previously thought, and that the development of pale skin pigmentation took place much more recently. The research into the origins and appearance of Cheddar Man suggests that the population of Western European hunter-gatherers of that period almost certainly looked similar to Cheddar Man, with dark to black skin. The earliest Europeans, just like the earliest Britons, could also be considered black people. Notions of Britishness and Englishness once more need to be re-thought.[11] The analysis of Cheddar Man also demonstrated significant scientific advances. Although the analysis of DNA has been possible for several years, techniques have markedly improved in the second decade of the twenty-first century and create the possibility for new revelations about Britain's ancient populations in the future.

For some time, it has been established that Britain was where the 'African emperor' Septimius Severus, who was born in Libya of Berber origin, was cremated. Britain was also governed by several other Africans during the Roman period. These include Quintus Lollius Urbicus, who came from what is today Algeria, was governor of Britain from 139 to 142 CE and supervised the building of the Antonine Wall in Scotland. Several other Roman governors also originated from modern-day Libya, Tunisia and Algeria, as did numerous military commanders and soldiers.[12] For some years, historians have known that Africans were part of the Roman army of occupation in Britain, especially during the period when Severus and his sons ruled the Roman empire.[13]

There was a unit of North African soldiers, known as the *Numerus Maurorum Aurelianorum*, stationed at the western end of Hadrian's Wall, near what is today Burgh by Sands in Cumbria, as is evident from several inscriptions found in the area and from Roman records. It is known that one of the black soldiers in this unit presented a garland of cypress boughs to Emperor Severus.[14] Archaeological evidence dating from the second and third centuries CE also includes pottery, and the especially distinctive 'Roman head pots', said to be unquestionably of North African design, that have been found at Chester, York and other sites, including some in Scotland. This shows not just that some of those serving in the Roman army of occupation were recruited from Africa but that it is likely that there were either 'soldier-potters' or other African potters accompanying the army.[15] Referring to samples of cooking vessels found near York, one expert concluded that they were made 'by Africans for the use of Africans'.[16] More evidence of an African presence in Roman Britain has been found from tombstones and other archaeological finds, including writing in what has been described as 'neo-Punic script'.[17] In short, there is evidence of the presence in Britain not only of African soldiers but also of civilians from what today are Libya, Tunisia, Algeria and Morocco.

Many of the most interesting recent discoveries have been made using the latest archaeological and scientific techniques. Some of these have been utilised to analyse human remains found in what was the Roman city of Eboracum, today York, where Emperor Septimius Severus died in 211. At the beginning of the twentieth century, people digging in a street in York discovered a 1,700-year-old stone coffin of a woman. She had been buried with jewellery, including jet and ivory bracelets, as well as other possessions and was undoubtedly of elite status. It was not until 2010 that archaeologists were fully able to analyse the skeleton, which they found to be of a young woman, probably between eighteen and twenty-three years old, and of North African origin.[18] The archaeologists were even able to make a reconstruction to show us what this African 'Ivory Bangle Lady' may have looked like.[19] This and other research has shown that those of African heritage, including African women of all classes, were a settled population before the arrival of the Angles and Saxons. Such findings prompted one leading archaeologist to conclude that 'analysis of the "Ivory Bangle Lady" and others like her contradicts common popular assumptions about the make-up of Roman-British populations as well as the view that African immigrants in Roman Britain were of low status, male and likely to have been slaves'.[20]

Another young woman from North Africa has been discovered by archaeologists and scientists analysing human remains from the Roman period kept at the Museum of London. Tests showed that the 'Lant Street Teenager', who was only fourteen at the time of her death, had been born in North Africa but probably had sub-Saharan African ancestry. The young woman had been living in London for only a few years, prompting questions about the circumstances of her migration. Another skeleton found in London is of a middle-aged African man who had probably grown up in London.[21] DNA analysis of such remains show the diversity of Roman towns and cities but also the fact that Africans could be found living in many parts of Britain. Recent analysis of human remains from the Roman era also suggests that not only those of North African origin found their way to Britain but also others from sub-Saharan Africa, such as 'Beachy Head Lady'. Beachy Head Lady was so named because her skeletal remains were first discovered near Eastbourne, in southern England. The remains are thought to date from the mid-third century CE, in the middle of the Roman period, and are of a young woman. Although she is thought to have grown up in the area, analysis of her remains suggests that she was of African origin. She was evidently from a part of Africa that was not included within the Roman empire, and she was probably either born in Sussex or brought to Britain at a very young age. Such evidence poses fascinating questions about the past and about the possibility of families of Africans living in Britain in ancient times.[22]

The early medieval period

Although we are learning more about the presence of Africans in ancient and Roman Britain, at present we have very little knowledge of this presence for almost one thousand years following the main Roman exodus. This is partly because an African presence is not immediately visible, although there are certainly a few pictorial representations, and partly because very little research has been carried out. Once again, DNA analysis of skeletal remains reveals that Africans were certainly living in Britain in the early medieval and medieval periods. In 2013, a skeleton found in a Gloucestershire river was shown to be that of a sub-Saharan African woman dating from between the late ninth and early eleventh century CE: that is, before the Norman conquest. At present, however, nothing more is known about how she arrived or her status. No doubt our knowledge will increase as more research is undertaken.[23] Another young African woman has been identified from a Saxon burial site at North Elmham in Norfolk, but again nothing more is known of the circumstances that placed her there.[24] In the past, such evidence of the presence of African women in early medieval England has been linked to slavery, or at least capture. Paul Edwards and others have suggested that this presence might be the result of Viking raids on North Africa, or on Muslim Spain, which, according to ancient annals in Irish and Arabic, brought African captives, 'blue men', to Ireland.[25] There now seems to be other corroborating evidence for these reports, although no evidence that Vikings brought enslaved Africans to England.[26] Others have suggested that the young woman at Elmham originated in ancient Ghana and was trafficked across the Sahara, but there is even less evidence to support this speculation.[27] It might just as plausibly be argued that these African women came of their own free will from Africa to Muslim Spain and from there to Britain. There is certainly evidence from coins, real and imitation, as well as from other sources, that trade between England and the Muslim world existed long before the Norman conquest.[28]

Earlier historical reports, such as those from the Venerable Bede, record that the North African abbot Hadrian was sent by the Pope to accompany the new Archbishop of Canterbury to England in 668 CE. Hadrian, it is reported by Bede, was initially asked to become archbishop himself but refused the post. He later become the abbot of St Peter and St Paul's in Canterbury. Bede described him as 'vir natione Afir', which has been translated as a 'man of African race'.[29] His exact origins are unknown, however, and some historians suggest that he was a Berber from what is today Libya. It is thought that Hadrian had a major influence on the structure of the Christian church in England, which he helped to reform, and on education and Anglo-Saxon literature. It is also thought that he brought with him some important North African literary works and introduced students to new ideas in various subjects from astronomy to philosophy.[30] Recent archaeological isotopic analysis of the human remains found at a seventh-century cemetery in Ely, at sites in Wales dated earlier than the seventh century and at a burial site in Northumberland, dating from the seventh to ninth centuries, have also identified skeletons of men, women and children that may have North African origins, suggesting that links between England and the African continent might have been more common than previously thought.[31]

There are several early medieval references to Africans in Britain. In the late twelfth century, a monk named Richard of Devizes produced his *Chronicon* or chronicle of the reign of Richard I. In one descriptive passage, he refers to his dislike of the city of London because 'all sorts of men crowd together there from every country under the heavens'. These include 'Moors' or 'Garamantes', a term specifically referring to Africans, who are the only 'sorts of men' described by geographical origin.[32] What is particularly interesting about Richard of Devizes' description is that it suggests that 'Moors' were fairly numerous in London and quite commonplace. A few years later, in 1205, King John 'gave a mandate to the constable of Northampton to retain Peter the Saracen, the maker of crossbows, and another with him, for the king's service and allow him 9d a day'.[33] 'Saracen' was a vague term but one that was often used interchangeably with 'Moor' and 'Ethiopian'. It is not clear if this mandate refers to two 'Saracens', or two crossbow makers, but it suggests that those of African heritage could provide useful skills. This reference is in stark contrast to the disparaging remarks of Richard of Devizes, who appears to regard Africans as a social nuisance and a blight on the city of London.

There is also the skeleton of 'Ipswich Man', found in the cemetery of Greyfriars monastery and buried between 1258 and 1300 CE. It seems likely that Ipswich Man was another North African, probably from Tunis, the capital of modern Tunisia. Historians think that this is the case because the Greyfriars monastery was built by Robert Tiptoft, a colleague of Richard de Clare, and both men went on a crusade together in 1270. In the *Flores Historiarum*, a medieval history, it states that de Clare brought 'four captive Saracens' with him to England from Tunis in 1272. It may be that the Ipswich Man was one of those four captured during the Crusades, but he is just as likely to have been a free man and possibly even a friar by the time of his death.[34]

One of the earliest pictorial depictions of an African man in England dates from the thirteenth century. It occurs in the *Domesday Abbreviato*, an abbreviated version of the famous Domesday Book, the survey of the country demanded by William the Conqueror in 1085. One of the illustrations in the *Domesday Abbreviato*, accompanying the capital letter for the entry for Derbyshire, shows a man of African descent; from his dress, he was probably someone of low or non-elite status. It is not known if this represented a living person, nor exactly why he is depicted. Perhaps his image suggests that Africans were not unknown to the artist or scribe.

Evidence of Africans in England during this period is often connected with slavery, but usually without compelling evidence. One of the earliest records of an enslaved African, however, is from the thirteenth century. It is recorded in the Calendar of Patent Rolls of Henry III for 21 June 1259 that the king, sitting at Windsor, had issued a:

> Mandate to all persons to arrest an Ethiopian of the name of Bartholemew, sometime a Saracen, slave [*servus*] of Roger de Lyntin, whom the said Roger brought with him to England, the said Ethiopian having run away from his said lord, who has sent an esquire of his to look for him: and they are to deliver him to the said esquire to the use of the said Roger.[35]

Unfortunately, the fate of Bartholemew is unknown, but it is important to note that this early record of an enslaved African is also a report of an African engaged in self-liberation. His act of resistance is one that would be adopted by other Africans held in servile status in Britain in later centuries.

The early modern and modern periods

The essays in this volume focus on Britain's history in the period after 1500, when much greater evidence exists demonstrating an African presence. However, for the early modern period, there is still a paucity of information, despite recent publications, and therefore Onyeka Nubia's essay focusing on the agency and self-naming of Africans in Tudor England is of great significance.[36] While the history of Africans in eighteenth-century Britain, such as the abolitionists and writers Olaudah Equiano, Quobna Ottobah Cugoano and others, is becoming better known, Molly Corlett's essay shows that there is still much to be learned, not least about the lives and agency of African children, women and men who actively strove to determine their own status in society. Hitherto, historians of the eighteenth century have recognised the significance of the abolitionist movement, but without always acknowledging its mass character and the role played by the everyday actions of Africans in Britain. Both essays show that the history of Africans in Britain cannot be correctly understood without viewing it in the context of Britain's relationship with Europe, Africa and the Americas, especially the exploitative and colonial relationships that began in the sixteenth century.

Britain's colonial relationship with Africa and the Caribbean and the racism that emerged alongside it provide the context for most of the remaining essays in this volume, which focus on the twentieth century. Men and women from Africa and the Caribbean worked, resided and agitated in Britain long before the arrival of the *Empire Windrush*. Black people participated in significant numbers in two World Wars, and John Siblon's essay analyses the enormous contributions made during World War One and the absence of memory and official memorials to reflect this great sacrifice. This absence has also been apparent during the commemorations of the centenary of this conflict, which have seen numerous attempts to present its history in a Eurocentric manner, as a war fought solely on European soil and involving only Europeans. The conflict between the groups of major imperial powers was unresolved by the war and the great loss of human life. Moreover, the system of colonialism that underpinned the conflict continued, and, in most cases, the colonial exploitation of millions of people in the colonies intensified. This was particularly the case during the 1930s, when the colonies bore the brunt of the economic crisis that engulfed the capital-centred economies in most of the world outside the Soviet Union. Many people in the colonies were inspired by the alternative economic and political system that was being constructed in the Soviet Union. The colonial system itself went into crisis, a situation exacerbated by Nazi Germany's demand for colonies and fascist Italy's invasion of Ethiopia.

Kesewa John's essay focuses on the anti-colonial journalism of Anglophone and Francophone Caribbean activists during the period leading up to and at the commencement of World War Two. It highlights the emergence of new forms of anti-imperialism and Pan-Africanism that later culminated in the Manchester Pan-African Congress, held only a few years later in 1945.

The remainder of the essays focus on the post-war period, which is often associated only with the arrival of the *Empire Windrush*. Kevin Searle's essay demonstrates that racism was an ever-present threat for migrants and residents from Africa and the Caribbean by focusing on events in Birmingham in 1949. Similar attacks occurred in Liverpool and London during the 1940s, long before the more infamous Notting Hill riots of 1958, when the involvement of Mosley's fascists was so evident. The racist attacks on African and Caribbean migrants in the post-war period led directly to the 1962 Immigration Act and still further attacks. These were met by concerted resistance and the activities of one of the main anti-racist organisers of the period, Claudia Jones. Jones was a Trinidadian Communist who had been imprisoned and then deported from the US for her membership of the Communist Party. As Kennetta Perry's essay shows, she then not only became one of the key anti-racist figures in Britain, campaigning against the 1962 Immigration Act and the ubiquitous colour bar, but also continued to campaign in solidarity with, and as part of, the civil rights movement in the US. The impact of racism is also the central theme of Carol Pierre's essay on community responses to the infamous New Cross fire in 1981, the tragic events in which thirteen young black people were killed. Although the authorities have never been able to identify the perpetrators of this crime, its impact continues, nearly forty years later. It has not been forgotten that initially the state authorities ruled out the possibility of any racist motive for such criminal activity, or that no condolences were sent from the royal family or the state to the families and communities involved.

From the late 1960s, black people in Britain became politically active in a host of new organisations, some of which were influenced by political developments related to the Black Power movement in the US and worldwide. W. Chris Johnson's essay charts the early years and activities of the Black Liberation Front in the 1970s, while Claudius Adisa Stevens analyses the influence of those Africa-centred organisations, beginning with the Pan-African Congress Movement, which arose during and after the mid-1970s. These essays again show the transnational – or perhaps rather the Pan-African – nature of Black British politics, which continues to have links with Africa, the Caribbean and North America. This Pan-African theme is a central concern of Esther Stanford-Xosei's essay, which looks at the important British contribution to the global African (Afrikan) movement for reparations. Although the essay comments on earlier historical manifestations of the demand for reparation for slavery and colonialism relating to Africa and its diaspora, it is chiefly concerned with highlighting the Pan-Africanist character of more recent struggles in which the author was a leading figure.

The post-war history of black people in Britain has often focused on those of Caribbean origin, but by the dawn of the twenty-first century the largest percentage of the black population originated from the African continent.[37] Africans had also migrated to Britain during the 1940s and even long before, but their histories have largely been forgotten or ignored. A few studies have been produced but there is a need for many more. Christopher Zembe's essay looks in great detail, as perhaps only an insider can, at the migrant experience of his compatriot Zimbabweans in Britain. He demonstrates how old national rivalries, exacerbated during colonial times and after, have continued to create divisions among Zimbabweans in Britain, but also how the younger generation, socialised and educated in different circumstances to their parents, are starting to adopt a different approach to the national question.

Notes

1 Special thanks to Kesewa John, who played a key role in organising this conference.

2 David Olusoga, *Black and British: A Forgotten History* (London: Pan Macmillan, 2016).

3 Joel A. Rogers, *World's Great Men of Color*, Volume II (London: Touchstone, 1996); Joel A. Rogers, *Nature Knows No Color-Line* (St Petersburg: Helga M. Rogers, 1980).

4 Folarin Shyllon, *Black Peoples in Britain, 1555–1833* (Oxford: Oxford University Press, 1977); *Black Slaves in Britain* (Oxford: Oxford University Press, 1974).

5 Ron Ramdin, *The Making of the Black Working Class in Britain* (Aldershot: Gower, 1987).

6 See, for example, Joan Anim Addo, *Longest Journey: A History of Black Lewisham* (London: Deptford Forum Publishing, 1995); Delia Jarrett-Macauley, *The Life of Una Marson 1905–1965* (Manchester: Manchester University Press, 1998); Gretchen Gerzina, *Black London: Life Before Emancipation* (New Brunswick: Rutgers University Press, 1995); David Dabydeen, J. Gilmore and Cecily Jones (eds) *The Oxford Companion to Black British History* (Oxford: Oxford University Press, 2007); Ray Costello, *Black Salt: Seafarers of African Descent on British Ships* (Liverpool: Liverpool University Press, 2012); Hakim Adi, *West Africans in Britain 1900–1960: Nationalism, Pan-Africanism and Communism* (London: Lawrence and Wishart, 1998); Gemma Romain, *Race, Sexuality and Identity in Britain and Jamaica: The Biography of Patrick Nelson 1916–1963* (London: Bloomsbury, 2016).

7 http://www.dailymail.co.uk/news/article-3393189/Plans-teach-GCSE-pupils-Africans-came-Britain-English-branded-pro-immigration-propaganda-critics.html, accessed 30 January 2018.

8 Stephen Oppenheimer, *The Origins of the British: The New Prehistory of Britain from Ice-Age Hunter Gatherers to Vikings as Revealed by DNA Analysis* (London: Robinson, 2007).

9 http://www.caitlingreen.org/2015/10/oxygen-isotope-evidence.html, accessed 30 January 2018.

10 http://www.telegraph.co.uk/science/2018/02/07/first-britons-black-natural-history-museum-dna-study-reveals/, accessed 7 February 2018.

11 http://www.nhm.ac.uk/discover/cheddar-man-mesolithic-britain-blue-eyed-boy.html, accessed 7 February 2017.

12 Lloyd A. Thompson, 'Africans in Roman Britain', *Museum Africum: West African Journal of Classical and Related Studies* I (1972), pp. 28–39.

13 R. W. Davies, 'Roman Cumbria and the African Connection', *Klio* 59 (1977), pp. 155–77.

14 Thompson, 'Africans in Roman Britain', p. 36.

15 Vivien G. Swan, 'Builders, Suppliers and Supplies in the Tyne-Solway Region and Beyond' in P. Bidwell (ed.) *Understanding Hadrian's Wall: Papers from a Conference Held at South Shields, 3–5 November 2006, to Mark the Publication of the 14th Edition of the Handbook to the Roman Wall* (South Shields: Tyne and Wear Archives and Museums, 2008), pp. 49–82.

16 Vivien G. Swan, 'Legio VI and its Men: African Legionaries in Britain', *Journal of Roman Pottery Studies* 5 (1992), pp. 1–33; Vivien G. Swan and Jason Monaghan, 'Head-pots: A North African Tradition in Roman York', *Yorkshire Archaeological Journal* 65 (1993), pp. 21–38.

17 Swan, 'Legio VI', p. 4.

18 S. Leach, H. Eckardt, C. Chenery, G. Müldner and M. Lewis, 'A Lady of York: Migration, Ethnicity and Identity in Roman Britain', *Antiquity* 84 (2010), pp. 131–45.

19 https://www.ourmigrationstory.org.uk/oms/roman-britain-the-ivory-bangle-lady; https://www.yorkshiremuseum.org.uk/collections/collections-highlights/ivory-bangle-lady/, accessed 25 January 2018.

20 https://www.reading.ac.uk/news-and-events/releases/PR270747.aspx, accessed 25 January 2018.

21 http://www.bbc.co.uk/news/science-environment-34809804, accessed 24 January 2018.

22 http://www.culture24.org.uk/history-and-heritage/archaeology/art474162-beachy-head-lady-was-young-sub-saharan-roman-with-good-teeth-say-archaeologists, accessed 31 January 2018.

23 http://www.ibtimes.co.uk/fairford-sub-sahara-africa-skeleton-gloucestershire-507102, accessed 31January 2018.

24 Paul Rich, 'The History of Blacks in Britain', *History Today* 31/11 (September 1981), p. 33.

25 Paul Edwards, 'The Early African Presence in the British Isles' in J. S. Gunadara and I Duffield (eds), *Essays on the History of Blacks in Britain* (London: Avebury, 1992), pp. 11–14.

26 http://www.caitlingreen.org/2015/09/a-great-host-of-captives.html, accessed 8 February 2018.

27 C. Wells and H. Cayton, 'Evacuations at North Elmham Park, 1967–1972' in *East Anglian Archaeology: Report No. 9* (Gressenhall: Norfolk Archaeological Unit, 1980), especially pp. 259–62, http://eaareports.org.uk/publication/report9/, accessed 8 February 2018.

28 Andrew Petersen, 'The Archaeology of Islam in Britain: Recognition and Potential', *Antiquity* 82/318 (December 2008), pp. 1080–92.

29 http://blogs.bl.uk/digitisedmanuscripts/2016/10/an-african-abbot-in-anglo-saxon-england.html#, accessed 10 February 2018.

30 http://blogs.bl.uk/digitisedmanuscripts/2016/10/an-african-abbot-in-anglo-saxon-england.html; https://www.publicmedievalist.com/mystery-stephen-african/, accessed 8 February 2018.

31 Sam Lucy et al., 'The Burial of a Princess? The Later Seventh-century Cemetery at Westfield Farm, Ely', *Antiquaries Journal* 89 (2009), pp. 81–141; S. E. Groves et al., 'Mobility Histories of 7th–9th Century AD People Buried at Early Medieval Bamburgh, Northumberland, England', *American Journal of Physical Anthropology* 151/3 (2013), pp. 462–76; K. A. Hemer et al., 'Evidence of Early Medieval Trade and Migration between Wales and the Mediterranean Sea Region', *Journal of Archaeological Science* 40/5 (2013), pp. 2352–9.

32 Onyeka, *Blackamoores: Africans in Tudor England, their Presence, Status and Origins* (London: Narrative Eye, 2013), p. 47.

33 Marika Sherwood, 'Black People in Tudor England', *History Today* 53/10 (October 2003), p. 40.

34 https://www.ourmigrationstory. org.uk/oms/the-ipswich-man, accessed 31 January 2018.

35 https://catalog.hathitrust.org/ Record/000270470, accessed 8 February 2018.

36 See also Miranda Kaufmann, *Black Tudors: The Untold Story* (London: Oneworld, 2017).

37 https://www.ons.gov.uk/ peoplepopulationandcommunity/ culturalidentity/ethnicity/ articles/ethnicityandnationalidentityin englandandwales/2012-12-11, accessed 19 September 2018.

1 | 'BLACKAMOORES' HAVE THEIR OWN NAMES IN EARLY MODERN ENGLAND

Onyeka Nubia

Warning: Parts of this chapter contain swearing and derogatory racial epithets, which some readers may find offensive.

'Free People name themselves: Slaves and Dogs are named by their masters.'[1]

African countrymen[2]

Africans were William Shakespeare's countrymen.[3] They lived in England 400 years ago. It was the same country where Henry Tudor usurped the crown from Richard III, at the Battle of Bosworth Field, in 1485. Henry reigned from 1485 to 1509, and Pero, or Pedro, Alvarez was present in London under his authority in 1490. Pedro was described in early modern records as a '*negro e forro*', which literally means a 'foreign or strange black'.[4] Pedro won his manumission (freedom) from Henry VII on 13 March 1490, and this was upheld by John II, King of Portugal.[5] During the reign of Henry VIII (1509–47), an African called 'Fraunces Negro' or 'Fraunces ye negro' worked in the royal stables.[6] His presence was noted in the subsidy rolls (records of taxation) for 1523.[7] When 'Bloody' Mary (Mary I) was queen, from 1553 to 1558, Africans lived in English cities, towns and villages, and one of them was an African man who was a pioneer in the needle-making industry:

> Spanish needles was first taught in Englande, by Elias Growse a Germaine, about the eight year of Queen Elizabeth, and in Queen Maries time, there was a Negro made fine Spanish needles in Cheapside, but would never teach his art to any.[8]

During the reign of Elizabeth I, 'the Virgin' Queen, from 1558 onwards, Africans and their families were a significant presence in Tudor England. And as Francis Drake and Walter Raleigh sallied forth to do battle with the Spanish Armada in 1588, two years earlier 'Christopher Cappervert a blackemoore' was buried in the churchyard of St Botolph without Aldgate, London, on 22 October 1586.[9] Africans lived and were baptised, married and buried in Tudor and Stuart England. When James I was crowned King of England in 1603 and Guy Fawkes tried to destroy Parliament in 1605, Africans such as Henrie Anthonie Jetto, 'A Blackemore', and his large extended family lived in Holt, Worcestershire and were a significant presence in their local community.[10]

This chapter is about the ethnicity of these Africans who lived in early modern England (from 1485 to the 1620s).[11] The term 'African' is used here to describe those people who had a direct connection to the continent of Africa and others who were of African descent and who, within a common vernacular,[12] may be called 'black'.[13] Where different issues apply to people with a mixed parentage or dual heritage, this will be stated.[14] In this chapter we shall explore whether Africans at this time had the capacity to choose descriptive 'names' and terms such as 'Blackamoore' or 'Negro' to describe their ethnicity. Since this is the focus, those academics conversant with African populations elsewhere may be particularly challenged by the findings included in this chapter.[15] But this has been written with a general readership in mind, and some explanations that academics would usually require have been redacted. For example, those who wish to explore further my methodology may find out more in my other works.[16]

'Sacred white' spaces

The early modern period is frequently written about by historians and others in reference to the Tudor and Stuart monarchs mentioned earlier.[17] An idea may then develop, which is often compounded by some academics,[18] that this period of English history was 'a sacred white space' where people of African descent were absent.[19] This is because the history of this era is usually characterised by the machinations of English noblemen, fratricide and internecine conflicts, the insidious and Machiavellian nature of foreign wars, the tempestuous nature of Tudor and Stuart politics, and the theological dissension of the times. These matters not only reflect the interests of modern historians in this period,[20] but, to a certain extent, they also echo the preoccupations of early modern historians, translators, and so on.

The English early modern writers such as Raphael Holinshed, John Stow, Edmund Howes and William Harrison were often sponsored by monarchs, the church and wealthy patrons when they wrote the history of their times.[21] Therefore, most of what they wrote tended to be about white, wealthy, Christian Englishmen. All other people, including women (of any class), the poor, religious and ethnic minorities, among others, were often part of the 'missing pages of history'.[22] Or, if they were mentioned, it seems that their inclusion was an afterthought, sometimes inserted into the margins or footnotes of these writers' works.[23]

Modern historians such as Imtiaz Habib, Gustav Ungerer and others may sometimes be influenced by this early modern trend. And when this is coupled with a postcolonial praxis,[24] it can lead to speculation that Africans in early modern England were the epitome of otherness and strangeness.[25] The term 'postcolonial' refers to the effects and legacies of colonialism, and the word 'praxis' means an 'accepted practice' or 'custom'.[26] Through this praxis, historians sometimes apply principles learned from a postcolonial interpretation of history and use this to decipher what happened in early modern England. This praxis can enable another concept: that Africans were not capable of exercising agency – and did not do so – over any part of their lives in early modern England. Africans automatically become slaves and transitory visitors, not living in English society but passing through as interlopers.[27] Unfortunately, a range of historians, including Peter Fryer, Kim Hall and others who write about black history, the renaissance, Shakespeare, women's studies, and so on,[28] may do this. This is despite these authors creating work that in many other ways is ground breaking and important.[29] I recognise the contribution of these writers, but question their findings on this topic.

The act of naming

The act of naming referred to in the title of this chapter is not a reference to the way in which people acquired personal names. Instead, it is a reference to 'names' used to describe ethnicity. Sometimes these discussions can become an analysis of etymology or semantics. However, this chapter builds on a body of work in which many etymological and semantic discussions have already taken place.[30] Therefore, the focus is on whether Africans in early modern England were capable of defining their own identity, and whether their definitions influenced how English people described them. An underlying theme is that Africans in the diaspora did not begin their exploration of identity in modern times, but long before.[31]

The 'Blackamoore' lives in early modern societies

In Tudor and early Stuart England, the archetypal 'Moor'[32] was a 'dark-skinned' African,[33] as stated by the English writer John Minsheu and many other early modern authors.[34] However, the word 'Moor' was already used in the English language before the early modern period.[35] Nevertheless, it was during this era that the word 'black' was added as a cognomen to create the term 'Blackamoore'. This descriptor then became the most popular term used generically to describe Africans. Prior to that, terms such as 'Aethiopian', 'Niger' and 'Garamantes' were often used to describe Africans, with 'Saracen' being a generic term that could include Africans.[36]

The term 'Blackamoore' was also the most frequently used descriptor of Africans in other early modern documents, such as letters and dictionaries, written by a range of different Englishmen such as George Best, John Minsheu, Barnabe Rich and others.[37] Furthermore, 'Blackamoore' was used in important official documents written at the end of the Tudor period. These documents include two letters signed on 11 and 18 July 1596, and a draft proclamation of 1601. Both letters were signed by Elizabeth I, but are unlikely to have been written by her, while the proclamation was an unsigned draft that was not supported by enforceable laws. These documents were instigated by Casper Van Senden, a Dutch slave trader working from Lubeck in Germany, but were drafted by an English adventurer, Thomas Sherley, and his son, with initial help from Robert Cecil (one of the most powerful men in England). Cecil later ceased his support, and they 'lost' Elizabeth I's 'pleasure' in their activities.[38] These documents ended up failing in their intention to legally or illegally treat Africans as slaves.[39] There are many important points about these documents, but based on our focus, we should note that these writers, even though they put forward negative ideas, still chose the most popular term, 'Blackamoore', to describe Africans.[40]

Africans were also called 'Blackamoores' in English parish records from the early modern period. These records included details of baptisms, marriages and burials of the people who lived in local parishes. Other terms used in the records included 'Moor', 'Black', 'Negro', 'Aethiopian' (Ethiopians) and 'Niger'.[41] These words described African men, as most ethnic sobriquets were (and are) masculine;[42] however, in early modern England they also applied to women and children when the English writer added additional phrases, as in the record for

'Sebrina a blackmore wench'. Sebrina was buried in St Andrew's parish in Holborn, London on 30 January 1590.[43] The word 'wench' did not have the same pejorative connotations as it does now, and tended to describe a young single woman.[44]

Where the African being baptised was a child, the recorders tended to write this in the record, either by calling the subject 'a child' or by inference, referring to them as the 'son' or 'daughter' of someone. Of course, where the latter terms were used, additional evidence is now needed to ascertain whether they really were a child. For example:

Sara the daughter of Henry Jetto A Blackemore servante to Sir Henry Bromley baptised (10 December 1598)

And her sister, baptised three years later:

The 29 June was Margaret daughter of Henry Jetto a Blackemore baptised (29 June 1601)

In these examples, both Sara and Margaret were children at the time of their baptisms and they were born in England; this was verified by other evidence included in Worcestershire parish records.[45] Where children of dual heritage were baptised or buried, they were sometimes described in reference to their Blackamoore father or mother.[46] English writers such as George Best and official recorders often remarked that these children resembled their African parent more than their white father or mother. Of course, for a child born to a white mother and an African father in an English parish, the mother had proved by the act of giving birth that the child was hers. For a white father, his fatherhood may be less obvious. In those cases, the recorders often noted the white parent as the 'supposed father'. Sometimes recorders used these terms to denote that the child was born out of wedlock, as in the Plymouth[47] records for 'Helene, daughter of Cristian the negro svant [servant] to Richard Sheere, the supposed father being Cuthbert Holman, illeg.', dated 2 May 1593.[48] Sometimes the father was a powerful person who did not claim the baptised child as his. In other words, the union was morganatic:[49] for example, 'Richard a Bastard the sonne of Joanne Marya a Blackemore and was not the wife of Thomas Smythe by the latter [?] was baptised the 15 day of August 1600'.[50] Thomas Smythe was an influential man in early modern England, and the relationship between him and Marya was indicated by the way in which he was described in the record.[51]

These records are an important resource for our understanding of Africans in early modern England. Parish records were legal documents created by recorders that were subject to inspection and review by church officials and public officers. As such, the statements written in these documents could be investigated for verification. We can assume that what recorders wrote in these documents was not a fantasy.[52] Moreover, the writers of these records were expected to interview or investigate the people they baptised, married or buried. These people often lived side by side with and knew the writers. The terms, sobriquets or even epithets in the records that revealed the subject's ethnicity had probably been extracted from a much longer conversation.[53] It seems highly likely that these conversations influenced the use of terms such as 'Blackamoore' in these documents.

New scholarship 'discovers' Blackamoores

Scholarship is beginning to emerge on Africans in early modern England. This scholarship primarily focuses on the evidence found in early modern parish records and other primary English documents. There are a small number of historians at the forefront of this research who are reshaping our perceptions of early modern English history.[54] I began my research almost thirty years ago and have found over 1,423 entries concerning Africans in English parish records. It is not possible in this chapter to reveal all this evidence, especially as some of this ground-breaking research has been revealed elsewhere. I acknowledge that, for first-time readers, this may be challenging, but nevertheless it is now appropriate to advance arguments on more challenging topics.[55] One of these relates to meanings connected to the word 'Blackamoore' that link it to specific 'nations' of Africans. But before we explore this, let us take a look at where we find evidence for Africans in early modern England.

In early modern England, there was not the pseudo-science of race, nor a coherent racist philosophy, although ideas of difference and inferiority did exist.[56] In this milieu, we may also consider that Africans were not segregated by law, state policy, convention or religious doctrine[57] from other peoples in Tudor and early Stuart society. So, primary evidence of these people can be found by meticulous examination of ordinary English records. One cannot resort to special 'slave registers' or 'coloured people's records', as in the

USA,[58] and so locating Africans in early modern records requires more diligence. For example, one is required to carefully read every page of every parish register within a given area. When one does, records such as these emerge from St Margaret's Church in Deptford, London: 'Cornelius Blacke a More.' He was a parishioner buried in the churchyard on 2 March 1593 or 1594.[59]

Parish records, unlike most of the official histories written at the time, were focused on recording local people no matter what their status was. Therefore, these records include people such as Maria Mandula, a person who would probably be missing from the writings of Holinshed et al. Mandula was buried in Calne in Wilshire on 10 December 1585. She was described as a 'stranger and Aethiops'. But she was domiciled,[60] resident and sufficiently part of her parish to be given a Christian burial despite being called 'a stranger' (a movable term describing people who were perceived as not being 'native').[61]

Blackness of the Blackamoore

The word 'Moor' means 'black', so why add the word 'black' to it? Could it be that this was initiated by Englishmen's contact with Africans in the diaspora? One explanation hitherto not analysed by modern historians is that Africans may have chosen to emphasise their own blackness and used this term to describe themselves. The term 'Blackamoore' could thus be seen as a statement of how they saw their identity, origins and nationhood, in a similar way as some people today choose the term 'Black African' to define their identity.[62] But to acknowledge that this type of etymological process was possible in early modern England offers a radical departure from scholarship on this issue. It suggests that Africans in early modern England had a 'black sense of self', perhaps inherited from elsewhere or developed while in England.[63] Perhaps this 'black sense of self' was hinted at through the fictional characters of early modern plays, with their 'dangerous' ethnology, such as Aaron in *Titus Andronicus*, the Prince of Morocco in *The Merchant of Venice*, and Eleazar in *Lust's Dominion*.[64] In all three examples the fictional portrayal by Englishmen of Blackamoore men 'prefer[ring]' their own colour 'against the whole world'[65] at least illustrates a trope in early modern thought.

There is more factual evidence, from England and Spain, about how Africans in the early modern period may have seen their own identity. One of the more seemingly anecdotal but interesting quotations comes from the Spanish physician Juan Huarte. He stated in 1588 that: 'Blacks pass their colour on to their descendants even in Spain away from their homeland.'[66] This statement on Africans in Iberia may appear like a passing comment (no pun intended), that can be dismissed accordingly. However, when these comments are placed within the context of what was happening in Iberia at the time they become very significant, not just because of what they reveal about Spain, but also because of how this may reflect on Africans in England too. In Spain, institutional persecution was aimed at eradicating not only Moorish traditions and cultures but also the Moor's skin colour. In Spain, the Moor's 'blackness' was synonymous with Moorish nationhood. This was evidenced by persecutions that included various systems of 'blue-blood inheritance' that systematically prevented the Moors in Spain from obtaining livelihoods, inheriting wealth, raising their own children or marrying each other. Those Moors who retained their colour developed an ethnology of blackness that resisted the negative inscription placed on their complexion from the society in which they lived. Moorish people originating from Iberia who held on to their colour, or even cultivated it, could be seen as acting with agency.[67]

This type of agency was alluded to by English writers from the fifteenth to the seventeenth century. One of them, Thomas More, in his *First Boke* (1557) stated that an:

> Inde[68] that never came out of *hys country* nor never had seen any white man or women in his life but innumerable people black he might ... [think] that it were against the nature of man to be white. Now ... nature seemeth to show him to behave ... that all men should be blacke.[69]

More refers to a 'black' person who has never come 'out of hys country'. But More had never travelled outside Europe and would therefore only have met or seen 'black' people in the diaspora, for example in Iberia and England. Either he was extrapolating this black 'sense of self' from these diasporian Africans, or he was fantasising about what he believed was their philosophy on blackness. Either way, he articulated that 'black' people were capable of having a sense of self and that this was an innate, natural perspective for 'black' people to have. Other early modern English writers also stated something similar.[70] For them, the idea of African identity was informed by African people's perception of it.[71]

A Moorish nation

The words 'Moor' and 'Blackamoore' were used generically to describe Africans. However, a less obvious meaning attached to these words was present in how they were used in early modern England. This meaning would seem to contradict what has been said about the word 'Blackamoore' being generic. But, in fact, it clarifies why these words became popular to describe Africans. This is that the words 'Moor' and 'Blackamoore' related to a particular 'nation' (or 'nations') of Africans in Iberia.[72] The English adventurer Thomas Sherley provides an indication of this. In November 1600, he complained that his plan of capturing Africans and exchanging them for English prisoners was defunct. But, indignantly, he remonstrated that 'all the *blackamoores* in England are regarded but only for the strangeness of their *nation*, and not for service to the Queen'.[73] There are many important implications in his statement, but, for our deliberations here, Sherley related the word 'blackamoores' to 'nation' and allegiance. Sherley inferred that the 'Moors' in Tudor England had a different sovereign lord to Elizabeth I. In other evidence, Sherley also made the link between the 'nation' of 'blackamoores' in early modern England and Spain.[74] Some of Sherley's statements were hyperbolic and exaggerated, but his decision to include these words reflected a perspective on the identity of Africans in Tudor England.[75]

Other parish records also indicate this, as in the record of the burial of 'Anne Vause a Black-more wife to Anthonie Vause, Trompetter of the said Country' (24 April 1618). The juxtaposition of the word 'Black-more' with 'said country' suggests that they are synonymous, and that Anne Vause's musician husband was a 'Black more' and that was why he came from the same 'said country' as she did.[76]

During the early modern period, the meanings of the words 'Moor' and 'Blackamoore' were introduced into the English language by Iberian people. Some of these people were Iberian Moors who lived in Europe in 'nations' that had been conquered by Spain and Portugal. The last independent Moorish kingdom, Granada, fell in 1492.[77] Of course, there were some early modern ideas about the Moors of Iberia that were negative, but they were often characterised during the early modern period as literate and urbane and as having a 'higher culture' than their white counterparts in Spain and Portugal.[78] Many Moors were multilingual and blessed with acumen and intellect. Of course, not every single African in the Iberian Peninsula was endowed with luminosity and savvy. Some Moors in Iberia were enslaved, and more were later to be reduced to that status through the ethnic policies of white Christian princes in Spain and Portugal. But this did not mean that the Moors lost their sense of identity or the remembrances of their 'nation's' glories. Identity would be the most fundamental aspect of their sense of nationhood, and they would retain this.[79]

It is highly likely that, long after 1492, many Moors considered themselves as still hailing from 'nations' that were part of Spain and Portugal only by conquest and sequestration. This is not speculation, as, among other concerns, the fear that the Moors were a 'nation within a nation' fuelled their continuing persecution in Spain and Portugal.[80] Ironically, this xenophobia in the fifteenth and sixteenth centuries may have encouraged Moorish communality and nationalism: they began to see themselves as one nation, in a way they may not have done before.[81]

When the words 'Moor' and 'Blackamoore' were used in early modern England, they came with these hidden meanings about nationhood. These meanings would have been ubiquitous among Spanish monarchs and their descendants in England, such as Catherine of Aragon, Mary I and Philip II. But it was Iberian Moors, arriving as they often did as adults, with memories of their past, living in English parishes, talking to parish priests, employed as servants to men of power, and having sexual relations with white English people, who provided the greatest source for this nomenclature.

Further indications are to be found in the records of 'Mary Filis of Morisco', who was baptised in St Botolph without Aldgate parish, London, on 3 June 1597. In her detailed records contained in the parish registers, she was described as 'Mary Filis, a black more, being abowt xx yeares owld and dwelling with Millicent Porter, a seamester'.[82] It is only when the *Memorandum Daybook* is examined do we find out why she was referred to in this way.

> *She said* [emphasis added] hir father's name was Filis of Morisco, a black more, being both a basket maker and also a shovell maker.[83]

This quotation is one of many that repeat the phrase 'she said', and it is the writer's attempt to show that the terms used to refer to Mary's colour, ethnicity and nationhood originated from her, not from the English writer. To be more precise, they came from the way in which

Mary described herself as 'a black more', and her father as 'a black more' and 'of Morisco'. Mary had the agency to name herself and describe her ancestry. She had been in England for fourteen years and could speak (and perhaps read) in English. Her statements about her father's colour and 'nation' were sufficiently probative for the recorder to borrow her words to describe her ethnicity. This pattern continued with all of her written records, including those in parish registers, bound[84] and unbound copies, and in the *Memorandum Daybooks*.[85]

In Mary's case, as with many other people of African descent present in early modern society, the term 'black more' was associated with the Moors of Spain. In Spain, these people were sometimes called 'Moriscos'. Mary's additional use of the word 'Morisco' underlined her connection to that culture and the national grouping of those particular Africans. In this example, the word 'Morisco' was self-actualised, or at least self-authenticated (it may have come from her father) – it was not a pejorative adjective.[86] In other words, Mary chose it and advocated it.

In Mary's record in 1597, Sherley's comment in 1600, the proclamation of 1601 and statements in Anne Vause's record in 1618, the word 'Blackamoore' described Africans but also related to an idea of nation. The evidence indicates that 'of Morisco' and the 'said country' seemed to be synonymous, or at least could be associated with the 'nation' in which the Moriscos in Iberia lived.[87]

These investigations of the term 'Blackamoore' reveal that at least some Africans in early modern England were capable of having a 'black sense of self', and that they had the capacity to influence their own ethnography. Early modern England has hitherto been portrayed as a 'sacred white space', but we have found that Africans who lived there were not all voiceless outsiders. It also shows us that, 400 years ago, there were people of African descent living in England who were capable of influencing how their identity was seen. And that many Africans were able to frame definitions of themselves that English people could absorb. Africans in Tudor England lived in a country that had not yet become the largest slave-trading nation in the world. When that happened, major changes were implemented in the way in which Africans were described, and in how they saw themselves. These changes saw a repression of self-authenticated black identities. Those European educators, politicians, priests and scientists, among others, who orchestrated this annihilation of self sought to make African people into perpetual slaves.

The intersection of modern ethnology

Of course, modern readers may be influenced by modern ethnology. In modern times, Africans in Britain have often been objectified by the terms and labels that have been applied to them. Certainly, from the 1960s to the early 1980s, Africans were alienated and othered by names and terms related to ethnicity. These terms included animalistic references such as 'Ape' and 'Monkey', which were intended to dehumanise them, while other terms related to colour, such as 'Black' and 'Coloured'. There were also words and epithets such as 'Coon', 'Foreigner', 'Golliwog', 'Immigrant', 'Negro', 'Nig Nog', 'Nigger', 'Pickaninny', 'Stranger', 'Spade' and 'Wog'. Some of these pervasive terms morphed into insults intended to demean the recipient labelled in that way. Other terms involved the mixing of different terms to form a multifaceted derogatory slur such as 'Black bastard, go the fuck back to Africa!' Other methods involved playing on ideas associated with certain racial epithets to create an etymological chimera, such as 'You ugly black coon'.[88]

The epithets used to describe Africans in modern Britain (1960s–1980s) were often influenced by ideas on race present in that society.[89] These ideas were predicated on the pseudo-science of race that developed in the eighteenth and nineteenth centuries, which contained theories that separated people into distinct racial groups based on genetic and somatic differences. The somatic differences included facial features, hair texture, skin colour and so on.[90] In modern Britain, the words used to describe Africans were actualised by people who classified themselves as white, and were an expression of white privilege.[91] In other words, only white authors had the authority to describe and define the ethnicity of Africans in Britain.

Africans in Britain from the 1960s to the early 1980s did not originate and rarely adopted the terms listed above as descriptions of themselves, with the obvious exceptions of the words 'coloured' and 'black'.[92] Some historians have speculated that this capacity to delineate between 'acceptable' and 'unacceptable' ethnology must be modern, and that Africans in early modern England would not have had the wherewithal to 'name themselves'. It is perhaps because of this modern history that we may now be reluctant to believe that, 400 years ago, Africans in England could have influenced their nomenclature. But that notion has more to do with the effects of modern racism on us than with the history of early modern England.

Notes

1 Raphael Philemon Powell, *Human Side of a People and the Right Name* (New York: Philmeon Co., 1937), n.p.; also quoted in Richard B. Moore, *The Name 'Negro,' its Origin and Evil Use* (Baltimore: Black Classic Press, 1960), p. 49.

2 A book about Africans in England with a similar title but different findings to those contained here is by Eldred Jones, *Othello's Countrymen: The African in English Renaissance Drama* (London: Oxford University Press, 1965), passim.

3 William Shakespeare (1564–1616). See George Bagshawe Harrison, *Shakespeare at Work 1592–1603* (London: Routledge, 1933), pp. 310, 311; Simon (Samuel) Schoenbaum, *William Shakespeare: A Compact Documentary Life* (Oxford: Clarendon Press, 1977), p. 125; Schoenbaum, *Shakespeare's Lives* (London: Clarendon Press, 1991), p. 688; Hugh Calvert, *Shakespeare's Sonnets and Problems of Autobiography* (Braunton: Merlin, 1987), pp. 203–6, 220; Brenda James, *Henry Neville and the Shakespeare Code* (Bognor Regis: Music for Strings, 2008), pp. 150–4; Robert Nye, *The Late Mister Shakespeare: A Novel* (London: Chatto and Windus, 1998), pp. 281–5, 289–97 (a fictional retelling of the Lucy Negro legend).

4 See primary records in Pedro De Azeved (ed.), *Archivo Historico Portuguez* (Madrid: Libano da Silva, 1903), p. 300; Antonio Vieyra and Jacinto Dias do Canto, *A Dictionary of the Portuguese and English Languages, in Two Parts* (1773; second edition: London: J. Collingwood, 1827), p. 351. However, this record does not mean that all Africans in early modern England were considered foreign or strange or needed to win their manumission.

5 Azeved, *Archivo Historico Portuguez*, p. 300.

6 Evidence in R. E. G. Kirk and E. F. Kirk (eds), *Returns of Aliens Dwelling in the City and Suburbs of London from the Reign of Henry VIII to that of James I*, Volume I (1902), p. 2; Volume III (1907), p. 301.

7 For more on these records, see Onyeka, *Blackamoores: Africans in Tudor England, their Presence, Status and Origins* (London: Narrative Eye, 2013), pp. xix–xxiv.

8 Quotation from William Harrison in Frederick James Furnivall and John Norden (eds) et al., *Harrison's Description of England in Shakespeare's Youth*, Volumes II and III (1577, 1584, 1877; new edition: London: New Shakespeare Society, 1878), p. 34. There is more evidence that confirms this African's existence, that he was from Spain, and that he was the 'first' person to manufacture 'Spanish needles' in England; see Onyeka, *Blackamoores*, pp. 133–5, 213.

9 Guildhall Library, GL Ms 9222/1, 22 October 1586.

10 Worcestershire Archive and Archaeology Service, Holt Parish Registers, ref. 985, p. 19; also see Onyeka, *Blackamoores*, pp. 239–42.

11 There is an acknowledgement that some historians include the eighteenth century when talking about the early modern period; see John Cannon, *The Oxford Companion to British History* (Oxford: Oxford University Press, 2002), introduction; James Sharpe, *Early Modern England: A Social History, 1550–1760* (London: Bloomsbury Academic, 1997), introduction; Alison Wall, *Power and Protest in England, 1525–1640* (London: Bloomsbury Academic, 2002), introduction. However, in this chapter I suggest a different historiography for the eighteenth century in relation to the ethnicity of Africans in England.

12 The ontology (ways of reasoning) and the semantics of etymology

(understanding the meaning of words) for this approach are not analysed here because I have already examined them; see Onyeka, *Blackamoores*, passim; Onyeka, 'What's in a Name: Africans in Tudor England', *History Today* 62/10 (October 2012), pp. 34–9, http://www.historytoday.com/onyeka/tudor-africans-whats-name#sthash.G2xe8vO4.dpuf, accessed 1 November 2018.

13 This use of the term 'African' is a standard approach used by many historians, including those influenced by African-centred historiography. I acknowledge the contribution of African-centred historians. For a definition of this historiography, see Molefi Asante's work: Molefi K. Asante and Ama Mazama (eds), *The Encyclopedia of Black Studies* (London: SAGE, 2005 [2004]), introduction; Molefi K. Asante, *Afrocentricity: Imagination and Action*, Dissenting Knowledges Pamphlet Series 12 (Penang: Multiversity and Citizens International, 2013), n.p.; Molefi K. Asante, *Afrocentricity: The Theory of Social Change* (Trenton: African American Images/Africa World Press, 2003 [1988]), passim; Molefi Asante, *Contemporary Black Thought: Alternative Analyses in Social and Behavioral Science* (New York: Sage, 1980), passim.

14 The term 'mixed race' has not been used in this chapter for a number of reasons. Firstly, it was not a term used in early modern England. Secondly, it is a term strongly associated with the idea of the pseudo-science of race and a postcolonial reading of ethnology. However, the term 'mixed relationships' is used in Onyeka, *Blackamoores*, pp. xxi–xxiii.

15 For example, those with groundations in the Americas or the Caribbean may feel challenged. More on these histories can be found in: Jack Forbes, *Africans and Native Americans: The Language of Race and the Evolution of Red-Black Peoples* (Urbana: University of Illinois Press, 1993 [1988]), passim; Kent Williams, 'African Heritage in Central America', http://www.bjmjr.com/afromestizo/imp_dates.htm, accessed 12 March 2006; Richard Price (ed.), *Maroon Societies: Rebel Slave Communities in the Americas* (New York: Anchor Books, 1973), pp. 11–15; Ira Berlin, *Many Thousands Gone: The First Two Centuries of Slavery in North America* (New York: Harvard University Press, 2000 [1998]), pp. 20–1; Richard Juang and Noelle Morrissette (eds), *Africa and the Americas: Culture, Politics, and History. A Multidisciplinary Encyclopedia* (Santa Barbara and Oxford: ABC-CLIO, 2008), pp. 277–9; Junius Rodriguez (ed.), *Slavery in the United States: A Social, Political, and Historical Encyclopedia*, Volume 2 (Santa Barbara and Oxford: ABC-CLIO, 2007), pp. 7, 13, 230–1, 541–3; Asante and Mazama, *The Encyclopedia of Black Studies*, pp. 188–9.

16 Onyeka, *Blackamoores*, pp. xxii–xxxv; Onyeka, 'The Missing Tudors: Black People in Sixteenth-Century England', *BBC History Magazine* 13/7 (July 2012), pp. 32–3; Onyeka, 'What's in a Name'.

17 For example: Geoffrey Rudolph Elton, *England Under the Tudors*, revised edition (London: Methuen, 1995 [1974]); Robert Tittler, *Townspeople and Nation: English Urban Experiences, 1540–1640* (Stanford: Stanford University Press, 2001); Robert Tittler and Norman Jones (eds), *A Companion to Tudor Britain: Blackwell Companions to British History* (Oxford: Wiley Blackwell, 2004).

18 Academics or academia is the name given to the senior administrators and sometimes policymakers in higher education who are part of mainstream universities, education institutes and places of learning. It can also refer to other people involved in academic pursuits connected to these establishments. The failure of

British academia not only to facilitate a thorough investigation of England's past but also to address issues regarding its own inclusiveness have been written about by many, including Jack Grove, 'Black Scholars Still Experience Racism on Campus', *Times Higher Education Supplement*, 20 March 2014, https://www.timeshighereducation. com/news/black-scholars-still-experience-racism-on-campus/2012154. article, accessed 7 January 2016; 'Staff and Students of Colour Speak out on Racism in Academia,' Black British Academics PhD Network, 17 October 2015, http://phdnetwork. blackbritishacademics.co.uk/2015/10/17/ staff-and-students-of-colour-speak-out-on-racism-in-academia, accessed 7 January 2016.

19 On 'sacred white spaces', see James W. Perkinson, *White Theology: Outing Supremacy in Modernity* (New York: Palgrave Macmillan, 2004), pp. 1–26, 184; Jarvis Williams, 'Are Ethnic Minorities Safe in Christian White Spaces', *The Witness*, 8 September 2016, https:// thewitnessbcc.com/ethnic-minorities-emotionally-safe-white-christian-spaces/, accessed 1 November 2018. On the pathology of exclusiveness associated with whiteness, see Neely Fuller, *The United Independent Compensatory Code/ System/Concept: A Textbook/Workbook for Thought, Speech and/or Action for Victims of Racism (White Supremacy)* (Washington, DC: NFJ Productions, 1984), passim; Nell Irvin Painter, *The History of White People* (New York and London: Norton and Company, 2004), passim.

20 The same trend is also present in popular books written on other time periods.

21 On these matters, see David Cressy, *Society and Culture in Early Modern England* (London: Ashgate, 2003), p. 1; Francis Bacon, *The Two Bookes of Francis Bacon of the Proficience and Advancement of*

Learning Divine and Humane (London: Henrie Tomes, 1605), p. 1; Antonia Gransden, *Historical Writing in England, c. 550–1307* (London: Routledge, 1996 [1970]), introduction.

22 The term 'missing pages' in relation to African history was coined by the African-American historian Arthur Schomburg in Benjamin P. Bowser, Louis Kushnick and Paul Grant (eds), *Against the Odds: Scholars Who Challenged Racism in the Twentieth Century* (Amherst: University of Massachusetts Press, 2002), p. 9.

23 See Stephen Alford, 'Politics and Political History in the Tudor Century', *Historical Journal* 42/2 (1999), pp. 535–48; Peter Holbrook, *Literature and Degree in Renaissance England: Nashe, Bourgeois Tragedy, Shakespeare* (Newark: University of Delaware Press, 1994), pp. 169–70; Louise Schleiner, *Tudor and Stuart Women Writers* (Bloomington: Indiana University Press, 1994), pp. 1–30.

24 The following authors are pioneers in many ways, although their work on Africans in Tudor England tends to fall into the postcolonial praxis: Faiza Ghazala, *A History of the Black Presence in London* (London: Greater London Council Ethnic Minorities Unit, 1986), pp. 7–8; Folarin Shyllon, *Black People in Britain* (Oxford: Oxford University Press, 1977), pp. 1–10; Paul Edwards and James Walvin, 'Africans in Britain, 1500–1800' in *The African Diaspora: Interpretive Essays* (Cambridge, MA: Harvard University Press, 1976), pp. 173–204; James Walvin, *Black and White: The Negro in English Society, 1555–1945* (London: Allen Lane, 1973), pp. 1–31; Madge Dresser, *Slavery Obscured: The Social History of the Slave Trade in an English Provincial Port* (Bristol: Redcliff Press, 2007 [2001]), p. 11; Imtiaz Habib, *Black Lives in the English Archives, 1500–1677: Imprints of the Invisible* (London: Ashgate, 2008);

Gustav Ungerer, *The Mediterranean Apprenticeship of British Slavery* (Madrid: Verbum Editorial, 2008).

25 *Oxford Dictionary of English* (Oxford: Oxford University Press, 2003), p. 1247 (quotations on otherness); on strangeness and otherness, see Ania Loomba and Jonathan Burton, *Race in Early Modern England: A Documentary Companion* (Basingstoke: Palgrave Macmillan, 2007), preface, introduction; Tony Bennett, Lawrence Grossberg and Meaghan Morris (eds), *New Keywords: A Revised Vocabulary of Culture and Society* (Oxford: Blackwell, 2005), pp. 249–50; Matthieu Chapman, *Anti-Black Racism in Early Modern English Drama: The Other 'Other'* (New York: Taylor and Francis, 2016), passim.

26 Imtiaz Habib uses it differently in *Shakespeare and Race: Postcolonial Praxis in the Early Modern Period* (Lanham: University Press of America, 1999), passim. In the English dictionary, the word 'postcolonialism' is defined as a 'theoretical approach in various disciplines that is concerned with the lasting impact of colonization in former colonies', and 'colonialism' as a 'policy or practice of acquiring full or partial political control over another country, occupying it with settlers, and exploiting it economically'; *Oxford Dictionary of English*, p. 340; 'praxis' is defined on p. 1383 (quotations included).

27 *Oxford Dictionary of English*, p. 1247 (quotations on otherness); on strangeness and otherness see Loomba and Burton, *Race in Early Modern England*, preface, introduction; Bennett et al., *New Keywords*, pp. 249–50; Chapman, *Anti-Black Racism*, passim.

28 Peter Fryer, *Staying Power: The History of Black People in Britain* (London: Pluto Press, 1984), pp. 135–46; Habib, *Black Lives in the English Archives*; Kim Hall in *Things of Darkness: Economies of Race and Gender in Early Modern England*, second edition (New York:

Cornell University Press, 1996 [1995]), passim; Ungerer, *The Mediterranean Apprenticeship of British Slavery*, p. 76; Gustav Ungerer, 'Recovering a Black African's Voice in an English Lawsuit' in J Leeds Barroll, *Medieval and Renaissance Drama in England* (Madison: Fairleigh Dickinson University Press, 2004), pp. 255–71; Gustav Ungerer, 'The Presence of Africans in Elizabethan England and the performance of Titus Andronicus, at Burley-on-the-Hill, 1595–96', *Medieval Renaissance Drama in England Annual* 21 (2008), pp. 19–56. Other historians with similar views include: Walvin, *Black and White*, pp. 1–16, 16–31; Shyllon, *Black People in Britain*, pp. 1–10; Edwards and Walvin, 'Africans in Britain', pp. 173–204.

29 See previous note.

30 Onyeka, 'The Missing Tudors', pp. 32–3; Onyeka, 'What's in a Name?', pp. 34–9; Onyeka, *Blackamoores*, pp. 41–90; Miranda Kaufmann, *The Black Tudors* (London: Oneworld, 2017), passim. This also includes a range of African-American and Caribbean historians: Edward Scobie, *Black Britannia: A History of Blacks in Britain* (Chicago: Johnson Publishing Company, 1972), pp. 190–203; Joel Augustus Rogers, *World's Great Men of Colour*, Volumes I and II (New York: Touchstone Books, 1995 [1931]), pp. 1–7; Joel Augustus Rogers, *Sex and Race* (Petersburg: Helga Rogers, 1941–42), Volume I, pp. 151–60, 196–220; Ivan Van Sertima (ed.), *African Presence in Early Europe* (New Jersey: Transaction Publishers, 1985), pp. 190–223.

31 On this quest for identity, see William Wright, *Black History and Black Identity: A Call for a New Historiography* (Westport: Greenwood Publishing Group, 2002), pp. 99–101; Rogers, *World's Great Men of Colour*, p. 94; Rogers, *Sex and Race*, pp. 86–8.

32 Moors were not automatically Muslims, and there were 'white' and 'tawny' Moors in Iberia; see Onyeka,

Blackamoores, pp. 41–54; Onyeka, 'What's in a Name?', pp. 34–9.

33 These dictionaries offer a contrary view: *The Oxford English Dictionary* (London: Oxford University Press, 1998), pp. 49, 401, 1058; *Oxford Dictionary of English*, pp. 1139, 1178; *Chambers Dictionary of Etymology* (New York: Harrap Publishers, 1988), pp. 676, 699. Of course, who is 'dark-skinned' and who is not is relative; see Asante and Mazama, *The Encyclopedia of Black Studies*, p. 370.

34 John Minsheu and Richard Percyvall, *A Dictionarie in Spanish and English, First Published by R Percivale Now Enlarged by J Minsheu* (London: E. Bollifaunt, 1599), p. 172. Other evidence can be found below and in Onyeka, *Blackamoores*, pp. 107–51.

35 There is an acknowledgement that during the Roman occupation of Britannia, and perhaps for some time afterwards, Roman and other writers used the word 'Mauros', a root word for Moor, to describe Africans.

36 On the use of some of these terms, see *The Calendar of the Patent Rolls, Henry III, 1258–1266* (London: HMSO, 1910), p. 28; Michael Ray in Michael Jones (ed.), 'A Black Slave on the Run in Thirteenth-century England', *Nottingham Medieval Studies* L1 (2007), pp. 111–19.

37 See George Best, *A True Discourse of the Late Voyages of Discoverie* (London: H. Bynyman, 1578), pp. 28–32; Minsheu and Percyvall, *A Dictionarie in Spanish and English*, p. 17. Interestingly, Minsheu links the word 'Negrillo' to 'Ethiopia' but still uses the word 'Moor' as well. Barnabe Rich, *The Famous Hystory of Herodotus, Conteyning the Discourse of Dyuers Countreys, the Succession of theyr Kyngs* (London: Thomas Marshe, 1584), passim; Joannes Leo Africanus, *A Geographical Historie of Africa*, translated by John Pory (London: G. Bishop, 1600), p. 6.

38 The quotation contains the words of Elizabeth I paraphrased by Thomas Sherley, 29 November 1600; see Thomas Sherley and Casper Van Senden, 'Cecil Papers Petition', Volume 10, p. 431. It is discussed further in Onyeka, *Blackamoores*, pp. 10–15, 22–7, 289–91.

39 Various authors, letter to lord mayors signed by Queen Elizabeth, 11 July 1596, National Archives, Kew, London, PC 2/21, p. 304; various authors, letter signed by Queen Elizabeth, 18 July 1596, National Archives, Kew, London, PC 2/21, f. 306; various authors, proclamation, c. January 1601, National Archives, Kew, London, *Tudor Royal Proclamations*, 1601/804.5–805. For more on this, see Onyeka, *Blackamoores*, pp. 1–40.

40 There is an acknowledgement that they also used the terms 'Moor', 'Black', 'Negro' and 'Neger'; see Onyeka, *Blackamoores*, pp. 1–40. However, it does not mean that the term 'Blackamoore' was automatically pejorative.

41 Parish records officially began in 1538, but some records exist before that date. For more on how ethnic terms were used in those records, see Onyeka, 'What's in a Name?', p. 62; Onyeka, *Blackamoores*, pp. 41–90, 107–52. Primary evidence is available in Guildhall Library (GL), London, GL Ms 9243–5, GL Ms 4310, GL Ms 9222.

42 On questions of gendering, ethnicity and other issues, see Cecily Jones, 'Contesting the Boundaries of Gender, Race and Sexuality in a Barbadian Plantation Society', *Women's History Review* 12/2 (2003), pp. 195–232.

43 St Andrew Holborn, GL Ms 6673/1, 30 January 1589/90.

44 On the word 'wench' and single women in Tudor society, see Michael Braddick and John Walter (eds), *Negotiating Power in Early Modern Society: Order, Hierarchy and Subordination in Britain and Ireland* (Cambridge: Cambridge University Press,

2001), pp. 65–9, 76–84, 87, 90; Marliss C. Desens, *The Bed-Trick in English Renaissance Drama: Explorations in Gender, Sexuality and Power* (Newark: University of Delaware Press, 1994), pp. 17, 34, 94; Laura Gowing, 'Gender and the Language of Insult in Early Modern London', *History Workshop Journal* 35 (1993), pp. 1–21.

45 Worcestershire Archive and Archaeology Service, Holt Parish Registers, ref. 985, p. 19; Henry Anthony Jetto, 21 March 1596, Baptism, Worcestershire Archive, Holt Parish Register, ref. 985, p. 19. His will is at 'Will of Henrie Jetto', will number 102, dated and signed on 20 September 1626, but executed 13 September 1638, Worcestershire Archive; see Onyeka, *Blackamoores*, pp. 239–41.

46 Jetto's children may be of dual heritage, as we do not know the ethnicity of Jetto's wife, Persida.

47 This is Plymouth, England.

48 Plymouth and West Devon Record Office, St Andrews/May 2/1593/MF1-4.

49 The word 'Morganatic' has a different etymological origin to the word 'Moor' and describes a marriage or union where one partner's spouse and children do not inherit. There is considerable research on this issue; see Kim Hall, 'Object into Object, Some Thoughts on the Presence of Black Women in Early Modern Culture' in Peter Erickson and Clarke Hulse (eds), *Early Modern Visual Culture: Representation, Race, and Empire in Renaissance England* (Philadelphia: University of Pennsylvania Press, 2000), pp. 346–80; Habib, *Black Lives in the English Archives*, pp. 100–12, 205; Ungerer, *The Mediterranean Apprenticeship of British Slavery*, pp. 75–6; Anthony Gerard Barthelemy, *Black Face, Maligned Race: The Representation of Blacks in English Drama from Shakespeare to Southerne* (London: Louisiana State University Press, 1987), pp. 22, 27, 40, 131–46, 197–8 (on beauty in interracial unions). Race is not listed as a bar in Tudor marriage ceremonies in Vivien Brodsky-Elliot, 'Single Women in the London Marriage Market: Age, Status and Mobility, 1598–1619' in R. B. Outhwaite (ed.), *Marriage and Society: Studies in the Social Mobility of Marriage* (London: Europa, 1981), pp. 81–100; David Cressy, *Birth, Marriage, and Death: Ritual, Religion, and the Life-Cycle in Tudor and Stuart England* (Oxford: Oxford University Press, 1997), pp. 298–307.

50 Bristol Record Office, Bristol, P/ST PJR/1/1/CMB 1576–1621, n. p. There is more detail on Marya in Onyeka, *Blackamoores*, pp. 228–31.

51 For more on whether African women such as Marya were discriminated against because of their gender and ethnicity in early modern England, see Onyeka, *Blackamoores*, pp. 226–38.

52 For more on this, see Onyeka, *Blackamoores*, pp. 41–90, 107–52. For the 'rules' of authenticity and record keeping in early modern England, see Andrew Gordon, *Writing Early Modern London: Memory, Text and Community* (New York: Palgrave Macmillan, 2013), passim.

53 Gordon, *Writing Early Modern London*.

54 Not all of the following historians agree about the status of the Africans whom they write about: Habib, *Black Lives in the English Archives*, passim; Kaufmann, *The Black Tudors*, passim; Marika Sherwood, 'Blacks in Elizabethan England', *History Today* 53/10 (2003), pp. 40–2; Lucy MacKeith, *Local Black History: A Beginning in Devon* (London: Archives and Museum of Black Heritage, 2003), p. 35; Rogers, *Sex and Race*, pp. 86–8; Mike Sampson, 'Friends of Devon Archives, the Black Connection', *Friends of Devon Newsletter* 25 (May 2000), pp. 12–15; Scobie, *Black Britannia*, pp. 190–203; Van Sertima, *African Presence in Early Europe*,

pp. 12–15; Ungerer, *The Mediterranean Apprenticeship of British Slavery*, passim. A longer list of authors is included in the bibliography of Onyeka, *Blackamoores*, pp. 297–340. A number of other authors are not included here because they have not yet engaged with the 'new evidence'.

55   The questions of what these names mean, why they were used and when have been analysed to some extent in Onyeka, 'What's in a Name?', pp. 34–9 and Onyeka, *Blackamoores*, pp. 41–90, and by others who have come to different conclusions; see Habib, *Black Lives in the English Archives*; Ungerer, *The Mediterranean Apprenticeship of British Slavery*; Kaufmann, *The Black Tudors*.

56   On race, see Peter Fraser, 'Slaves or Free People: the Africans in England 1550–1750' in Randolph Vigne and Charles Littleton (eds), *From Strangers to Citizens: The Integration of Immigrant Communities in Britain, Ireland, and Colonial America, 1550–1750* (Eastbourne: Sussex Academic Press, 2001), pp. 254–61; Chancellor Williams, *The Destruction of Black Civilisation: Great Issues of a Race from 4500 BC to 2000 AD*, third edition (Chicago: Third World Press, 1987), pp. 176–95, 243–72 (on how racism was enforced and maintained); Andrew Valls (ed.), *Race and Racism in Modern Philosophy* (New York: Cornell University Press, 2005), passim.

57   This matter is controversial because of ideas such as the 'Curse of Ham'. See Onyeka, *England's Other Countrymen* (London: Zed Books, 2019), passim.

58   In the US, especially in the southern states, during the eighteenth and nineteenth centuries special laws, conventions and customs separated Africans from Europeans; see Juang and Morrissette, *Africa and the Americas*, pp. 277–9; Rodriguez, *Slavery in the United States*, Volume 2, pp. 7, 13, 230–1, 541–3; Asante and Mazama, *The Encyclopedia of Black Studies*, pp. 188–9.

59   Local History and Archives Centre, Lewisham, London, A78/18M/A1/1; Lewis Leland Duncan and Oswald Barron (eds), The Registers of All the Marriages, Christenings and Burials in the Church of St Margaret's Lee in the County of Kent, From 1579–1754 (Lee: Lewisham Antiquarian Society, 1888), p. 40.

60   'Domiciled' refers to treating 'the country ... as [her] permanent home, or [having a] substantial connection with [it]' (*Oxford Dictionary of English*, pp. 515, 1171; definitions of 'native', etc.). On who was 'native' and 'liege', see Lien Luu, *Immigrants and the Industries of London, 1500–1700* (Aldershot: Ashgate, 2005), pp. 142–4.

61   Wiltshire and Swindon Records Office, Wiltshire Family History Society, *Calne Parish Register. Volume 1: 1538–1602* (London: A. Webb, 1944), n.p. (10 December 1585).

62   As used in Cheikh Anta Diop's, *The Cultural Unity of Black Africa: The Domains of Patriarchy and of Matriarchy in Classical Antiquity* (Chicago: Third World Press, 1962); originally published as *The Cultural Unity of Negro Africa* (Paris: Presence Africane, 1959), passim; Dickson A. Mungazi, *The Mind of Black Africa* (Westport: Praeger, 1996), passim.

63   The idea of a 'black sense of self' is evinced by pride, confidence, self-esteem, etc.; see, Richard L. Allen, *The Concept of Self: The Study of Black Identity and Self Esteem* (Detroit: Wayne State University, 2001), pp. 67–106.

64   Christopher Marlowe or Thomas Dekker, *Lust's Dominion or the Lascivious Queen, a Tragedie* (London: Printed for F. K., 1657), passim; Christopher Marlowe and George Robinson (ed.), *The Works of Christopher Marlowe: Lust's Dominion; or, The Lascivious Queen*. Volume II (London: W. Pickering, 1826), passim.

65   Such ideas also appear in Christopher Marlowe, *The Famous*

Tragedy of the Jew of Malta (London: Nicholas Vavasour, 1633), Act 2, n.p.; *Tamburlaine the Great* (London: Marlowe, 1592), pp. A3, D4, E4, F2, F3, F4, G1–2; *The Tragedy of Dido Queen of Carthage* (London: Thomas Nash, 1594), passim; William Shakespeare, *Othello*, in Richard Proudfoot, Ann Thompson and David Scott Kastan (eds), *The Arden Shakespeare Complete Works* (Walton-on-Thames: Thomas Nelson and Sons, 1998), pp. 939–78; *Titus Andronicus*, pp. 1123–50 (quotations); *The Merchant of Venice*, Act II, Scene I, Line 1–46, pp. 835–6, Act II, Scene VII, Line 1–79, p. 840.

66 Juan Huarte, *Examen de Ingenios Para las Ciencias* (1588), p. 250, quoted in Jonathan Schorsch, *Swimming the Christian Atlantic: Judeoconversos, Afroiberians, and Amerindians in the Seventeenth Century* (Leiden, Boston and Biggleswade: Brill Extenza Turpin), p. 361.

67 Of course, readers may need more evidence on the Iberian experience, and this can be found in Onyeka, *Blackamoores*, pp. 107–51, which also contains a list of primary and secondary sources on this matter.

68 The term 'Inde' was generic enough to include all 'people of colour', including Africans, as discussed in more detail in the following: Sidney Lee, 'Caliban's Visits to England', *Cornhill Magazine* 34 (1913), pp. 333–45; James Laurence Bolton (ed.), *Alien Communities of London in the Fifteenth Centuries* (Stamford: Richard III and York History Trust with Paul Watkins, 1998), pp. 29, 42.

69 Thomas More and William Rastell (ed.), *The Works of Sir Thomas More, Knyght ... The First Boke* (London: John Cawod and Richard Tottell, 1557), pp. 126–7.

70 These include Francis Bacon, 'Experiment Solitary Touching the Coloration of Black and Tawny Moors', *Novum Organum* (1620) in James Spedding (ed.), *The Works of Francis Bacon Collected and Edited by James Spedding, Robert Leslie Ellis, and Douglas Denon Heath* (London: Longman and Co., 1857), p. 473; Thomas Browne, *Pseudodoxia Epidemica: or, Enquiries into Very Many Received Tenents and Commonly Presumed Truths* (London: Edward Dod, 1646), p. 332.

71 In this idea, Tudor writers were influenced by Neoplatonic teachings, some aspects of Roman natural law, and medieval ideas of 'Universals' – that all living things have their own 'name' and 'substantiality'. See Paul Vincent Spade (tr./ed.), *Five Texts on the Mediaeval Problem of Universals: Porphyry, Boethius, Abelard, Duns Scotus, Ockham* (Indianapolis: Hackett, 1994), passim.

72 *The Oxford English Dictionary*, p. 1058.

73 Thomas Sherley and Casper Van Senden, 'Cecil Papers Petition: Merchant of Lubeck to the Queen', Volume 14, p. 143.

74 Various authors, proclamation, c. 1601: 'the great Numbers of Negroes and blackamoors which (as she is informed) are carried into this realm since the troubles between her highness and the King of Spain'.

75 The words 'nation'/'nations' are within quotation marks because by the end of the fifteenth century Moorish people no longer lived in Iberia in independent nations. They were part of 'white' Christian kingdoms that became Spain and Portugal. For how English people saw 'nation', see Andrew Boorde, *The First Boke of the Introduction of Knowledge. The Whych Doth Teach a Man to Speake and Parte of All Maner of Languages and to Know the Vsage and Fashion of all Maner of Countries ...* (London: William Copeland, 1550), pp. 88–9; *Oxford Dictionary of English*, p. 1170, 'large body of people united by common descent ... inhabiting a particular state or territory'.

76 GL Ms 9222/1, Parish Register, p. 560, 24 April 1618. A similar view on this is offered by Habib, *Black Lives in the English Archives*, pp. 135–6; Kaufmann, *Black Tudors*, pp. 30, 53, 55, 124; Within the reading of early modern parish records, these terms used in this way are rare. Another interpretation is possible of their meaning, but unlikely. This matter is analysed in a little more detail below, and the wider issues are explored in Onyeka, *Blackamoores*, pp. 41–90, 107–52.

77 On the Moors, see Onyeka, *Blackamoores*, pp. 107–51; Van Sertima, *African Presence in Early Europe*, pp. 12–15; Mary Floyd-Wilson, *English Ethnicity and Race in Early Modern Drama* (Cambridge: Cambridge University Press, 2003), pp. 1–13.

78 The quotation is from Ieronimo Conestaggio, *The Historie of the Uniting of the Kingdom of Portugal to the Crowne of Castill*, translated by Edward Blount (London: A. Hatfield for E. Blount, 1600), pp. 6–7, 39. On this 'higher culture', see Philippus van Limborch, *The History of the Inquisition* (London: Simpkin and Marshall, 1816), p. 128; A. C. de C. M. Saunders, *A Social History of Black Slaves and Freedmen in Portugal 1441–1555* (Cambridge: Cambridge University Press, 1982), pp. 29–33, 59–60, 87, 149; Ruth Pike, 'Sevillian Society in the Sixteenth Century: Slaves and Freedmen', *Hispanic American Historical Review* 47/3 (1967), pp. 345–59.

79 Quotations from Abentarique, *The History of the Conquest of Spain by the Moors. Together with the Life of the Most Illustrious Monarch Menesh Almanzar and of the Several Revolutions of the Mighty Empire of the Caliphs and of the African Kingdoms ... Now made English* (London: Fleach, sold by T. Fox, 1687), preface; Stanley Lane-Poole, *Story of the Moors of Spain* (London: Fisher Unwin, 1887), pp. 54, 217; Jean Pierre Claris de Florian and Robert Heron (tr.), *Gonsolvo or Cordova or The Conquest*

of Granada (London: Morison and Son, 1792), p. 97; Van Sertima, *African Presence in Early Europe*, pp. 144–76.

80 The Moors were part of several different independent kingdoms (nations), the last of which – Granada – became the refuge for Moors who still wanted sovereign independence. It then became the seat for Moorish nationalistic aspirations; see Janet Lloyd, *The Spanish Inquisition: A History* (London and New Haven: Yale University Press, 2006), pp. 44–6, 54, 105; John Robert Scott, *A Dissertation on the Expulsion of the Moors from Spain and the Protestants from France and the Low Countries* (Dublin: Joseph Hill University Press, 1779), p. 7.

81 Caelius Augustinus Curio, *A Notable History of the Saracens ...* (London: William How and Abraham Veale, 1575), pp. 31, 46–51, 67, 68, 79; see also Jacob van Maerlant, 'Charlemagne Killing a Moorish Leader', image on vellum, 32 by 233 cm, in *Spiegel Historiael* (West Flanders: publisher unknown, 1325–55), n.p.; Anne Marsh-Caldwell, *The Song of Roland, as Chanted Before the Battle of Hastings, by the Minstrel Taillefer* (London: Hurst and Blackett, 1854), passim; Ivan Van Sertima (ed.), *Golden Age of the Moor* (Piscataway: Transaction Publishers, 1992), p. 372; John Bagnall Bury, *The Cambridge Medieval History*, Volume II (London: University Press, 1964), pp. 374–5.

82 GL Ms 9223, Paper Baptism Register, 3 June 1597.

83 GL Ms 9223, Parish Clerk Memorandum Daybook, St Botolph without Aldgate, 1597, 69/Bot2/A01/Ms 9234/6, pp. 257–8.

84 GL Ms 9220, Parish Baptism Register, p. 90, 3 June 1597.

85 Memorandum daybooks were compiled by parish priests, recorders or other literate people in the

parish as an additional record of local events; see Onyeka, *Blackamoores*, pp. xix–xxiv.

86   A different view on the meaning of the word 'Morisco' in Mary's record is offered in Kaufmann, *Black Tudors*, pp. 134–68, but we are in agreement that she had the capacity to name herself.

87   On the Moors, see Onyeka, *Blackamoores*, pp. 107–51; Van Sertima, *African Presence in Early Europe*, pp. 12–15; Floyd-Wilson, *English Ethnicity and Race in Early Modern Drama*, pp. 1–13.

88   On the insidious uses of these terms, see Various Authors, *Parliamentary Debates (Hansard): House of Commons Official Report*, Volume 65 (London: Her Majesty's Stationery Office, 1983), p. 547; Keith Allan and Kate Burridge, *Euphemism and Dysphemism: Language Used as a Shield and a Weapon* (Oxford: Oxford University Press, 1991), pp. 120–3. The etymology of these sorts of 'names' is discussed in Richard B. Moore, *The Name 'Negro', its Origin and Evil Use* (Baltimore: Black Classic Press, 1992), passim.

89   On racism in post-war Britain there are a multitude of texts; a useful one is Paul Gilroy's *There Ain't No Black in the Union Jack: The Cultural Politics of Race and Nation* (Chicago: University of Chicago Press, 1991), passim.

90   The idea of 'race' is complex and seen by some as controversial. Where the word is used now by historians it tends to be as Jonathan Schorsch does in *Swimming the Christian Atlantic*, p. 5 (6): 'Without wishing to enter into an enormous and dangerous topic, race/ethnicity is real, i.e., "natural" insofar as different population groups often manifest different biological conditions [genotype]: immunities to particular diseases or lack thereof, manifest specific patterns of disease (lactose intolerance, sickle cell anaemia, Jays-Sachs disease, etc.). Different population groups may also manifest statistically-notable somatic uniqueness [phenotype]: eye shape, particularly light skin, height, etc.'

91   On 'white privilege', see Painter, The History of White People, passim; Perkinson, *White Theology*, pp. 1–26; Fuller, The United Independent Compensatory Code/System/Concept, passim.

92   'Coloured' was a term still used by people of African descent to describe their ethnicity in the 1960s, although 'black' became more popular in the decade. For more on 'black' etymology, see Moore, *The Name 'Negro'*, passim.

2 | BETWEEN COLONY AND METROPOLE

Empire, race and power in eighteenth-century Britain

Molly Corlett

In the spring of 1779, a bill to dissolve the marriage between Captain Thomas Edwards and his wife was read in the House of Lords. This was the only way to secure what we understand by 'divorce' – a separation that allowed both parties to remarry – in the eighteenth century. Captain Edwards had already convinced two courts that Judith, his wife, had been sexually unfaithful. But Judith protested that the earlier verdicts had been unjust. It was by 'false Evidences of her own Slaves, Mustees and Mulattoes', she claimed, that 'her said Husband has obtained a Divorce from the Petitioner, in the Commissary Court of *Surrey*'. She went on to complain that he had 'possessed himself of the Petitioner's Jewels and other Valuables, her separate Property, the Gifts of her former Husband and Relations'. This included over £500, which her two eldest daughters had raised 'from the Sale and Hire of several Negro Servants, left to them by their said Father', with 'the Slave *Ann Williams*, Evidence in Behalf of Captain *Edwards*, being One of such Slaves'.[1]

The partial transcription of this case in the printed House of Lords journal – the only surviving source for the Edwards' marital drama – tells us nothing about the lords' reaction to Ann Williams. Seven years earlier, Lord Mansfield had ruled that the formerly enslaved James Somerset could not be forcibly sent back to the colonies.[2] While slave owners panicked, abolitionists and London's black population rejoiced; it was widely believed, in North America as well as in Britain, that slavery had been outlawed in the metropole.[3] But in lawsuits like this, which were not directly concerned with slave ownership, the Mansfield judgment went unmentioned. The power of white masters/ owners over their black servants/slaves was discussed in passing, taken up as an issue when it related to the main facts of a case and dropped when it did not. Although only a handful of late eighteenth-century adultery cases feature black servants, this material gives us an insight into black lives in Britain which is missing from other sources. Yet for the same reason – because they are not designed to tell their readers about race in eighteenth-century Britain – these records are in many ways frustrating, with their silences and omissions as significant as the incidental detail they do provide.

Recent work on Britain's black population has interpreted archival silences optimistically. In contrast to the earlier scholarship of Folarin Shyllon, who argued for an essential continuity between British racism in the early modern period and British racism in the present day, subsequent studies have questioned the significance of racial difference in eighteenth-century England, Scotland and Wales.[4] In her study of Britain's black presence between 1780 and 1840, Norma Myers suggests that 'the mass of both the black and the poor white population underwent similar experiences'.[5] Peter King and John Carter Wood argue that racial prejudice played no significant role in Old Bailey cases.[6] And, most strikingly, Kathleen Chater's recent study concludes that slavery impacted 'very little on the lives of the overwhelming majority' of black people in eighteenth-century England and Wales, who are best seen as 'just one of the many minorities who make up the rich mix of British ancestry'. She maintains that 'their very invisibility is further evidence they were neither slaves nor stigmatised outsiders'.[7] Yet scholars who focus on representations of blackness – sources that do talk explicitly about racial difference – continue to paint a bleaker picture. In this work, the late eighteenth century figures as a turning point: at this point, debates between abolitionists and pro-slavers came to shape racial categories in Britain.[8] Similarly, historians who focus on the eighteenth-century British Empire, rather than on Britain or England in isolation, have emphasised the transatlantic dynamics that shaped black lives in the metropole.[9]

When we consider this wider transatlantic context, Ann Williams' appearance in court becomes exceptional. The humanity of enslaved women, Marisa Fuentes argues, has been obscured not just by scant source material but also by 'the violence in and of the archive ... [They] appear as historical subjects through the form and content of archival documents in the manner in which they lived: spectacularly violated, objectified, disposable, hypersexualised, and silenced.'[10] In Barbados, the focus of Fuentes' work, neither slaves nor free people of colour could testify in court.[11] Trevor Burnard has pointed out that it was much harder to prove (white women's) adultery in eighteenth-century Jamaica than in Britain: the workers who saw illicit intimacy in the household were slaves, and so were barred from appearing as witnesses.[12] Ann's relationship with her mistress had been forged in Antigua, where she could not have testified in court. As a result, her testimony belonged to both metropole and colony – a duality to which this chapter will repeatedly return. By reading depositions in adultery cases alongside advertisements for black runaways, this chapter brings together empirical presence and representation, empire and metropole.

Runaway advertisements existed because eighteenth-century servants and apprentices, as well as slaves, were thought to 'belong' to their masters. This meant that dependants of all kinds could be forcibly retrieved if they attempted to leave, and that masters could place notices to this effect in local and/or London newspapers. Between 1691 and 1776, at least 222 advertisements for black runaways were placed in the London papers.[13] The vast majority of these runaways were young black men, although eighteen were women or girls. As with adultery cases, this genre was not defined by race, yet the presence of black subjects unavoidably altered its terms and implications. Both types of source documented the lives of black people in Britain, while making significant and strategic choices about how they represented those lives; both described colonial power alongside British experience. These sources point to the continued vulnerability of formerly enslaved people. Their silences are best understood as a product of Britain's particular relationship to slavery – a relationship based on simultaneous distance from and proximity to its slave-holding colonies, and framed by both complicity and disavowal.[14]

The status of black servants

In eighteenth-century slave societies, 'the master–slave relationship provided the model for all social relations: husband and wife, parent and child, employer and employee'. The British Atlantic world was also home to 'societies with slaves', where slavery existed as 'just one form of labor among many'.[15] Yet England, Scotland and Wales belonged to neither of these categories. Although owners brought their colonial slaves to Britain, slavery figured as a rhetorical device rather than a legitimate option in discussions of domestic labour relations. This did not necessarily mean that slavery in Britain was illegitimate: it just meant that it could not be understood in solely metropolitan terms. In this context, the line between slavery and domestic service was often left unclear. This could be either useful (allowing formerly enslaved people to transition to freedom) or dangerous (meaning that free servants could be forced back into bondage). In a 1745 issue of the *Daily Advertiser*, a would-be master announced that he was looking for a 'Young Negro or Mulatto Fellow' who might be either free or enslaved. 'The Owner of such a one may hear of a purchaser, by applying to Mr. Baker, at Lloyd's Bar,' he offered, 'or such a Fellow who has the Disposal of himself, may be treated with, applying to the same Place and Person.'[16] To respond to this advertisement as a free man would mean accepting a position, and by implication a type of treatment, deemed suitable for a slave.

By the early 1760s, Sir John Fielding was warning that London's black population made it:

> their Business to corrupt and dissatisfy the Mind of every fresh black
> Servant that comes to England; first, by getting them christened
> or married, which they inform them makes them free, (tho' it has
> been adjudged by our most able Lawyers, that neither of these
> Circumstances alter the Master's Property in a Slave.)

This was troubling because, even though baptism did not change the legal status of a slave, it 'gets the Mob on their Side, and makes it not only difficult but dangerous to the Proprietor of these Slaves to recover the Possession of them'.[17] As the chief magistrate at Bow Street, Fielding had practical experience of black runaways. Nine runaway notices between 1754 and 1764 directed readers to him, as did an advertisement for the sale of a thirteen-year-old black boy.[18] His warning was probably exaggerated (there is no sign of a sympathetic mob in these records), but it was not uninformed. Significantly, it implied that popular understandings of slavery mattered as much as – and sometimes more than – the legal status of colonial slaves in Britain. In this context, thinking about how black footmen and maids represented themselves, and how they were represented by others, becomes crucially important.

Because runaway advertisements expressed normative ideas about blackness and slavery, they guided their readers' perceptions of race. In December 1743, for example, a seven-year-old 'Negro Boy' was brought into the Cross Keys Alehouse in the City of London. He told people there that his name was Dover. Three days later, a notice in the *Daily Advertiser* explained that he had 'not yet been claimed by the Owner, nor advertised; if the Owner will come to the Cross Keys, he may have him again, paying the Charges'.[19] The notice implicitly told its audience that this child's age, name and race marked him out as a slave. Runaway advertisements were, then, significant in two ways. First, they described (and were part of) a power struggle between advertiser and advertised.[20] Second, they taught contemporaries about racial power relations. Metropolitan newspaper readers learned that black servants' hair was said to be 'Wooley', that their skin was described as ranging from 'Coal Black' to 'yellowish', and that their masters called them by classical or place names.[21] They heard that, before coming to Britain, runaways had served their masters as domestics or sailors or – occasionally – crafts-men.[22] And they were asked not only to accept colonial categories, but to actively uphold this racial order by retrieving black runaways. A 1763 advertisement for a fourteen-year-old girl, born in Barbados but 'lately come from Philadelphia', recognised that members of the metropoli-tan public might feel charitably towards her. But it also assumed that, for readers, her mistress's property rights would take precedence over sympathy. 'If anyone has taken her in out of Compassion, it is hoped they will return her,' it requested, given that she was 'private Property'. Anyone who saw her asking for charity ought to bring her to Sir John Fielding's house, where they could collect a guinea reward.[23]

These notices reminded their readers that blackness meant a his-tory of colonial slavery. Even where runaways took on the trappings of freedom to disguise themselves, they could still be recognised – advertisers suggested – by enduring marks of servitude. A Welsh gentleman explained that a slave whom he called Windsor, but who could now be expected to 'take on him the name of Henry Win', had likely removed the lace from his livery hat, 'the better to disguise him'. He was still identifiable, though, because 'on his left Shoulder is his Master's Plantation Mark in the West-Indies'.[24] A young man from Martinique was thought to have 'changed his livery coat for a white coat' in 1765, 'and by this endeavours to pass himself for a free black'. But if readers looked out for 'a real black, with every mark of the Negro visible to be seen', speaking a combination of good French and broken English, he might be found.[25] When runaways took on Christian names after escaping, they were primarily referred to by their old names.[26] In 1710, the *Daily Courant* published a notice about a young black man who had run away on Christmas Day. He had tried to board a ship at Chatham, had been identified, discharged and brought back to his master, and had run away again that same night. Readers were told to look for the baptism certificate which he carried with him. He must have been holding on to this certificate because of the common opinion that baptism made slaves free, believing or hoping that it would save him from re-enslavement. His master's advertisement denied this logic. The certificate did not protect him; instead, it meant that he could be recognised and returned. The identity that it claimed for him, meanwhile, was ignored. He was 'known about York-Buildings by the Name of Kingston', the advertisement explained, marking him out as a slave or former slave. Even though he was likely going by his Christian name, his master did not include it in the advertisement.[27]

Christening mattered in this way because black servants were inherently at risk. Across the British Atlantic world, baptism was thought to provide tentative protection against slavery and/or abuse. The correspondence of Sir William Stapleton, the absentee owner of a plantation in Nevis, brings out some of the tensions caused by this view. In 1725, the driver (a slave who assisted the white overseer) on his estate, who he trusted and depended on, was accused of taking part in a slave conspiracy. Stapleton's agents had to contend with the 'several p[e]r[s]ons here that has laid themselves under the strongest obligation to destroy him', infuriated by the spectre of slave insurrection. They sent Frank (the driver) to live with Stapleton in England, and discussed christening him so that he would be protected by the church when he returned. But this was risky territory: later in the century, a Nevis rector would warn that 'When a Slave is once Christened ... he conceits that he ought to be upon a level with his Master'. In the end, Frank was not christened, and the 'very ungreatfull rogue' ran away again as soon as he was brought back to Nevis.[28] In Britain, christening was more directly – if inaccurately – linked to freedom. Joseph Alamaze, a black footman who allegedly seduced a married white woman after meeting her at a dancing class, had been brought to England as the slave of a merchant. A witness who had lived next door but one from them at the time explained that the merchant had moved to Florida in about 1769, leaving Joseph 'with a brother of his in England; soon after which, he got himself christened'.[29] He was employed as a free servant for a decade after this, although he would later be seized by a press gang at the request of his lover's husband.[30] John Webb, another young black footman, was severely beaten after running away to get himself christened in 1783.[31] A member of counsel in the case suggested that John's master had been particularly angry because 'at that time there used to be an idea pretty prevalent, that when a black was made a Christian he became a free man'.[32] He had been known only as 'Jack' before his christening, and his master continued to refer to him in this way afterwards.

By looking at both advertisements and witness testimony, we can compare masters' printed assertions of power with the more uncertain claims made by witnesses. Advertisers claimed that their 'Property' was protected by law in Britain, threatening to prosecute white gentlemen or captains who took on a runaway.[33] They also threatened literate servants. 'As the above-mentioned Negro can read,' a 1771 description of a runaway called Harry concluded, 'if he does not return in a short Time after this Publication, other Measures will be pursued, which may be dangerous to him.' Harry had been caught stealing from his master before, and had 'a solemn, or rather sullen Countenance'. The advertiser explained that he had 'formed some bad Connexions, and is not willing to return to his native Country, Antigua', then warned other gentlemen against 'admitting a dangerous, treacherous Servant into their Employ, who has been spoiled by Indulgence'.[34] Similarly, a 1769 advertisement described a 'Young Negro Man, called Jeremiah or Jerry' who was partially literate, played the violin, and had often accompanied his master to the spas at Bath and Bristol. 'As the said Negro knows his master's affection for him,' it went on to offer, 'if he will immediately return, he will be forgiven, if freedom be what he wishes for, he shall have it, with reasonable wages.' But if he did not take advantage of 'this present forgiving disposition in his master, he may be assured that more effectual measures will be soon taken'.[35] Jeremiah's lack of freedom was openly admitted, while Harry was described only as a servant. But he was a 'servant' who had grown up in a slave society, and his master was trying to take him back.

Advertisers could choose how they represented the master–servant relationship. In witness testimony, on the other hand, competing representations were voiced by different parties. In the most detailed of the adultery cases, litigants, witnesses and lawyers disagreed about whether John Webb – a nineteen-year-old who had been born in coastal West Africa and then forcibly shipped to Kingston, Jamaica – remained a slave.[36] His mistress wrote that he 'remained with [her husband] as his Sailor, his Servant, and, *in the Operation of his servile Mind, his Slave*', suggesting a psychological rather than legal definition of slavery.[37] Elsewhere, she claimed that John had been a gift from another naval captain to her husband.[38] Her nursery maid agreed that John was a slave, although the other servants did not. John himself insisted that he was free.[39] Although the case began in 1785, thirteen years after the Mansfield judgment, John Webb's master threatened in print that he 'could most certainly have turned him over to any ship

that was going to the East or West Indies, without the smallest difficulty'.[40] One witness claimed that John was 'absolutely frightened and
fearful of being flogged if he contradicted his then Master ... and perhaps he said sent back to the West Indies where he had formerly been
a slave'.[41] Other testimony revealed that he had not received wages
from his master.[42] All of this emerged only because it was relevant
to the separation case between John's master and mistress, and even
once it had been said (on oath), it was largely ignored: the lawyers and
judge resolutely overlooked and/or mischaracterised the power relations involved. Nobody suggested that John Webb could not be a slave
because slavery did not exist in England.

This case also exposed a broader undercurrent of racial hostility. A
fellow servant described 'two or three little Boys' throwing pebbles at
John as he led his master's coach across Rochester Bridge one day: they
had been 'laughing and making their sport of him because he was a
Black'.[43] In addition, he had been 'several times illtreated by People in
the Streets'.[44] Meanwhile, the coachman testified that his mistress had
'always appeared to him ... rather to dislike and be afraid of the said
John Webb, which he attributed to his being a black' – a suggestion
that likely tells us at least as much about the coachman's own perceptions of race.[45] In this context, the 'invisibility' of racial abuse in other
types of source does not prove that black people 'were neither slaves
nor stigmatised outsiders during the long eighteenth century, when
the British slave trade was being conducted'.[46] There was little legal
or cultural clarity about the status of servants who either were or had
once been slaves. This meant that some black people in Britain could
redefine themselves through christening, renaming and escape, while
others were left open to abuse.

Colonial power in the metropole

The 'social and security structure' of Barbados, the first colonial slave
society, amounted to 'a terror network which spanned the island' by the
eighteenth century.[47] But in 1762, the former president of the council
of Barbados found that he could rely on no such structure in Britain. A
runaway livery servant, described as his property, was returned to him
early that year. But in March, an advertisement explained that he had
'absconded again, since a Reward was given for taking him'. 'If he will
come of his own Accord, he shall be forgiven,' his master claimed, 'and
meet with the useful Clemency he has had shewn him.'[48] Three days

later, a second advertisement added that he was 'well known at Bath and Bristol, and was inticed away by some Blacks' – the stuff of Fielding's nightmares.[49] Colonel Valentine Morris, an Antiguan planter and justice of the peace, asserted his power with similar caution in the metropolis. In 1723, an act of the council and assembly in Antigua ordered that several runaway slaves were to be put to death if they did not return within a month. Morris was one of the owners named.[50] Three years earlier, however, he had tried to recover a black livery servant who had run away from his London lodgings. In his English advertisement, he said only that anyone who brought him back would receive a guinea. '[I]f the said John Buff will return to his said Master within a week,' he added, 'he shall be well receiv'd.'[51] Threats that were enshrined in law in the colonies could not be openly voiced in London papers.

Yet this tells us little about the experience of black servants who did not run away, but remained subject to oppressive colonial masters. At this point, we can return to 'the Slave *Ann Williams*' – and to her mistress, Mrs Judith Edwards. Judith was the daughter of Andrew Lesley, former president of the council of Antigua. Her first marriage had been to an Antiguan planter called Charles Williams; this was where Ann's (alleged) surname came from. After Charles' death, Judith had come to England for the education of her daughters. In 1771, still in England, she had married Captain Thomas Edwards. Their marriage had quickly broken down, and she was now accused of having a child by the second of two extramarital lovers. Like many Leeward Islands planters, Charles Williams had died thousands of pounds in debt.[52] In turn, Judith was grievously indebted. Her illegitimate child had been born in King's Bench, a debtors' prison, and the 'Sale and Hire of several Negro Slaves' that she described was likely a way to pay off creditors.[53]

The Edwards' marital dispute had already been heard in the church court, which could grant permission for a couple to separate. It was here that the 'false Evidences of [Judith's] own Slaves, Mustees and Mulattoes' had allegedly swung the case against her. But to secure a divorce, Captain Edwards had to get a private bill passed by the House of Lords. This was the legal context that brought Ann before the lords in 1779. The House of Lords journal, based on manuscript minutes taken in court, recorded both the questions put to her and her answers. She was introduced as '*Ann Dennis*, a Black Woman'. First, she was asked if she was a Christian and could swear her testimony on oath:

yes, she said, 'she had been christened when young, and brought up as such'. Because she had to explain how she knew Judith Edwards, she went on to relate part of her own history:

> That she had known Mrs. *Edwards* from a Child; that she had, before her Marriage with Mr. *Edwards*, been married to a *Mr. Williams*, by whom she had Two Children, both of whom are now living; that she knew Mr. *Edwards* at *St. Vincents*; that she, the Witness, upon Mr. *Edwards* leaving *St. Vincents* was a free Woman, but that Mrs. *Edwards* broke open her Chest and stole her Freedom thereout, and then sold her for a Slave ... that she, the Witness, did not live with Mrs. *Edwards* when her Husband went from *St. Vincents* ... Being asked, What Capacity she lived in with Mrs. *Edwards* at *St. Vincents*; said, she was sent for to nurse the Children.

Ann was unable to offer a chronology for the story that she told, 'she never having been learnt the Days of the Week, Month or Year'. But she had come to London with her mistress in 1766, moving across the city four times between October that year and March 1777.[54] Their most recent landlady, Elizabeth Hayes, incidentally described the presence in her household of 'a Black Woman Servant called *Nanny*, who is *Ann Williams* (the Deponent's Fellow Witness)'. At one point, when Judith had disappeared into her bedchamber with her lover, Elizabeth had been 'left alone in the Dining Room with *Ann Williams* (the Black) and the little Girl (Miss *Edwards*)'. In September 1777, Judith had abruptly moved out of the house to conceal her pregnancy; after this, 'her Daughters and the Black Woman staid' until close to the end of the contract in December. Elizabeth also recalled Judith, her daughters, her lover, her brother and Ann going out to the theatre that spring.[55]

After this, '*Ann Dennis* was again called in'. It became clear that she had set the case in motion: the captain's lawyer referred to her as 'a material Witness' and also called her Ann Dennis rather than Ann Williams. Until Captain Edwards' lawyer had summoned her, Ann claimed, she had said nothing about his wife's affair to him. She had, however, reported it to both his sister-in-law and Judith's sister. She was asked why she had done this, and 'said, because she thought it right; that she told it to Mrs. *Walkin*, Mrs. *Edwards's* Sister, who knew that she the Witness was Mrs. *Edwards's* Maid, and that she thought she had a Right to clear herself'. Mary Walkin testified next: she explained that 'she first heard of the *West India* Story [about Judith Edwards' first affair] from *Ann Dennis'*, and after this 'she the Witness told Mr. *Edwards* ... that his Wife was gone off with Child; that the Black Woman told her so'.[56] Ann was at the centre of the case and was taken seriously as a witness to her mistress's adultery. But she was repeatedly othered as 'the Black' or 'the Black Woman'; two different names were used for her without acknowledgement, let alone explanation; and her slave status was overlooked, even though relationships of dependency were often questioned in English courts.

When Ann testified on oath that her mistress had stolen her 'Freedom' – this must have meant a freedom certificate – she was answering questions put to her by her mistress's counsel. She was not asked when she had become free, what her relationship to Charles Williams had been, to whom she had been sold, how she had ended up back in Judith's service, or where the surname 'Dennis' came from. The case was about adultery, not slave status. But the representation of Ann in the House of Lords journal is more broadly characteristic of how we encounter black subjects in these sources. The archival silences here are not those of eighteenth-century Barbados. Ann could testify against her mistress before some of the most powerful men in Britain, and, in the process, disavow what was likely her former owner's name. Her testimony was recorded and reproduced in the same way as anyone else's. But this meant that its ambiguities were also recorded and reproduced. Because racial power relations in Britain were uncodified and rarely discussed, and because popular understandings of slavery could matter as much as legal precedent, black servants in Britain were in an inherently precarious position. The abolitionist movement tried to make these power dynamics visible, forcing the reading public to confront their own complicity in the slave trade and colonial violence. But these sources suggest that enslaved and formerly enslaved people remained vulnerable.

Conclusion

Recent work on Britain's eighteenth-century black population downplays the significance of colonial dynamics. Yet most black people in Britain worked as servants or sailors, serving masters with colonial experience or at least colonial knowledge. Black servants' transatlantic histories stayed with them, too: the fraught politics of naming and christening, the physical and psychological marks left by slavery, their unwanted ties to past owners. The experiences of enslaved and formerly enslaved people were different everywhere in the British Atlantic world, ranging from freedom and self-sufficiency to abject servitude, from hawking or artisanal work to field labour. The question is not whether black lives in Britain were the same as black lives in Antigua or Bridgetown or New York, but where Britain fits into this wider context. This means asking both what the metropole meant to colonial subjects, and what the colonies meant in Britain.

Often, points of interracial contact in Britain were also points of contact between colony and metropole. In 1753, for instance, an apprentice visited 'the West India Ship' moored on Newcastle's quayside and viewed '2 or 3 Tortesses alive, a Parrott & Parrokett, a Negro Boy, Munkey & pine apples'. This taught him to view the boy as a commodity and, in his own words, a 'curiosity which I was a stranger to'.[57] Later in the century, ideas about blackness became more closely linked to the political debate over slavery. The uncertain relationship between Britain and its colonies was thrust into public view, with people on both sides of the debate forced to reassess their loyalties. William Dickson, who had been secretary to the governor of Barbados for over a decade, bridged the gap between metropolitan and colonial sensibilities. In Barbados, where planters referred to their island as 'Little England' and viewed themselves as devoted English subjects, the growth of abolitionism came as a shocking betrayal.[58] Dickson's *Letters on Slavery* similarly described it as 'an island, for which, as an ancient, valuable and loyal British colony, I cannot but express my regard'. But his experience there had steered him towards abolitionism, and he went on to catalogue the savagery of Barbadian plantation life.[59] Significantly, he maintained that it made little sense to blame West Indians alone: 'the whole British nation ... ought to be considered as particeps criminis [partners in crime]'.[60] Viewed from this perspective, the ambiguities of slavery in Britain begin to look like both a form of collusion and a starting point for historical enquiry.

The two types of source on which this chapter has focused – runaway advertisements and witness testimony – can be usefully read from this perspective. Both tell us about black men and women who were possibly free (their status was left unclear) or tenuously free (their status was fragile). Both describe colonial power relations that were imported into the metropole – modified to fit their new legal and societal context, but left essentially intact. And both leave out, pass quickly over, or fail to address the contradictions and uncertainties that shaped black lives in Britain. It is this context that explains the divergent experiences of Britain's eighteenth-century black population, the ambiguities of our surviving sources, and the starkly different claims of literary scholars and a genealogist such as Kathleen Chater. It is also this context that connects eighteenth-century black history to the longer story of race and the British Empire.

Notes

1 'House of Lords Journal Volume 35: February 1779 21–30' in *Journal of the House of Lords. Volume 35: 1776–1779* (London: 1767–1830), pp. 583–99. *British History Online*, http://www.british-history.ac.uk/lords-jrnl/vol35/pp583-599, accessed 18 December 2017.

2 Folarin Shyllon, *Black Slaves in Britain* (Oxford: Oxford University Press, 1974), pp. 175–6.

3 Simon Schama, Rough Crossings: Britain, the Slaves and the American Revolution (London: BBC Books, 2009), p. 70.

4 Folarin Shyllon, *Black People in Britain, 1555–1833* (London: Oxford University Press, 1977); Shyllon, *Black Slaves in Britain*.

5 Norma Myers, *Reconstructing the Black Past: Blacks in Britain, 1780–1830* (London: Frank Cass, 1996), p. 1.

6 Peter King and John Carter Wood, 'Black People and the Criminal Justice System: Prejudice and Practice in Later Eighteenth- and Early Nineteenth-century London', *Historical Research* 88/239 (2015), p. 108.

7 Kathleen Chater, *Untold Histories: Black People in England and Wales During the Period of the British Slave Trade, c. 1660–1807* (Manchester: Manchester University Press, 2011).

8 George Boulukos, *The Grateful Slave: The Emergence of Race in Eighteenth-century British and American Culture* (Cambridge: Cambridge University Press, 2008), pp. 77, 99.

9 Kathleen Wilson, *The Island Race: Englishness, Empire and Gender in the Eighteenth Century* (London: Routledge, 2003), p. 48.

10 Marisa J. Fuentes, *Dispossessed Lives: Enslaved Women, Violence, and the Archive* (Philadelphia: University of Pennsylvania Press, 2016), p. 5.

11 Fuentes, *Dispossessed Lives*, pp. 4, 62.

12 Trevor Burnard, '"A Matron in Rank, A Prostitute in Manners": The Manning Divorce of 1741 and Class, Gender, Race and the Law in Eighteenth-century Jamaica' in Verene Shepherd (ed.), *Working Slavery, Pricing Freedom: Perspectives from the Caribbean, Africa and the African Diaspora* (Oxford: Oxford University Press, 2002), pp. 138–9.

13 I searched for the keywords 'negro' and 'black servant' on the seventeenth- and eighteenth-century Burney Collection database.

14 Cf. Catherine Hall, *Civilising Subjects: Metropole and Colony in the English Imagination, 1830–1867* (Oxford: Polity Press, 2002), p. 10.

15 Quoting Ira Berlin, *Generations of Captivity: A History of African-American Slaves* (London and Cambridge MA: Belknap Press of Harvard University Press, 2003), p. 9. Cf. Hilary Beckles, *The First Black Slave Society: Britain's 'Barbarity Time' in Barbados, 1636–1876* (Kingston: University of the West Indies Press, 2016), pp. 1–2.

16 *Daily Advertiser*, 15 August 1745.

17   John Fielding, *Extracts from Such of the Penal Laws* (London: Printed by S. Richardson and C. Lintot for A. Millar, 1761), p. 143.

18   *Public Advertiser*, 29 October 1757; *Public Advertiser*, 22 November 1758; *Public Advertiser*, 12 February 1760; *Public Advertiser*, 13 December 1760; *Public Advertiser*, 30 October 1762; *Public Advertiser*, 15 January 1763; *Public Advertiser*, 6 June 1763; *Gazetteer and New Daily Advertiser*, 5 May 1764; *Public Advertiser*, 6 November 1764; *Public Advertiser*, 22 June 1754.

19   *Daily Advertiser*, 31 December 1743.

20   Simon P. Newman, *Embodied History: The Lives of the Poor in Early Philadelphia* (Philadelphia: University of Pennsylvania Press, 2003), p. 83.

21   See, for example, *Public Advertiser*, 9 March 1758; *British Journal*, 26 December 1724; *Public Advertiser*, 17 June 1761.

22   For carpenters, see *Public Advertiser*, 17 June 1761, *Gazetteer and New Daily Advertiser*, 12 October 1763; for a glazier and tinker who had run away in Virginia, see *Daily Post*, 17 December 1724. A thirty-year-old enslaved man was described as 'Master of the Trade of a Baker', while a twenty-year-old who ran away in South Wales was said to have 'work'd at the Ship Carpenters Business': *Gazetteer and New Daily Advertiser*, 15 May 1764; *Daily Journal*, 12 April 1753.

23   *Public Advertiser*, 15 January 1763.

24   *Public Advertiser*, 16 April 1757.

25   *Gazetteer and New Daily Advertiser*, 31 October 1765.

26   *Daily Advertiser*, 30 July 1744; *Gazetteer and New Daily Advertiser*, 21 February 1765; *Public Advertiser*, 27 June 1771; *Daily Advertiser*, 28 January 1761; *London Evening Post*, 13–15 September 1770; *Daily Courant*, 5 October 1714.

27   *Daily Courant*, 23 January 1710.

28   Keith Mason, 'The Absentee Planter and the Key Slave: Privilege, Patriarchalism, and Exploitation in the Early Eighteenth-century Caribbean', *William and Mary Quarterly* 70/1 (2013), pp. 86, 93–9.

29   *The Cuckold's Chronicle: Being Select Trials for Adultery, Incest, Imbecility, Ravishment, &c* (London: H. Lemoin, 1793), Volume 2, pp. 315–16.

30   *The Cuckold's Chronicle*, pp. 325–6.

31   Lambeth Palace Library (hereafter LPL), VH 80 44/11, fo. 17b.

32   *The Arguments of Counsel in the Ecclesiastical Court, in the Cause of Inglefield* (London: J. Murray, 1787), p. 24.

33   See, for example, *Lloyd's Evening Post*, 9–11 March 1767.

34   *Public Advertiser*, 17 April 1771.

35   *Gazetteer and New Daily Advertiser*, 10 March 1769.

36   I am currently working on an article about this case, and so deal with it only in passing here.

37   Ann Inglefield, *Mrs. Inglefield's Justification, Containing the Proceedings in the Ecclesiastical Court, Before the Right Worshipful Peter Calvert* (London: J. Sewell and J. Bew, 1787), p. xxx, emphasis added.

38   LPL, VH 80/44/7, fos. 2a–b.

39   LPL, VH 80 44/11, fo. 4b; VH 80 44/9, fo. 1a-3b.

40   Captain John Nicholson Inglefield, *Captain Inglefield's Vindication of His Conduct* (London: J. Murray, 1787), p. 43.

41   LPL, VH/80/44/32, fos. 15b–16a.

42   LPL, VH 80 44/11, fo. 17b.

43   LPL, VH/80/44/32, fo. 14b.

44   LPL, VH 80 44/21, fo. 10b.

45   LPL, VH 80/44/11, fo. 56a.

46   Chater, *Untold Histories*, p. 240.

47   Beckles, *The First Black Slave Society*, p. 160.

48   *St James's Chronicle or the Evening Post*, 13 March 1762.

49   *St James's Chronicle*, 16 March 1762.

50 *The Laws of the Island of Antigua: Consisting of the Acts of the Leeward Islands ... and the Acts of Antigua* (London: Samuel Bagster, 1805), pp. 215–16.

51 *Daily Post*, 22 February 1720.

52 Elsa V. Goveia, *Slave Society in the British Leeward Islands at the End of the Eighteenth Century* (New Haven: Yale University Press), p. 107.

53 'House of Lords Journal', p. 595.

54 'House of Lords Journal', p. 603.

55 'House of Lords Journal', pp. 604–5.

56 'House of Lords Journal', p. 605.

57 Peter Wright, *Life on the Tyne: Water Trades on the Lower River Tyne in the Seventeenth and Eighteenth Centuries, a Reappraisal* (London: Routledge, 2016), p. 77.

58 Beckles, *The First Black Slave Society Slave Society*, p. 176.

59 William Dickson, *Letters on Slavery* (London: J. Phillips, 1789), p. 5.

60 Dickson, *Letters on Slavery*, p. 91.

3 | 'RACE', RANK, AND THE POLITICS OF INTER-WAR COMMEMORATION OF AFRICAN AND CARIBBEAN SERVICEMEN IN BRITAIN

John Siblon

Introduction

The centenary of World War One has led to renewed reflection on its impact, not just on British history, but also on global history. Historians such as David Olusoga, Santanu Das and others have written books and presented TV programmes that have ensured that a less Eurocentric narrative is beginning to emerge, one that has been widened to include the participation of non-combatants, faiths, genders and ethnicities.[1] There is still much work to be done, however, regarding the service of groups who have been previously written out of the narrative of the war or who have had their contributions marginalised. Two such groups, I would argue, are African and Caribbean peoples.

The aim of this chapter is twofold. Firstly, it provides a brief overview of black African and Caribbean deployment in different theatres of war; and, secondly, it surveys the post-war rituals, monuments and war cemeteries to establish whether Black British and colonial war service was commemorated to the same extent as white servicemen and women in Britain.[2] I argue that our present-day remembrance of black colonial war service was mediated in the immediate aftermath of the conflict by politicians who used memorial culture and other means to symbolically and politically relegate black ex-servicemen to an inferior position in society. They did so to calm imperial anxieties about the social advancement of subject peoples. Unlike previous histories of black peoples in the British Army, I want to include black African and Caribbean colonial forces in a single analysis as I believe this will help explain the official 'race thinking' behind their deployment.[3] I also believe that by studying the construction of the memory of the war it is possible to build a more comprehensive picture of whether the conflict in any way changed the perceived lower status of African and Caribbean peoples in the imperial racial hierarchy.

Black war service in the multiple theatres

Black servicemen have a long tradition of military service in the British Army and Royal Navy going back to the eighteenth century.[4] In the 'enlistment' section of the 1914 version of the *Manual of Military Law* it stated that 'aliens' could enlist in the army at a proportion of one to every fifty British subjects but should not be permitted to attain the status of an officer; that 'any negro or person of colour, although an alien, may voluntarily enlist' on the above terms; and that 'aliens' could hold honorary commissions on the basis that they do not 'exercise any actual command or power'.[5] These orders meant that blacks could serve in the lower ranks of the British Army or colonial forces, as they had done since the Napoleonic Wars.[6] In 1902, the Committee of Imperial Defence had issued a memorandum which stated that the 'main burden of a great struggle between the British Empire and one or more states of European race or descent must be borne by white subjects of the king', adding: 'Military contingents therefore of other than men of European descent need not be considered.'[7] It was intended that black colonial forces would not be involved in a 'white man's war' in Europe. As the British Empire expanded in Africa, the West India Regiment (WIR) had been displaced, in the eyes of military planners, by African 'martial races', who the planners felt were more suited to policing threats of revolts in the newly acquired colonies than the less 'martial' Caribbeans.[8] Such views of the black soldiers of empire were based on Western notions that all individuals were born with innate, biologically determined characteristics. Any differences between human groups were ascribed to inherited traits and much effort was put into classifying peoples into different groups or 'races'. British colonial and military officials applied 'racialised' thinking to 'negroes' in particular, who they believed were innate 'savages' and suited to the military but not on an equal footing with whites.[9] Such official attitudes to Caribbean servicemen partly explain the initial reluctance to accept black volunteers in the British Army, despite offers after the declaration of war in 1914. Yet African soldiers were not considered for service in Europe either.

For some British military and colonial officials (as well as German ones) it was unthinkable for black soldiers to fight alongside whites in Europe and even to kill them, as they believed this would damage the notion of 'white solidarity' among the colonial powers; better for whites to kill each other than to employ blacks to do this.[10] The French, however, held a different view. They were happy to use North and West African troops in combat, albeit to preserve the lives of white French troops. The British reluctantly employed Indian troops on the Western Front before sending the bulk of the Indian army to serve in Mesopotamia and East Africa for the rest of the war.[11] Officials used pseudo-science to explain their disinclination to use black soldiers in Europe. 'Negro' soldiers, they explained, were best suited to fighting only in tropical climates. In temperate regions, where they were susceptible to diseases bought on by cold weather, they were best suited for labour or ancillary roles.[12] This attempt to explain military deployment as determined by biology was the essence of 'racial' thinking at that time.

As the war progressed, however, for political reasons and due to manpower shortages, British officials tempered their attitudes to the non-recruitment of blacks and allowed men from the newly formed British West Indies Regiment (BWIR), the Bermuda Militia Artillery (BMA), the South African Native Labour Corps (SANLC), the Cape Auxiliary Horse Transport Corps (CAHTC) and the Cape Coloured Labour Corps (CCLC) to serve on the Western Front on a strictly non-combatant basis and on condition that they had to be under the leadership of white officers.[13] These men served as labourers, digging trenches, laying cables, loading shells, guarding ammunition dumps, tending animals and constructing railways. Later, they would be joined in Europe by over 200,000 Labour Corps from across the British Empire: Egypt, India, Fiji, Mauritius and the Seychelles.[14] Thousands of colonial African and Caribbean volunteers served in the Royal Navy and Merchant Navy in the lowest ranks and with inferior status.[15] Many Black Britons had also volunteered and been accepted into the armed services.[16] It is estimated that, in Liverpool, 15 per cent of all Black British and colonial subjects joined up – a much higher rate than comparable groups.[17] It is incorrect, therefore, for historians to portray events in Europe and other theatres as 'a white man's war'.

Outside Europe, in the West and East African theatres, black African formations such as the King's African Rifles (KAR) and the West African Frontier Force (WAFF) served as combatants against African *Askaris* and also on condition that they were led by white officers.[18] The fighting in the African theatre would not have been possible without an army of over a million African carriers, porters, guides and camp followers, including females, on both sides. Small detachments of Caribbeans from the WIR, the BWIR and the Cape Corps (CC) were engaged in combat in West and East Africa and in Mesopotamia. The racially codified military deployment in these theatres ensured that black and 'coloured' servicemen killed mainly Africans or those from within the Ottoman Empire.

Recent histories have emphasised the fact that many Black Britons served in fighting British regiments. They have pointed to a number of black servicemen and a handful who attained the rank of officer as evidence that there was no colour bar or barrier to recruitment except in the officer class.[19] Other historians have conceded that official prohibition of black enlistment was not absolute but have cautioned that officials consistently sought to undermine black enlistment where possible.[20] It may never be known how many Black Britons or colonials served in the British Army in British units. The black population in Britain was around 10,000 at the start of the war and swelled as the war progressed.[21] Figures for the colonial contingents are more accurate. What is clear is that during the war blacks and whites served alongside each other in different theatres and, in some cases, there is evidence that these encounters changed the perceptions of individuals of different 'races' for the better.[22]

These cultural encounters ended abruptly after the fighting ended. The SANLC was disbanded in 1918 and the CAHTC and CC suffered a similar fate in 1919. The BWIR and the WIR had both mutinied at their wartime mistreatment; the BWIR was disbanded in 1919 and the WIR, with over 130 years of history, was disbanded in 1927.[23] This did not prevent Caribbean ex-servicemen venting their frustration at the colonial authorities over their racist mistreatment and deployment; veterans participated in a number of disturbances across the islands in 1919.[24] Meanwhile, in Britain, any goodwill towards African, Caribbean, Arab and Asian seafarers soon evaporated after demobilisation, as whites violently attacked black colonial seamen whom they blamed for the lack of jobs in an industry that had retracted sharply on conclusion of hostilities. There were a number of 'race riots' in port cities across Britain in 1919 and five people were killed during the violence.[25] The armed services were becoming white again. This was the context in which government and military officials met to discuss commemoration of the national and imperial war effort.

The Peace Day Parade of 1919

In 1919, the British War Cabinet appointed a Peace Celebrations Committee to organise official celebrations of the end of the war. Sir

Gilbert Grindle, representing the Colonial Office, argued against invit-ing blacks to a proposed victory march in July 1919 on the basis that it would be 'inviting trouble'.[26] He was supported by another member of the Colonial Office, Sir Henry Lambert, who pointed out the official government policy after the 'race riots' was to repatriate black African and Caribbean seamen and their wives. The use of the words 'inviting trouble' suggests that the Colonial Office had problematised all black ex-servicemen despite evidence showing that black seamen were the victims of violence.[27] The many instances of rioting involving white dominion troops in London were overlooked.[28] A decision was taken that black troops and seamen should not be invited to the London march.

Even when officials changed their views, after pressure from the Dominions and the India Office, to include white dominion and Indian military representation, the Colonial Office held firm; African and Caribbean peoples were still not invited.[29] The official programme for the Peace Day celebration of 19 July 1919 shows that the Americans and the Allies led off the parade. The French contingent included a company of *Zouaves* and *Tirailleurs* from France's North and West African territories. The dominions were represented by Australians, New Zealanders, Canadians and white South Africans.[30] Indian troops had not arrived in time for the parade but some Indian officers were in the procession. The Peace Day Parade was an important event in the construction of the memory of the war. No Black British colonial troops had been invited to the victory march and an order of prece-dence was established that laid the framework for official remembrance rituals in the succeeding years. The first Armistice Day ceremony in November 1920 was presided over by virtually the same officials who had arranged the 1919 exclusion and so a 'tradition' of excluding black servicemen was established.[31]

The Cenotaph and the Tomb of the Unknown Warrior

The exclusion of black ex-servicemen in London in 1919 can be extended to those who had died in the war. During the Peace Day celebrations, troops had marched past a temporary structure of an empty tomb, a cenotaph, designed by Sir Edwin Lutyens to represent a dead British serviceman.[32] After the march past was over, 400,000 people visited the Cenotaph to grieve and pay homage to the dead of the conflict.[33] There were calls from the public for the Cenotaph to become a permanent feature in Whitehall. They desperately needed a place to mourn those whose bodies lay in cemeteries overseas that were not easily accessible.[34] The government agreed to a permanent Cenotaph which would be unveiled on Armistice Day 1920.

Was the Cenotaph conceptualised as an inclusive imperial memorial or a national one? If it was an imperial monument, then dead African and Caribbean servicemen might conceivably be among those mourned by the public. If it was conceived as a national monument, then it is possible to see how only white British servicemen were mourned. Historians have described nation states as 'imagined communities' and 'Britishness' as an identity imposed on diverse communities. During wartime, this 'British' identity became more defined and Black Britons, despite their service, were perceived as having a 'lesser' British identity.[35] In 1920, when discussing the unveiling of the Cenotaph in Whitehall, a Cabinet official reminded those present that 'the Cenotaph was an imperial monument commemorating men of many races and creeds'.[36] After the unveiling, Lloyd George wrote to Lutyens and thanked him for designing a 'shrine not only for the British Isles but also for the whole of the British Empire'.[37] One cannot know with any certainty which 'empire' Lutyens wanted to be represented in the Cenotaph. Historians have noted that his designs included European classical forms in the service of the British Empire, such as the Viceroy's House in New Delhi, which was constructed to dominate the skyline and to remind Indians of the dominance of the British and the lesser place of Indians in the colonial hierarchy.[38] It is conceivable that, while Lutyens did take into consideration the contributions of Indians and Africans in the war, 'empire' meant the continued dominance of the British over subject peoples. In this way of thinking, Asians, Caribbeans and Africans were not considered present in the 'community of sacrifice'.[39] Over time, as Britain lost its empire, the Cenotaph lost the imperial connection and became a symbol of the nation state.

The decision to symbolically bury a British serviceman in Westminster Abbey on the same day as the unveiling of the Cenotaph was made in October 1920. A request was made by the Dean of Westminster, Herbert Ryle, for a public funeral in the Abbey with a surrogate body in Britain for those families who were unable to visit the war cemeteries in France and Belgium.[40] The Cabinet agreed to this on the basis that no one person was being favoured in the proposed public ceremony, as the identity of the soldier would be unknown. They believed that the public would appreciate the opportunity to honour an anonymous body of a fighting man in the absence of gravesites in Britain. They could believe that the body in the coffin might be a relative. Six bodies without identifying marks were exhumed from locations in Ypres, Arras, the Somme, Cambrai, the Aisne and the Marne. The bodies were placed in coffins and taken to Ypres, where a blindfolded officer selected an anonymous coffin containing a body to be transported to England for burial.[41]

At the time, many people believed that the body of the Unknown Warrior could be any soldier of any 'race' from within the British Empire who had served on the Western Front. *The Times* newspaper proclaimed that the body 'may have been born to a high position or to low; he may have been a sailor, a soldier, an airman; an Englishman, a Scotsman, a Welshman, an Irishman, a man of the Dominions, a Sikh, a Gurkha. No one knows.'[42] Adrian Gregory has pointed out that the body could not have been from the Navy, Air Force or a dominion, and could not have been a black colonial, Indian, Kitchener volunteer, conscript or territorial.[43] This was because the Memorial Services Committee was determined that there should be a 'British' character to the commemoration. When Herbert Ryle had suggested exhuming a body, he made it clear that he wanted to bury the bones of a body from a specific location and only from 1914.[44] This meant that the selected body of the Unknown Warrior, despite conveying anonymity in terms of name, rank and regiment, could only be white and British. It is plausible to suggest that Ryle knew that, by limiting the scope of where the body was obtained by year and location, the consequence would be that a white British corpse would be honoured. If this is the case, then the nationality of the body, despite serving its purpose as a surrogate to mourn and grieve, was unknown to the public but not wholly unknown to Cabinet officials.[45]

The 'One Million Dead of the British Empire' memorial

In 1923, the Imperial War Graves Commission (IWGC), which had been established in 1917 to care for the war graves and memory of the dead and missing of the British Empire, responded to requests from the dominion governments for a greater acknowledgement of their war losses.[46] In response, they commissioned a series of tablets dedicated to the war dead of the British Empire to be erected in cathedrals throughout France and Belgium and in Westminster Abbey. The tablets were designed, in a hierarchical style, with the

Figure 3.1 The coffin of the Unknown Warrior in Westminster Abbey. Photograph courtesy of the Commonwealth War Graves Commission.

British coats of arms surrounded by the coats of arms of India, Canada, Australia, Newfoundland, New Zealand and South Africa. The Caribbean colonies were contributors to the Commission, but, despite paying a contribution towards the cost of the tablets, they were not represented on them, and neither were Britain's African colonies.[47] This omission appears to represent a continuation of the official policy of excluding black colonial troops in commemorative practice. The tablet, titled the 'One Million Dead of the British Empire', was erected in Westminster Abbey in 1926 in time for the Imperial Conference of British and dominion leaders later that year.

An interesting exchange of letters in 1932 between the IWGC and an ex-sergeant from the BWIR, T. A. Daley, casts some light on official attitudes of the time regarding colonial commemoration. Daley wrote of his disappointment at not seeing the Caribbean and other colonies represented on the tablets in Westminster Abbey and Notre Dame Cathedral. Daley suggested that the Caribbean colonies could be inscribed retrospectively on the tablet. The issue was debated at the highest level and Major-General Sir Fabian Ware, the vice chairman of the IWGC, corresponded with Sir Algernon Aspinall, the secretary of the West India Committee. In the correspondence, it was acknowledged by the Commission that Caribbean governments were contributors to the cost of the memorials. Aspinall, supporting the

Figure 3.2 A replica of the 'One Million Dead of the British Empire' tablet. Photograph courtesy of Westminster Abbey Library.

IWGC, wrote back to Daley, stating that there was 'no room' to put the colonies on the tablet; that Britain had a 'special relationship' with the dominions; and that all colonies were represented on the tablet by the British coat of arms. Daley responded to Aspinall:

> No mention whatever is made of the loyal colonies, as if they do not constitute part of the British Empire. No stranger to the fact can be expected to see in these memorials that the British West Indies and the other colonies played any part in the war: nor could future generations reading the plaques be expected to draw any other conclusion that in the Great War of 1914–1918, the British West Indies and the overseas colonies of the Mother Country were conspicuous by their absence.[48]

Unfortunately, the correspondence ends at this point. The memorial still remains on public display in Westminster Abbey without acknowledgement of the colonies' contribution.

The Royal Navy and Merchant Navy memorials

For bodies that were missing or buried at sea, memorials to the missing were constructed in military cemeteries. An imperial order of precedence appears on all these memorials. Reading left to right, the names of British servicemen are always first and arranged by Navy, Army and Air Force, followed by names from the dominions and India, which had not then achieved dominion status, and lastly those from the colonies. This is a hierarchy of rank, but I argue that it intersects with one of 'race'. In 1920, discussions began between the Commission and the Admiralty over the design and construction of naval memorials for the missing. The first discussion between the two branches resulted in a decision to erect memorials in the main naval ports of Chatham, Portsmouth and Plymouth; the second discussion was to clarify policy regarding the commemoration of dominion sailors, Chinese, Indian 'Lascars', African 'Seedie Boys' and 'Kroomen'.[49] It was suggested in 1921 that white and dark-skinned sailors should be commemorated in separate locations. Chinese sailors would be commemorated in Hong Kong, 'Lascars' in Bombay, and 'Seedie Boys' and 'Kroomen' in Aden.[50] White British and dominion sailors could be commemorated in Britain.

By 1922, it was clear that the IWGC wanted all the names of African, Caribbean and Asian seamen, whether in the Royal Navy or Merchant Navy, commemorated away from Britain. Henry Chettle, the Director of Records at the IWGC, calculated the total deaths of 'native' merchant seamen as 2,255. He estimated that 490 were Chinese and the remainder (1,765) Indians or West Africans. He could not distinguish, however, between the Indian, East African or West African names, so the proposal for an Aden memorial for 'Seedie Boys' and 'Kroomen' was abandoned, and, instead, a decision made to commemorate Chinese seamen in Hong Kong, and all other 'native' seamen in Bombay. Chettle was aware that this would result in African and Caribbean sailors having their names on the proposed memorial in India. He discussed with the Management Committee the idea that the names of West Africans (and Caribbeans) be 'allowed to slip in' on the joint memorial in Bombay.[51] The Admiralty accepted this decision, which meant that black seamen from the Royal Navy and the Merchant Navy would not be commemorated in Britain.

The decision to separately commemorate African, Asian, Arab and Caribbean sailors on memorials away from Britain was not an oversight but an objective of the IWGC and the Navy. By 1923, the Admiralty commissioners had responded favourably to the Commission suggestion that 'Native Ratings' be excluded from the Royal Navy memorials proposed for Chatham, Portsmouth and Plymouth. Officials in the Navy concurred with the proposal that 'all men of colour serving under any form of Naval engagement, including those in the Merchant Marine Reserve should be commemorated separately with other natives who died whilst serving in His Majesty's Forces'.[52] In the three coastal locations in Britain, the names of sailors who died in the war are commemorated first by year and then by rank alphabetically on the memorials. Some of the first names on the Portsmouth memorial, for example, are from HMS *Good Hope*, which was sunk at the Battle of Coronel in November 1914 with the loss of 916 lives. A look at the muster roll of HMS *Good Hope* shows that twenty-six stokers on the ship were Caribbean, mainly from St Lucia, but also from Barbados and Antigua.[53] The names of the white British stokers from HMS *Good Hope* are inscribed on the Portsmouth memorial but not the names of the Caribbean stokers who died alongside them. They are commemorated by name on the memorial in Bombay: a black memorial 'space' far from Britain.[54]

Figure 3.3 The Tower Hill memorial. The name 'Acquah' derives from Ghana. Photograph by John Siblon.

In 1923, the IWGC met to discuss constructing a memorial to the Mercantile Marine missing or buried at sea. The Commission made clear that the proposed memorial was for only 11,900 Europeans: meaning white seamen.[55] Tower Hill was eventually chosen as the location for the memorial, which was unveiled on 12 December 1928. Dominion representatives from South Africa, Australia, New Zealand, Canada and Newfoundland were invited but not representatives from India or the colonies. This was most likely because it was imagined and constructed as a white European memorial. However, a close look at the roll of honour or the physical memorial reveals many Asian, Arab and African names: a direct challenge to the whiteness of the memorial.

These names were most likely those of 'native' crew who served in the Atlantic Ocean theatre and were not separated into a distinct register like the East Africans, 'Lascars' and Chinese who died in the Indian and Pacific Ocean theatres, and so they were commemorated by name as 'British' on the Tower Hill memorial despite the original intentions of the Commission. It may be that officials in the IWGC knew that there were black seamen on the register but could not find a way of separating their names from those of white seamen. The records are silent on this contestation. Recently, historians have tried to present the memorial as a site conveying the British identity of West Africans and Bangladeshis who have a long-standing presence in the area.[56] The reality is that IWGC officials had attempted to exclude both these groups but were not successful on this occasion.

Africans and Caribbeans in cemeteries in Britain

The existence of cemetery plots in Britain with headstones for colonial servicemen from the Caribbean and South Africa appears to signify the enactment of the egalitarian principle of commemoration of individuals regardless of 'race, rank or creed' promoted by the IWGC.[57] In Seaford, Sussex, nineteen BWIR men are buried with headstones in the local cemetery. Their commemoration is nevertheless situated within a hierarchy of creed, 'race' and rank, as the Caribbean men were Christian and so their bodies were considered worthy of full commemoration in preparation for an afterlife. The IWGC had classified 'West Indian Natives i.e. negroes in West Indian Regiments' such as the BWIR and the WIR as 'Christians and Church of England', and so they could be buried individually in cemeteries among British and dominion soldiers in Commission plots or inscribed by name on memorials to the missing due to their religion.

Hollybrook memorial to the missing

Despite their designation as Christian, the BWIR were still subject to a hierarchical arrangement based on 'race' and rank on memorials in Britain. In Hollybrook Cemetery in Southampton there is a memorial to the missing, unveiled in 1930, inscribed with the names of Army and Air Force personnel from across the British Empire who died at sea in warships, military transports and hospital ships. British names are followed by white dominion names, and then those of the 'coloured' CAHTC and the 'native' SANLC. The naming of the lighter-skinned CAHTC before the darker-skinned SANLC reveals the hierarchical ordering by 'race' on the memorial, as 'coloured' was considered higher than 'native' or 'negro' in the perceived imperial racial hierarchy. The lower status on the memorial of both the 'coloured' and 'native' South Africans was not only due to their skin colour but also due to their designation as Labour Corps, who were at the lower end of the military hierarchy.[58] Here 'race' and rank intersect; native and coloured South Africans were assigned to the Labour Corps because of their skin colour, demonstrating how 'race' was often viewed as more significant than rank in military commemoration.

Figure 3.4 A 'race' and rank order of precedence exists on the Hollybrook memorial. Photograph by John Siblon.

The last names in the memorial hierarchy, due to their colonial status, were those of fifty-eight men of the BWIR.[59] Their position in this hierarchy was co-determined by their racial status and their military status.[60] Other racial signifiers on the memorial include the inscriptions 'Native' and 'Cape Auxiliary', which operated as recognition of both war service and position in a racial classification. The memorial is known today as the location where Lord Kitchener is commemorated, but also because the names of 615 men of the SANLC, who died when the SS *Mendi* transport ship sank in the English Channel in February 1917, are included on the memorial. The prominent position given to the names of the men who lost their lives on the SS *Mendi* suggests an instance of non-hierarchical commemoration of Africans. However, naval vessels also have an order of precedence. As they were on a troop ship, their names should have been on the upper level of the memorial, but their names are written separately on the lower level, serving as an example of the problematic nature of intersecting commemoration. The *Mendi* memorial has become a significant site of memory in South Africa and Britain.[61] Missing from the histories of the tragedy and its commemoration are at least twenty-five West African seamen who were part of the crew of the *Mendi*.[62] Their names are not on the memorial or on the Commonwealth War Graves Commission (CWGC) website. The omission may be because the collision was deemed to be due to 'maritime peril' rather than enemy action, and so the crew were not considered 'war dead'. The West Africans have not received the same attention from historians as the South African dead, suggesting a hierarchy of remembrance.[63] Finally, other CAHTC and SANLC personnel who did not perish on the *Mendi* have their names commemorated at the far right of the memorial, low down in the imperial military hierarchy due to their 'race' and rank.

South African Native Labour Corps graves as signifiers of racial status

There is further evidence that 'native' South Africans buried in cemetery plots were subject to a 'race' and rank hierarchy in Britain. Many bodies of SANLC men from the *Mendi* were washed ashore, recovered, and then buried. In Milton Road Cemetery in Portsmouth, six SANLC servicemen are buried in three graves. Around the graves are plenty of empty spaces, meaning that there was space for single burial plots. Directly opposite the three graves in the cemetery is that of a

Figure 3.5 SANLC graves at Milton Road Cemetery: those with multiple burials are marked with wreathes. Photograph by John Siblon.

Figure 3.6 Reproduction of a single grave for SANLC men at Noordwijk General Cemetery. Photograph by John Siblon.

white South African officer who drowned on the *Mendi*. He has his own plot with an individual headstone. In Littlehampton, Sussex, the bodies of all the other servicemen in the cemetery have their own plots with headstones, but three SANLC men are buried in just one plot sharing a single headstone.[64] In the Netherlands, there are four SANLC men buried in just one grave in Noordwijk General Cemetery.[65] The frequency of the multiple burials in a single plot for a distinct corps of a different colour, in different countries, cannot be merely coincidence. It appears to be a marker of racial status signifying the difference in perceived status between the 'native' labourers and other white servicemen, to remind visitors to cemeteries in Britain of their lower status in the racial hierarchy in South Africa and the British Empire.

Conclusion

Public acknowledgement and commemoration of black war service is a relatively recent phenomenon in Britain. The Memorial Gates on Constitution Hill, London, which are dedicated to 'Commonwealth' servicemen and women of both World Wars, were unveiled only in 2002. The four columns on the memorial are inscribed with the words 'The Caribbean' and 'Africa'. Caribbean ex-servicemen and women, among others, had to lobby for the memorial in Central London. In 2017, the African Caribbean War Memorial was unveiled in Brixton by the Nubian Jak Community Trust. The names of African and Caribbean regiments who served in the World Wars are inscribed on the memorial.[66] Retrospective memorialisation is thought necessary due to the lack of monuments and inclusive commemoration in Britain. The lack of commemoration can be traced back to imperial 'race' policy, which was enacted to keep darker-skinned subjects of the British Empire in their place in a constructed hierarchy. During the war, the policy had to be adjusted to necessitate victory, but, on conclusion of hostilities, there was a determined attempt by officials to revert back to the pre-war racial-imperial status quo. The enactment of this 'race' and rank policy designed to exclude or marginalise black war service is still visible and written in stone in cultural sites of memory around Britain.

Notes

1 David Olusoga, *The World's War* (London: Head of Zeus Ltd, 2014); Santanu Das (ed.), *Race, Empire and First World War Writing* (Cambridge: Cambridge University Press, 2011); Timothy C. Winegard, *Indigenous Peoples of the British Dominions and the First World War* (Cambridge: Cambridge University Press, 2012).

2 I use the term 'black' to describe African and Caribbean servicemen. This relates to skin colour but also overcomes the problematic use of the term 'colonial', which was first used to describe all subject peoples of the British Empire but which later described those from the African, Asian and Caribbean 'dependent' territories as opposed to those from the dominions. In British colonies, the term 'native' or 'negro' was used to describe most black African servicemen and 'coloured' to describe Caribbean

or lighter-skinned servicemen from the Cape region of South Africa. These terms will be used in the chapter, but to show how military and governmental bodies envisaged Africans and Caribbeans as racially classified bodies.

3 Paul B. Rich, *Race and Empire in British Politics* (Cambridge: Cambridge University Press, 1990), p. 2.

4 David Killingray, 'Race and Rank in the British Army in the Twentieth Century', *Ethnic and Racial Studies* 10/3 (1987), pp. 276–7.

5 War Office, *Manual of Military Law* (London: HMSO, 1914), p. 471. 'Alien' in this sense meant anyone born outside Great Britain, but its meaning had been extended to include black people.

6 Brian Dyde, *The Empty Sleeve: The Story of The West India Regiments of the British Army* (London: Hansib, 1997).

7 Memorandum by the Colonial Defence Committee (CDC), 'Colonial Troops for Imperial Service in War', June 1902 prepared by Lt. Colonel E. A. Altham and J. E. Clauson, Secretary of the CDC, The National Archives (TNA) (UK), War Office (WO) 32/8304.

8 Sam C. Ukpabi, 'Recruiting for the British Colonial Forces in West Africa in the Nineteenth Century', *Odu: A Journal of West African Studies* 10 (July 1974), pp. 79–95.

9 Gavin Schaffer, 'Racializing the Soldier: An Introduction', *Patterns of Prejudice* 46/3–4 (2012), pp. 209–13.

10 Christian Koller, 'The Recruitment of Colonial Troops in Africa and Asia and their Deployment in Europe during the First World War', *Immigrants and Minorities* 26/1–2 (March–July 2008), p. 126.

11 Koller, 'The Recruitment of Colonial Troops', pp. 111–33.

12 David Killingray, 'All the King's Men? Blacks in the British Army in the First World War, 1914–1918' in Rainer Lotz

and Ian Pegg (eds), *Under the Imperial Carpet: Essays in Black History 1780–1950* (Crawley: Rabbit Press, 1986), p. 175.

13 The use of native African troops in combat was considered later in the war but never agreed. See David Killingray, 'The Idea of a British Imperial African Army', *Journal of African History* 20/3 (1979), pp. 421–36.

14 John Starling and Ivor Lee, *No Labour, No Battle: Military Labour during the First World War* (Stroud: Spellmount, 2009).

15 Jacqueline Jenkinson, *Black 1919: Riots, Racism and Resistance in Imperial Britain* (Liverpool: Liverpool University Press, 2009), p. 2.

16 Stephen Bourne, *Black Poppies: Britain's Black Community and the Great War* (Stroud: History Press, 2014); Ray Costello, *Black Tommies: British Soldiers of African Descent in the First World War* (Liverpool: Liverpool University Press, 2015).

17 Jacqueline Jenkinson, '"All in the Same Uniform?" The Participation of Black Colonial Residents in the British Armed Forces in the First World War', *Journal of Imperial and Commonwealth History* 40/2 (June 2012), pp. 207–30.

18 Hew Strachan, *The First World War in Africa* (Oxford: Oxford University Press, 2004).

19 Bourne, *Black Poppies*, pp. 39–40.

20 Jenkinson, '"All in the Same Uniform?"', p. 214.

21 Eric Storm and Ali Al Tuma (eds), *Colonial Soldiers in Europe, 1914–1945: 'Aliens in Uniform' in Wartime Societies* (London: Routledge, 2015), p. 97.

22 Anna Maguire, 'Colonial Encounters', *History Today* 65/12 (December 2015), pp. 39–44.

23 Richard Smith, *Jamaican Volunteers in the First World War: Race, Masculinity, and the Development of National Consciousness* (Manchester: Manchester University Press, 2004), pp. 136–7.

24 Glenford Howe, *Race, War, and Nationalism: A Social History of West Indians in the First World War* (Jamaica: Ian Randle Publishers, 2002), pp. 182–94.

25 Jenkinson, *Black 1919*.

26 Minute by Sir Gilbert Grindle, 'Peace Celebrations Report', 9 May 1919, TNA (UK), CO 323/804/14.

27 'Peace Celebrations Report', 9 May 1919, TNA (UK), CO 323/804/14.

28 Jerry White, *Zeppelin Nights: London in the First World War* (London: Vintage, 2015), pp. 208–9.

29 'Ministry of Works, Ceremonial – Part 2 – Peace Celebrations 1919', 23 June 1919, TNA (UK), Works 21/74.

30 *The Times*, 21 July 1919, p. 15.

31 'Arrangements for Conveying Body of Unknown Warrior from France to London', 8 November 1920, TNA, WO 32/3000.

32 Allan Greenberg, 'Lutyens's Cenotaph', *Journal of the Society of Architectural Historians* 48/1 (March 1989), p. 7.

33 George L. Mosse, *Fallen Soldiers: Reshaping the Memory of the World Wars* (Oxford: Oxford University Press, 1990), p. 96.

34 Dan Todman, *The Great War: Myth and Memory* (London: Hambledon Continuum, 2005), p. 50.

35 Jenkinson, '"All in the Same Uniform?"', p. 207.

36 'Conclusions of the Cabinet Meeting', 14 October 1920, TNA, CAB 23/22/17.

37 House of Lords Record Office, Lloyd George Paper, 17 November 1920, F/95/52.

38 Robert Grant Irving, 'Architecture for Empire's Sake: Lutyens's Palace for Delhi', *Perspecta* 18 (1982), p. 14.

39 David A. Johnson and Nicole F. Gilbertson, 'Commemorations of Imperial Sacrifice at Home and Abroad: British Memorials of the Great War', *History Teacher* 43/4 (August 2010), p. 581.

40 Joanna Bourke, *Dismembering the Male: Men's Bodies, Britain and the Great War* (London: Reaktion Books, 1996), p. 236; Adrian Gregory, *The Silence of Memory* (Oxford: Berg, 1994), p. 23.

41 Gregory, *The Silence of Memory*, p. 25.

42 'In the Abbey: the Warrior Laid to Rest', *The Times* supplement, 12 November 1920, p. ii.

43 Gregory, *The Silence of Memory*, p. 25.

44 Herbert Ryle, 'Unknown Warrior', 19 October 1920, TNA, Work 20/1/3.

45 'Conclusions of Cabinet Meeting', 15 October 1920, TNA, CAB 32/22/18.

46 In 1960, the IWGC became the Commonwealth War Graves Commission (CWGC).

47 CWGC, 24 January 1923, WG 1734/Pt 1.

48 'Omission of British West Indies from Tablets in Cathedrals: Complaint by Mr T. Daley', 22 October 1932, CWGC, WG 1734/3/1.

49 'Memorial to Those Lost at Sea during the War 1914–1918', Naval Memorials General File, 22 April 1921, CWGC, WG 1087/Pt 1.

50 F. R. Durham to F. Ware, Naval Memorials General File, 14 July 1921, CWGC, F845/1.

51 H. F. Chettle to F. R. Durham, 'Naval Memorials: Native Ratings', 7 November 1922, CWGC, WG 1087/11.

52 Secretary of Admiralty to Secretary IWGC, 'Naval Memorials: Native Ratings', 20 February 1923, CWGC, WG 1087/11.a.

53 Muster roll of HMS *Good Hope*: sunk 1 November 1914, TNA, ADM 116/1354.

54 Even today, the twenty-six men are hard to trace on the CWGC site as they are listed as either 'Indian' or 'British' on the web page for the Bombay World War One memorial: http://www.cwgc.org/find-a-cemetery/cemetery/

2111731/BOMBAY%201914-1918%20 MEMORIAL,%20MUMBAI, accessed 6 November 2018.

55 'Minutes of a Meeting of the Committee on Memorials to the Mercantile Marine', 1 October 1923, CWGC, SDC 79.

56 See Bourne, *Black Poppies*, pp. 126–33 for the black presence in London's docklands. For Asian seamen on the memorial, see http://blogs. iwm.org.uk/research/2013/03/south-asian-seamen-in-the-two-world-wars/, accessed 6 November 2018. For African seamen, see http://www.jeffreygreen. co.uk/065-the-sinking-of-the-falaba-march-1915, accessed 6 November 2018.

57 Gavin Stamp, 'The Imperial War Graves Commission', *Journal of the Society for the Study of Architecture* 33/1 (2008), p. 11.

58 For a brief description of the CAHTC, see Winegard, *Indigenous Peoples of the British Dominions*, pp. 172–3.

59 http://www.cwgc.org/ find-a-cemetery/cemetery/142019/ HOLLYBROOK%20MEMORIAL,%20 SOUTHAMPTON, accessed 6 November 2018.

60 Mike Hawkins, *Social Darwinism in European and American Thought, 1860–1845: Nature as Model and Nature as Threat* (Cambridge: Cambridge University Press, 1997), pp. 191–240.

61 Albert Grundlingh, 'Mutating Memories and the Making of a Myth: Remembering the SS *Mendi* Disaster, 1917–2007', *South African Historical Journal* 63/1 (2011), pp. 20–37.

62 J. Gribble and G. Scott, *We Die Like Brothers: The Sinking of the SS* Mendi (Swindon: Historic England, 2017).

63 http://www.fjordr.com/fjordr-blog/the-worlds-war-on-the-east-coast, accessed 6 November 2018.

64 http://www.cwgc.org/ find-a-cemetery/cemetery/44826/ LITTLEHAMPTON%20CEMETERY, accessed 6 November 2018.

65 http://www.cwgc.org/ find-a-cemetery/cemetery/54237/ NOORDWIJK%20GENERAL%20 CEMETERY, accessed 6 November 2018.

66 http://memorialgates.org/; http://www.bbc.co.uk/news/uk-england-london-40372063, both accessed 6 November 2018.

4 | 'YOU ASK FOR BREAD, THEY GIVE YOU HOT LEAD'

When Caribbean radicals protested against conscription for colonial subjects

Kesewa John

Political writings, such as those found in *International African Opinion*, *The Black Man* and *The Keys*, publications produced by African and Caribbean political observers and actors in Britain in the decade before World War Two, clearly demonstrate that, for contemporary observers, the official start of hostilities in 1939 was a long time coming. It was also obvious to them that World War Two was inextricably linked to larger questions about the world order and, of personal interest to them, African peoples' designated place within it.[1] Identifying themselves as a conquered but not vanquished colonised people, their analyses of the events leading to the war provide a largely forgotten yet invaluable insight into an oft-told story. This chapter does not assert that these mainly Caribbean thinkers were always correct in all their evaluations, but that they were extremely astute, and by seriously examining their version of events, a fuller picture of the war's preamble emerges.

The radicals whose ideas will be discussed here were peers from very similar social backgrounds. They were born into the few African middle-class families in colonial Caribbean societies, and were often the grandchildren of those who had personally experienced enslavement – and, in the case of Amy Ashwood Garvey, the terrible middle passage too. They were educated, highly articulate, well-travelled, politically engaged and fiercely proud; they would be considered unapologetically black in today's parlance. Almost all were born between 1895 and 1905, and thus, in the immediate decade before the war began, they were in their thirties. *Labour in the West Indies*, the 1938 pamphlet by St Lucian scholar Arthur Lewis, described the social stratification of their respective native countries:

The bulk of the population – 80% or more – are of African descent … the East Indians constitute about 12% of the population … The White population is relatively small, averaging about 3% of the total … but this tiny white element dominates every aspect of West Indian life.

Economically and politically the white man is supreme; he owns the biggest plantations, stores and banks, controlling directly or indirectly the entire economic life of the community. It is he who the Governor most often nominates to his councils, and for his sons that the best government jobs are reserved. Socially, the whites in general constitute the aristocracy. They run their own clubs from which non-whites are excluded, and it is they who constitute the 'Court' life of 'His Majesty's Representative' the Governor.[2]

Their life experiences of colonial British schooling and colonial rule as dark-skinned African-descended peoples during their formative years thus supported the development of an intimate understanding of imperial power and politics.[3] Why these effective political agitators did not believe that people from colonised countries should serve militarily in World War Two at its outset and why they published well-circulated articles to discourage potential recruits are the central questions this chapter will address.

The chapter initially offers a brief biography of the prominent Trinidadian activist and Communist George Padmore, widely considered the leading member of this network of radicals, and the organisations with whom he worked most closely. The chapter continues with the declaration of war articulated by Prime Minister Neville Chamberlain. It then outlines the arguments of two key articles that appeared at least six times, and on both sides of the Atlantic: in the black press in the UK, the US and the Caribbean in 1938 and 1939. These writings challenged the assumption that support in the form of military service from the people of the colonies – by which they meant the majority, Lewis's disempowered 92 per cent – would be forthcoming. The concluding thoughts suggest why cataloguing black dissent is essential for constructing an understanding of both Black British political history and British history more generally.

George Padmore: another Trinidadian Internationalist

Born Malcolm Nurse, Padmore was born into a radical-thinking middle-class family in colonial Trinidad and Tobago in 1903.[4] By 1939, George Padmore was an established anti-imperialist with a global audience. After working as a journalist in colonial Port of Spain, he spent five years studying in the US, where he became increasingly involved with the Communist Party of the USA. In 1929 the party sent him to a conference in Moscow, and, once in Russia, Padmore was tapped as someone who could lead the Communist International's work on what was then known as 'the Negro Question'. He never returned to the USA, although he maintained both familial and professional ties there.[5]

The Communist International was the global umbrella organisation for national Communist parties (such as the Communist Party of Great Britain and the *Parti Communiste Français*), and it had inscribed supporting freedom movements in the colonies into its membership charter in 1921. Number eight of the twenty-one conditions for admittance to the Communist International stated:

> Parties in countries whose bourgeoisie possess colonies and oppress
> other nations must pursue a most well-defined and clear-cut policy
> in respect of colonies and oppressed nations. Any party wishing
> to join the Third International must ruthlessly expose the colonial
> machinations of the imperialists of its 'own' country, must support –
> in deed, not merely in word – every colonial liberation movement,
> demand the expulsion of its compatriot imperialists from the colonies,
> inculcate in the hearts of the workers of its own country an attitude of
> true brotherhood with the working population of the colonies and the
> oppressed nations, and conduct systematic agitation among the armed
> forces against all oppression of the colonial peoples.[6]

A party activist and experienced journalist, George Padmore was soon editor of the *Negro Worker*, the Communist Internationalist trade union newspaper written for working-class black people all over the world. Through its pages, Padmore was responsible for detailing the black condition in Africa, the Caribbean, the US and Europe, and the many struggles for justice of 'Africans at home and abroad'.[7] As he was also the head of the International Trade Union Committee's Negro Work, George Padmore had a front-row seat to the rise of fascism in Germany. He was a Communist Party activist, an immigrant, and a dark-skinned black man who by 1933 had been living in Hamburg for a few years. When Adolf Hitler became chancellor of Germany in early 1933, it took only two weeks for his offices to be raided and Padmore to be deported back to the UK as a British colonial citizen, after spending 'three months in a Nazi prison'.[8]

The International African Service Bureau

George Padmore, however, had grown increasingly disenchanted with the organised Communism of the Soviet Union. In the September

1933 issue of the *Negro Worker*, he included a farewell message to readers. Padmore spent most of the following two years building his own worldwide network. He did this while working among black-led Parisian Pan-Africanist organisations, whose more arts-oriented members conceptualised *négritude*, the black pride movement that electrified the black French-speaking world in the 1930s and 1940s.[9] By 1935, George Padmore was living in London, where he remained for the following two decades. He had reconnected with his childhood friend C. L. R. James, who in turn introduced him to Amy Ashwood Garvey, now proprietor of the International Afro Restaurant at 62 New Oxford Street, serving the social needs of London's black community. Following the Italian invasion of Ethiopia in 1935, James and Ashwood Garvey had established the African-led British section of the global campaign supporting Ethiopia's claim to sovereignty – the International African Friends of Ethiopia (IAFE). Broadening their scope, in March 1937 they founded the International African Service Bureau, a Pan-African organisation that effectively replaced the IAFE. The Bureau (as it will be referred to henceforth) was created because:

> no people, race or nationality, has been oppressed, exploited or humiliated, as the black people for centuries past up to the present day, and the Bureau was formed to assist by all means in our power, the unco-ordinated struggle of Africans and people of African descent against the oppression from which they suffer in every country.[10]

The executive committee included Amy Ashwood Garvey, co-founder of the legendary Universal Negro Improvement Association with ex-husband Marcus, fellow Trinidadian and black Marxist philosopher C. L. R. James, future first president of an independent Kenya Jomo Kenyatta, Sierra Leonean trade unionist I. T. A. Wallace-Johnson, Ras Makonnen, a Guyanese Pan-African activist with a broad portfolio including publisher and restaurateur, Barbadian seafarer Chris Braithwaite aka Jones, who presided over the Colonial Seamen's Association, pioneering Trinidadian calypsonian Sam Manning, and the Grenadian Theophilus Albert Marryshow, an elected representative on the Legislative Council of Grenada, newspaper editor and elder to the group. The Bureau was proactive in its internationalism; it maintained a French section, and Émile Faure, a prominent Senegalese activist based in Paris, sat on the executive committee.

With a Caribbean and African leadership, the Bureau was determined to demonstrate the self-determination it preached. Its active membership was:

> open to all Africans and peoples of African descent, regardless of nationality, political creed or religious faith, who accept its aims and abide by its Constitution. Associate membership is open to Europeans and members of other races who sympathise with the aims and objects of the Bureau and desire to demonstrate in a practical way their interest in Africans and peoples of African descent.[11]

Close connections to political activists throughout the Caribbean, Africa, Latin America and the US were evident through the reach of the Bureau's publications, and the letters and articles detailing the work and struggles of African people in these parts of the world. *International African Opinion* was but one of several journals, including *Africa and the World*, *African Sentinel*, *Colonial Bulletin*, and single-issue pamphlets such as *Hands Off the Protectorates* and *The West Indies Today*. The anti-conscription position of the Bureau in response to the anticipated World War Two was in the main a commonly held, if now forgotten, left-wing viewpoint. It was shared with contemporary white British members of parliament, future cabinet ministers, and prominent writers and intellectuals such as George Orwell, Fenner Brockway, Leonard Woolf and Arthur Creech Jones, as well as many members of the Independent Labour Party (ILP) with whom the Bureau enjoyed a close working relationship.[12]

The declaration of war

Prime Minister Neville Chamberlain's declaration of war against Germany, announced on 3 September 1939, was broadcast over the radio, and was made on behalf of both Britain and France:

> I am speaking to you from the Cabinet Room at 10, Downing Street. This morning the British Ambassador in Berlin Nevile Henderson handed the German Government a final note stating that unless we heard from them by 11 o'clock, that they were prepared at once to withdraw their troops from Poland, that a state of war would exist between us. I have to tell you now that no such undertaking has been received, and that consequently this country is at war with Germany. You can imagine what a bitter blow it is to me that all my long struggle to win peace has failed. Yet I cannot believe that there is anything

more or anything different that I could have done and that would have been more successful ... His action shows convincingly that there is no chance of expecting that this man will ever give up his practice of using force to gain his will. He can only be stopped by force, and we and France are today, in fulfilment of our obligations, going to the aid of Poland, who is so bravely resisting this wicked and unprovoked attack upon her people.

We have a clear conscience. We have done all that any country could do to establish peace. The situation in which no word given by Germany's ruler could be trusted and no people or country could feel itself safe has become intolerable. And now that we have resolved to finish it, I know that you will all play your part with calmness and courage. At such a moment as this the assurances of support that we have received from the Empire are a source of profound encouragement to us. When I have finished speaking certain detailed announcements will be made on behalf of the Government ... Now may God bless you all. May He defend the right. It is the evil things that we shall be fighting against – brute force, bad faith, injustice, oppression and persecution – and against them I am certain that the right will prevail.[13]

Upon this pronouncement, the Bureau responded quickly, lobbying sympathetic MPs while carefully coordinating counter-discourses. Their priority was to challenge the narrative and insist that imperial powers ought not expect loyalty from their colonial subjects. The Bureau seized on the acknowledgement in the declaration of war that imperial governments were not intending to defeat Germany using only citizens born and raised in the imperial metropoles; they explicitly anticipated the assistance of troops from the colonies. From the outset, the military service of people from the colonies was calculated as necessary for a victorious outcome for both Britain and France. With no intention of aiding imperialist governments whose moral and political legitimacy they had been challenging for years, a direct response was issued.

Manifesto Against War

The *Manifesto Against War* originally appeared in the October 1938 issue of *International African Opinion*. Searing, unequivocal and unapologetic, the manifesto clearly aimed to pre-emptively disrupt discourses presuming the loyalty of people from colonised countries in the event of war. The significance of the *Manifesto Against War* is underlined in its preface in *International African Opinion*:

During the international crisis, when war seemed almost unavoidable, the Executive Committee [of the Bureau] held emergency meetings in order to formulate policies in keeping with the expressed wishes of its affiliate bodies, especially the French section, who would have had to bear the brunt of the fighting against the onslaught of the German troops westward to the frontiers of France. From every corner of the colonial world, communications poured into the headquarters of the Bureau and the tenor of all of them was opposition to any war fought by imperialist powers for a re-division of territory, a war in which the black peoples would be used only as cannon fodder, and from which it was a foregone conclusion they would gain nothing ... In keeping with the virtual mandate of the people to whom they are ultimately responsible, the Bureau issued on Sunday, September 25, 1938, the following manifesto which was widely distributed and reprinted in several English journals.[14]

Like the declaration of war, the *Manifesto* was ultimately a collectively created document: the product of several meetings, international correspondence and a shared policy position. The text's main objective was an articulation of the belief that a coming war would be a war over colonies, regardless of the reasons articulated by the governments involved; colonial subjects would be pawns twice over if they participated – once as cannon fodder, twice because they would be propping up those who held them down, the Bureau argued. The *Manifesto* highlighted the fact that Britain, France, Belgium and the Netherlands – 'the Allied powers' – were the primary proprietors of the largest international empires. Among 'the Axis' was a pervasive shame from failed imperial experiments: Italy's attempts at further imperial expansion via colonising Ethiopia in 1896 had been thwarted by the army of Emperor Menelik II, and Germany's colonies had been redistributed, mainly between Britain and France, as part of the Treaty of Versailles settlement. This was the true but unspoken context. Eight years earlier, in 1931, Japan had invaded Manchuria, and in late 1934 Italy re-launched another attempt to colonise Ethiopia. To the Bureau, it was therefore abundantly clear that the war was about colonies; the 'haves' of Britain, France, Belgium and the Netherlands versus the 'have nots' of Germany, Italy and Japan:

The British and French are no more concerned about the Poles than they were about the Czechs. What they ARE concerned about is the preservation of their colonial empires and the monopoly they enjoy in the exploitation of cheap coloured labour ... what Britain in particular is worried about, is the menace which German imperialism represents to her commercial interests. The politicians at Downing Street, who represent the Federation of British Industries and the Financiers of the City – the real rulers of the Empire – are afraid that if Hitler is not checked NOW, he might, after consolidating his position on the continent, demand the return of the former German colonies, which can be transferred only at the expense of Britain and France, who with Holland, Belgium and Portugal, control most of the colonial world. This then is the essence of the quarrel between Nazi Germany and the so-called Democracies.[15]

Rejecting the explanations offered in the prime minister's declaration of war, the *Manifesto* proposed far less noble intentions, and a certain amount of distasteful undeclared self-interest, in the Allied powers' determination to fight Germany militarily. According to the *Manifesto*, people from the colonies should not get involved in the war, at a minimum because it would be fought on dishonest premises:

Is it not strange that Mr Chamberlain denounces the wrongdoings of Hitler but remains silent about Mussolini's 'brute force, bad faith, injustice and oppression' towards Abyssinians and Albanians? Surely justice, like freedom, is indivisible. If Britain wants to win the respect of her subject peoples then her statesmen must be consistent in their advocacy of justice and fair play, even at the risk of offending Mussolini. This kind of duplicity only serves to emphasize the moral bankruptcy of those who talk about ridding the world of 'evil things'. We too want to rid the world of evil things, but this will never be until we have got rid of the system of imperialism, the most evil thing of all.[16]

The 'encouragement' Prime Minister Chamberlain referred to having received can be queried; it probably originated with colonial officials for whom, as European people tasked with administering their respective countries' colonies, loyalty from afar was second nature. The Bureau was adamant that the interests of colonial subjects were most definitely *not* aligned with those of the British government: 'Brothers and sisters of African descent, what democracy, what liberties, what rights have we got in this "glorious" British empire that calls us to shed our blood in its defence?'[17] The *Manifesto* did not mince its words, and offers a radically different interpretation of the causes of World War Two.

Ideas travel

An incredibly useful document, the *Manifesto*'s history is also circuitous. Originally released as a statement on 25 September 1938, which was reprinted by several UK newspapers, it was published in the October 1938 edition of *International African Opinion*. An almost identical version was republished in *Guiana Review*, the official newspaper of a local Guyanese trade union, on 23 April 1939.[18] Archival sources contain yet another version, modified in 1939 after the declaration of war, which was published in the US in November 1939, under its subtitle 'The Second World War and The Darker Races', in *The Crisis*, the main publication of the National Association for the Advancement of Colored People. The version published in Guyana contains an additional sentence – 'It would appear that the main function of the British press is to PRESS down on those who don't think'[19] – a critique that was omitted from the UK edition, presumably to avoid the ire of British media outlets which they hoped would republish the *Manifesto*. The *International African Opinion* version contains the phrase 'what rights have we got in these glorious Empires of Britain, France, Belgium, Portugal etc', whereas the *Guiana Review* version speaks only of the British Empire in the same phrase. They are otherwise identical. The version of the *Manifesto* rewritten after the declaration contains enough differences to be considered a complete reworking of the original document. Amended a year after the first version was released, this *Manifesto* is a reply to the declaration of war:

> What is the war about? This question is on the lips of every colonial – black, brown, yellow. While most Negroes, like the common people of England, are bewildered over the issues involved, about one thing they seem clear. And that is, the war, notwithstanding the protestations of statesmen, is certainly not one for democracy.
>
> When we consider the autocratic manner in which colonies are administered, be they under so-called democratic or totalitarian regimes, it should cause no surprise the colonial peoples have not been consulted as to whether they want to fight or not. All that they have been told is that this war is the noblest that has ever been embarked upon, for it is to save Poland, a Fascist State, from the big bad Fascist wolf Adolf Hitler. But this is sheer humbug ... They most certainly have not gone to war to defend Democracy which they themselves deny to hundreds of millions of coloured peoples in Africa, India, and the West Indies, Indo-China, Morocco, Tunis, Algeria and other territories too numerous to mention ... Nor are they at war to uphold

international law and order, or even to rid the world of those 'evil things – brute force, bad faith, injustice, persecution, and oppression' which Mr Chamberlain, in his speech of self-righteous indignation denounced over the radio as war was declared ... Behind all the shibboleths of 'brute force and oppression' which the British and other imperialists have been practicing upon their coloured subjects for centuries, is the long-standing conflict between bandit nations for colonies as markets, sources of raw materials and cheap labour, spheres for the investment of finance capital, and naval, military and air bases. It is for possession of these things that the war is being fought.[20]

A refusal to offer support to imperialist powers in the war, however, was not a call for apathy. On the contrary, those not fighting for the imperialists were urged instead to join the struggle for the freedom of the colonies. Connected to a global movement against imperialism, the Bureau declared itself for democracy, freedom and independence for *all* peoples – not only those recently affected by Germany's change in government and foreign policy aims:

It is not too late for our British masters to make good their lofty pretensions. If the British and the French imperialists, and all those who are taken in by their diplomacy, really want to convince the colored races – and for that matter the white working classes – that they are really concerned about ridding the world of 'evil things,' now is an excellent opportunity for them to start putting their own empires in order. Let them extend *Democracy* to their colonies. Let Mr Chamberlain get up at Westminster, and Mr Daladier in the French Chamber of Deputies, and issue a declaration to the world granting their colonies *self-government.* Such a revolution in international relations would not only be a moral victory for the democracies, but a bloodless one. Such a gesture, coming at this time, would rally reinforcement to the democratic front by giving hundreds of millions of subject peoples something tangible to defend. It would cut the ground from under Hitler's feet ... But will Mssrs Chamberlain and Daladier accept our challenge? Or shall our suspicions be confirmed – that their democratic statements are just a facade for their real imperialist aims?[21]

The Bureau's response highlighted the hypocrisy of Britain's and France's willingness to fight for the freedom of some people, with the full force of their respective militaries, while actively opposing the freedom of others:

You, in the West Indies, after a hundred years of so-called emancipation, are still denied the most elementary rights of human beings. When you ask for bread, they give you hot lead. The conditions you live under are Colonial Fascism.[22]

'Hot lead' here is bullets, overused by the colonial authorities in the severe repression of striking workers throughout the English-speaking Caribbean during the Labour Rebellions that fundamentally shook the region in the 1930s, leading to the birth of the modern Caribbean. For contemporary readers well-acquainted with the events, the hypocrisy of British claims of fighting *for* anybody's right to democracy would have been quite apparent. The *Manifesto* thus outlined why the Bureau and its affiliates were highly doubtful that Britain's and France's declared reasons for war with Germany reflected the real source of the conflict. It was this political perspective that Martinican *négritude* thinker Aimé Césaire later elaborated upon, when he stated in *Discourse on Colonialism*:

It would be worthwhile to study clinically, in detail, the journey of Hitler and Hitlerism, and reveal to the very distinguished, very humanist, very Christian middle class person of the twentieth century, that carried within them is a Hitler that they are unaware of, that Hitler lives within them, that Hitler is their demon that, if they rail against it, it's for a lack of logic and that deep down, what they don't forgive Hitler for, it is not for the crime itself, the crime against humanity, it is not the humiliation of humankind in and of itself, it is the crime against the white man, it's the humiliation of white people, and to have applied to Europe the colonialist methods which until now had only been known to the arabs of Algeria, the coolies of India, and the negroes of Africa.[23]

The *Manifesto Against War* remains remarkable as evidence of a politically astute, organised, confident group of Caribbean thinkers identifying themselves as African and determined to make their voice and political demands clearly heard in interwar Britain, in her colonies, and throughout the colonised world.

Why colonial/West Indian workers opposed conscription

The earliest opposition to colonial subjects' participation in the war may have come from the Malian Tiémoko Garan Kouyaté, the leading black Communist in the Francophone world. At a 1932 trade union meeting at a French port, he discouraged black seafarers from joining a new war; their main responsibility, he argued, was to refuse to serve French imperialism and instead to fight for freedom for the colonies, according to the report filed by police spies following the prominent activist.[24] Seafarers were an important contingent of black workers in early twentieth-century Europe: they were a highly unionised element of the working class and they often settled in port towns – to this extent, they were among the founders of Britain's earliest black communities. Sedition laws curbing free speech in French and British colonies alike were liberally applied and radical newspapers such as *International African Opinion* were frequently banned by colonial authorities. As regular travellers between the colonial world and the imperial metropoles, black seafarers were crucial in smuggling copies of criminalised anti-imperialist literature into ports via the ships on which they worked.

Chris Braithwaite aka Jones was an active member of the seafaring community and was involved in political organisations throughout the 1930s. As a member of the Communist Party of Great Britain, he had been involved in founding the Negro Welfare Association, and, after leaving the party, he later established the Colonial Seamen's Association.[25] Braithwaite was the Bureau's organising secretary and a powerful public speaker. Under his alias Jones, Chris Braithwaite authored 'Why Colonial Workers Oppose Conscription', the second document to be discussed here. A shorter article than the *Manifesto*, it explained simply that:

> We have no faith in Capitalist governments, whether they call themselves democratic or fascist. They are all imperialists and as such the exploiters and oppressors of colonial peoples. Therefore we are determined never again to allow ourselves to be used as cannon fodder by either camp in the coming war.[26]

Like the *Manifesto*, the article evokes the failure of the League of Nations to support Ethiopia when invaded by fellow member state Italy, unkept promises made to soldiers from the colonies who participated in World War One, and the opportunity a war for Britain represented for peoples in and from British colonies working for national independence: 'The Imperialists' difficulties must be our opportunities to strike a blow for freedom.'[27] Published just two months before the official declaration of war, it also challenged the veracity of the arguments being made to justify a future war, stating unequivocally:

In the West Indies the elementary principles of democracy are denied the native masses. Therefore we oppose Conscription ... it is sheer impudence on the part of the British ruling classes to appeal to colonial workers to help them defend their ill-gotten gains.[28]

The ideological similarities between the two texts are unsurprising; Chris Braithwaite and George Padmore were both prominent activists for the same Bureau. They shared a political outlook, so a similar interpretation of the events leading to World War Two is expected. More noteworthy is that 'Why Colonial Workers Oppose Conscription' appears almost simultaneously in two different Caribbean newspapers – on two different islands. The text first appeared in the 1 July 1939 issue of *The People*, published in Trinidad and Tobago. Titled 'Why West Indian Workers Oppose Conscription', it then resurfaced in the 15 July 1939 issue of the *Barbados Observer*. Local newspapers with a radical outlook in the Caribbean, it would appear, were in close contact with the Bureau.

Historians of early trade union movements in the Caribbean, such as Rhoda Reddock, Bukka Rennie and Kelvin Singh, have long established that *The People* was a crucial voice in Trinidad and Tobago's early trade union history. The editor, Leonard Fitzgerald Walcott, was a Garveyite: that is, a follower of the black nationalist and self-help teachings of Marcus Garvey. Founded in 1933, in its early days *The People* covered and supported Andrew Arthur 'Captain' Cipriani and the Trinidad Workingmen's Association, which advocated publicly for the masses of Trinidad and Tobago in their defence of 'the barefoot man'. Like many Trinibagonians, however, Walcott was disappointed with Cipriani's increasingly obvious paternalism. As mass working-class movements steadily grew in Trinidad and Tobago as the decade progressed, Walcott and the paper shifted their support to groupings militating for more radical social change. The paper regularly reported on the activities of the Negro Welfare Cultural and Social Association – linked to London's own Negro Welfare Association – led by Elma Francois,[29] and supported the workers led by Uriah Butler when they engaged in huge strikes in the oilfields of Trinidad in 1937. Walcott himself eventually joined political forces with the militant trade unionist lawyer Adrien Cola Rienzi; *The People* urged its readers to support Rienzi's election bid, and emphatically celebrated his electoral victory.[30]

The *Barbados Observer* was also a well-known newspaper sympathetic to the plight of the working classes of Barbados and the world. The *Observer* was edited for forty-four years by its founder, Algernon

Wynter Crawford. Like Walcott, Crawford was an early supporter of progressive causes. Earlier in the decade Crawford had been close to Grantley Adams, whose pre-1937 political position challenged a long-undisturbed colonial parliament that claimed almost 300 years of representative democracy for the minority who met the property and income requirements for suffrage. Like Walcott in Trinidad, Crawford was deeply affected by the labour rebellions in his country. Crawford, and the *Barbados Observer*, became sharply critical of the colonial authorities, reporting on the violent excesses of the colonial police force and querying the colony's capacity for justice in social and political life, despite the appearance of a local political infrastructure tasked with responsibility for this. Following the violent repression of peaceful protest in the summer of 1937, some of which he witnessed from his office in the capital, and which the paper reported on extensively, Crawford became a founding member of the Barbados Progressive League. This became the Barbados Labour Party and Crawford was later elected to office. Despite a long career in politics, including time in the cabinet of the first prime minister after independence, Errol Barrow, Crawford edited the *Barbados Observer* until it ceased production.[31]

It is noteworthy that this transatlantically published article is by Chris Braithwaite. Leslie James' work has detailed the reach of George Padmore's journalism, whose writings were published across the Caribbean, in the US, Africa and Europe. Scholars including James, Polsgrove and Hayes Edwards have considered this a consequence of his peripateticism.[32] Yet it would appear that a relationship existed between the editors of newspapers in different colonies, and with London: this is neither the first nor the only occasion on which identically worded articles appeared in *The People* and the *Observer* – it happened on several occasions throughout the decade. While the exact nature of these radical publishing relationships is not clear, it is evident that ideas circulated widely. From London to Guyana, from Trinidad to Barbados, newspapers published articles supporting the idea that Caribbean people should not serve in imperial armed forces; instead, they should fight for their own freedom from colonial rule.

Belonging to British history

Thus far it has not been possible to ascertain exactly how many colonial subjects did not sign up to serve in the British and French militaries in line with the exhortations of the International African Service

Bureau and its partner organisations throughout the world. Thousands of Caribbean men and women served in World War Two in the British armed forces. Indeed, the majority of the those arriving on the *Empire Windrush*, considered the first of a generation of post-war Caribbean migrants arriving in Britain, were former servicemen who were returning to the UK.

Examining the alternative discourses of Caribbean radicals on the roots of World War Two gets to the crux of why Black British History is not only a subject worthy of academic enquiry, but essential to a fuller understanding of British history. In considering the writings of people who identified themselves as the marginalised, the oppressed, and in lending equal weight to their version of events, it is possible to reassess what we think we know about the past. World War Two is an example of a narrative that is central to contemporary British ideas about 'the nation'. It is oft-repeated and unequivocal: Hitler was an evil monster, who Britain defeated in a just war in order to save the Jews of Germany, because Britain is a superior country whose values include fair play and tolerance. The eloquence of George Padmore, Chris Braithwaite and their colleagues, and their determination to create an independent political identity for themselves, offers an entirely different interpretation of the events leading to the outbreak of World War Two. In plain but impassioned words, colonial subjects who wished to play no part in representing Britain in what they referred to as a war for colonies posed the elephantine question: how can Britain go to war to defend democracy which 'they themselves deny to hundreds of millions'?[33] They were among those who believed, rather, that a war for Britain and France meant that their oppressors were distracted, and that they faced a unique historical opportunity to win the fight for their own freedom.

Taking the rhetorical floor, the Bureau put forward an alternative thesis: the war was in fact about who controlled the colonial world. They noted that Britain, France and their allies – the Netherlands, Belgium and Portugal – were the proprietors of the world's major empires. They also observed that since the mid-1930s the German government had with increasing frequency been demanding the return of the colonies dislodged as part of the Versailles settlement. Pointing out that in the preceding decade, Japan had invaded China and Italy had invaded Ethiopia, a clear, alternative division in the fascist–democratic line being propagated was apparent: those who perceived themselves to have sufficient access to colonies, and those who did not.

Both the *Manifesto* and 'Why Oppose' outline the political demands of a group of people from colonies, who articulated a discourse about Britain and her empire that confronted head on the notion of empire as a consensual family network implied in Prime Minister Chamberlain's declaration of war. That newspaper articles detailing their positions were republished in the Caribbean and further afield indicates a transnational network of Caribbean activists determined to speak truth to power. They also present a certain challenge; in the current political era, when a strand of anti-racist discourse argues that contemporary British citizens of colour are due their place within the national fabric *because* their ancestors fought in the wars, what place do those whose ancestors actively opposed those wars merit? Few would dream of suggesting that ILP member George Orwell's claim to Britishness is dependent on his adherence to current definitions of mainstream political ideologies. However, this, according to certain political discourses, is demanded of those who boldly declared themselves 'victims of imperialism'.[34]

The recent furore over grime artist Stormzy's message to Prime Minister Theresa May on live television is an example of the logical conclusions of such discourses about belonging. The following day, politically conservative newspapers lambasted Stormzy, the son of African immigrants, for a lack of 'gratitude'.[35] Stormzy had used his platform as a popular musician to highlight the plight of people who had lost their homes in the Grenfell fire, and who had still not been rehoused eight months later. Many people campaign on issues around the handling of the Grenfell Tower tragedy and in support of those living with the consequences. Stormzy's very right to criticise an inept government response, however, was challenged by those who consider his place within the national fabric of Britain debatable because his parents were not born in Britain, but in Ghana. One 'progressive' response to conservative racists is to overemphasise the 'loyalty' of Britain's immigrants and immigrant-descended populations. Implicit in this approach is an acceptance of the insidious idea that dissent is a gift, not a universal right. It is a dystopic stance worthy of the most terrifying Orwellian fiction. It is partly why the Caribbean radicals on whose writings this chapter has focused have been part of the strange silences of history dissected in Haitian historian Michel-Rolph Trouillot's classic work.[36] It robs us all of a fuller understanding of the past and condemns us to an infinitely intellectually narrower present and future.

Writing the history of Britain's black radicals and examining their political analyses is invaluable because, to paraphrase British feminist scholar Sara Ahmed, those who do not inhabit a norm see it more clearly.[37] As this chapter has demonstrated, the marginal position of Caribbean radicals in the 1930s enabled them to clearly perceive the veiled justifications for war in 1939. It was from this same position that this same group of activists from Britain's colonies would effectively construct a manifesto for decolonisation at the 1945 Pan-African Congress in Manchester, and organise the end of the British Empire.[38]

Notes

1   George Padmore, 'Ethiopia in World Politics', *The Crisis*, New York, May 1935, p. 133.

2   Arthur Lewis, *Labour in the West Indies: The Birth of a Worker's Movement* (London: Victor Gollancz, 1939), pp. 11–12.

3   The influence of colonial education in Jamaica on Amy Ashwood Garvey's politicisation is discussed by Tony Martin in *Amy Ashwood Garvey: Pan-Africanist, Feminist and Mrs Marcus Garvey No.1 or a Tale of Two Amies* (Dover: Majority Press, 2007). For C. L. R. James' discussion of childhood and schooling in colonial Trinidad and Tobago in Port of Spain and its intersections with politics, see *Beyond a Boundary* (London: Serpent's Tail, 1963). James and Padmore were playmates as children as their fathers were friends.

4   For more on the connection between pioneering Pan-Africanist Henry Sylvester Williams and George Padmore, son of Ivan Nurse, see Marika Sherwood, 'Pan-African Conferences, 1900–1953: What Did "Pan-Africanism" Mean?', *Journal of Pan African Studies* 4/10 (January 2012).

5   For a recent biographical treatment of George Padmore, see Leslie James, *George Padmore and Decolonization from Below: Pan-Africanism, the Cold War, and the End of Empire* (London: Macmillan, 2014).

6   'Terms of Admission into the Communist International'. The terms are attributed to Lenin and were adopted by the Second Congress of the Communist International in 1920. V. I. Lenin, *Collected Works*, 4th English edition (Moscow: Progress Publishers, 1965), Volume 31, pp. 206–11. Lenin Internet Archive: https://www.marxists.org/archive/lenin/works/1920/jul/x01.htm 2002, accessed 4 April 2018.

7   This term was used synonymously with the terms 'Africans' and 'African-descended peoples' and the now-dated 'Negro' in the publications with which Padmore was involved to refer to all diasporic Africans, including Caribbean people of African descent, and African people in or from Africa.

8   George Padmore, 'The Second World War and the Darker Races', *The Crisis*, New York, November 1939, p. 7.

9   See Brent Hayes Edwards, *The Practice of Diaspora: Literature, Translation, and the Rise of Black Internationalism* (Cambridge MA: Harvard University Press, 2003).

10   'Editorial', *International African Opinion*, London, July 1938, p. 2.

11   The General Secretary (I. T. A. Wallace Johnson), 'The International Africa Service Bureau', *African Sentinel*, London, October–November 1937, p. 4.

12   'General Strike in Case of War: ILP Resolution', *The Voice of St Lucia*,

Castries, 23 March 1935; George Orwell 'Why I join the ILP', *New Leader*, London, 1938. C. L. R. James was the chair of the Finchley (London) branch of the Independent Labour Party (ILP) between 1935 and 1936. For a recent work on C. L. R. James' time and politics in Britain in the 1930s, see Christian Hogsbjerg, *C. L. R. James in Imperial Britain* (Durham NC: Duke University Press, 2014). For a recent discussion of the ILP of the 1930s, including its relationship with the Labour Party, see Gidon Cohen, *Failure of a Dream: The Independent Labour Party from Disaffiliation to World War II* (London: I. B. Tauris, 2007).

13 http://www.bbc.co.uk/archive/ww2outbreak/7957.shtml, accessed 13 January 2018.

14 'Politics and the Negro', *International African Opinion*, London, October 1939, p. 9.

15 Padmore, 'The Second World War and the Darker Races', p. 7.

16 Padmore, 'The Second World War and the Darker Races', p. 7.

17 'Politics and the Negro', p. 9.

18 Manpower Citizens Association produced the *Guiana Review* from the mid-1930s and then the *Labour Advocate* in the 1940s. Manpower was explicitly formed to unionise Indo-Guyanese workers not yet engaged with Guyana's trade union movement. The newspapers published articles and adverts in Hindi and campaigned on legalising Muslim and Hindu marriages in order to increase its profile among Indo-Guyanese workers, as well as work-related issues. Manpower's establishment was encouraged by Hubert Critchlow, the pioneering Afro-Guyanese trade unionist and Communist who had created the first legal trade union in the Caribbean in 1919. It is probable that Critchlow met with Padmore on a political trip to Europe in the early 1930s.

19 'Guianese Writes from Abroad. Endorses International African Service Bureau. The Manifesto Against War', *Guiana Review*, Georgetown, 23 April 1939, p. 9.

20 Padmore, 'The Second World War and the Darker Races', p. 7.

21 Padmore, 'The Second World War and the Darker Races', p. 7.

22 'Guianese Writes From Abroad', p. 9.

23 Aimé Césaire, *Discours sur le Colonialisme* (Paris: Presence Africaine, 1956), pp. 13–14, author's translation.

24 See File 3SLOTFOM/36 at Archives Nationales d'Outre Mer, Aix-en-Provence. The French state kept colonial subjects in France under intense surveillance and their political groups and associations were thoroughly infiltrated. Reports from the vast network of police spies survive in the SLOTFOM files, and can be found under the heading 'Ministère des Colonies [Ministry of Colonies], Service de Liaison avec les Originaires des Territoires d'Outre Mer [Linking Service with Those Originally from Overseas Territories]'.

25 For more detail on the life and work of Chris Braithwaite aka Jones, see Christian Hogsbjerg, *Mariner, Renegade and Castaway: Chris Braithwaite* (London: Redwords, 2013).

26 Chris Jones, 'Why Colonial Workers Oppose Conscription', *The People*, Port of Spain, 1 July 1939, p. 9.

27 Jones, 'Why Colonial Workers Oppose Conscription', p. 9.

28 Jones, 'Why Colonial Workers Oppose Conscription', p. 9.

29 For the life and work of Elma Francois, see Rhoda Reddock, *Elma Francois: The NWCSA and the Workers' Struggle for Change in the Caribbean in the 1930s* (London: New Beacon Books, 1988).

30 Our Political Correspondent, 'The People's Candidate Scores a Smashing

Victory', *The People*, Port of Spain, 29 January 1938, p. 7.

31   For the life and work of Algernon Wynter Crawford, see Woodville K. Marshall, *I Speak for the People: The Memoirs of Wynter Crawford* (Kingston: Ian Randle, 2003).

32   See James, *George Padmore and Decolonization from Below*; Carol Polsgrove, *Ending British Rule in Africa: Writers in a Common Cause* (New York: Manchester, 2009); Hayes Edwards, *The Practice of Diaspora*.

33   Padmore, 'The Second World War and the Darker Races', p. 7.

34   Padmore refused to undertake British military service in World War Two, privately stating in a letter to the Minister of Labour and National Service: 'I think it is a piece of bold effrontery to expect a victim of Imperialism, who is excluded from all the lofty declarations of the Atlantic Charter, to contribute to the perpetuation of my own enslavement.' For the full text, see Roi Ottley, *No Green Pastures* (London: John Murray, 1952); cited in James, *George Padmore and Decolonization from Below*. More publicly, he also authored an article 'Why I Oppose Conscription', *New Leader*, London, 21 June 1939.

35   See Yomi Adegoke, 'Minority Brits Don't Have to Be "Grateful" for Living in the UK', 14 April 2018 (https://www.the-pool.com/news-views/opinion/2018/15/Yomi-Adegoke-on-ethnic-minority-brits-and-being-grateful), for further discussion on the Stormzy 'controversy' and the racism in expecting gratitude from UK citizens and residents. For discussion of the gratitude discourse in the broader context of British imperialism, also see Nilesh Shukla, 'No I'm Not Grateful for Colonialism, and Here's Why', *Guardian*, London, 6 May 2018.

36   Michel-Rolph Trouillot, *Silencing the Past: Power and the Production of History* (Boston: Beacon Press, 1995). Another reason is the fallacious 'origin myth' of Britain's black community being born with the arrival of the *Empire Windrush*. Thus, as Trouillot argues, the history that cannot be conceptualised is archived, written and transmitted with immense difficulty: as a consequence, the very presence of Black Britons prior to 1948 is constantly contested.

37   'Brick Walls: Racism and Other Hard Histories', address given by Sara Ahmed at Birkbeck Race Forum, London, May 2016.

38   See Hakim Adi and Marika Sherwood, *The 1945 Manchester Pan-African Congress Revisited* (London: New Beacon Books, 1995).

5 | BEFORE NOTTING HILL

The Causeway Green 'riots' of 1949

Kevin Searle[1]

The dominant narrative of post-war 'race' relations in Britain begins with the *Empire Windrush* bringing the earliest Caribbean workforce, and the anti-black riots of 1958 on the streets of Nottingham and Notting Hill signalling the first major instances of 'race-related' public disorder.[2] But there was an earlier phase to this history – one that saw flashpoints between workers of different nationalities housed in Ministry of Labour hostels during the late 1940s. It was in fact the 'racial' policies of such hostels and their handling of potential enmities that may well account for later long-term black settlement patterns. This chapter examines this neglected aspect of Black British History, concentrating on events at Causeway Green, West Midlands, in 1949, when European volunteer workers turned on Jamaicans, attempting to run them out of the hostel, which resulted in restrictions on the number of black workers allowed to stay in government hostels at any one time.

This chapter is based largely on research into the collections of local newspapers held at Birmingham Central Library and grey material at the National Archives.[3] It explores the disturbances at Causeway Green, as well as responses from the community and official agencies, which would attempt to remove the black tenants and implement a restrictive quota system for them across the hostels.

Post-war Britain faced a massive shortage of labour – estimated at 1,346,000 at the end of 1946[4] – and the government tapped a number of sources of labour, including ex-prisoners of war (POWs), Polish ex-servicemen and eventually the European Voluntary Workers (EVW) scheme. There were an estimated 7,000 Polish workers labouring in the mines, foundries and factories of the Midlands,[5] the majority of whom had come under this scheme, which ran until the early 1950s and recruited Eastern European refugees from the displaced persons camps in Germany and Austria to work in a particular range of industries that were experiencing labour shortages. The scheme was deeply discriminatory: given the Poles' status as aliens, they could be directed to, and kept within, certain undermanned and frequently undesirable sectors of employment, a status that clearly differentiated them from Caribbean migrants. As British citizens, Caribbean workers were exempt from such controls. Thousands of West Indians had come to Britain during the war, either as volunteers in the armed forces or as technicians, and while a few remained, the majority returned home. It was the shortage of opportunities, and the underdevelopment of the islands under colonial rule, that provided the impetus for many more to seek employment in the 'mother country' in the late 1940s.[6]

The housing of a number of the new migrant workers in the vicinity of their employment was organised by the National Service Hostels Corporation (NSHC), set up in 1941 by Ernest Bevin, the Minister of Labour and National Service, to 'cater for the needs of workers employed away from home during the Second World War'.[7] After the war, the main function of the NSHC was to provide accommodation for both British and migrant workers on important reconstruction work. It was inevitable, given that Caribbean, Polish, Irish and other labourers would all work together, that they would therefore be housed together in the rather basic but necessary hostels.[8]

Earlier NSHC disturbances

The records of the NSHC report disturbances at their hostels from 1946. The West Bromwich hostel, home to predominantly Irish and Caribbean tenants, witnessed some disorder on 25 December 1946, instigated by the Irishmen's dislike of black men dancing with white female members of staff at the Christmas party.[9] Letchworth hostel in Hertfordshire saw a disturbance in late February 1947, following, 'a "round robin" signed by 350 white trainees demanding the instant removal of all black personnel from the Centre'. There, it was 'believed that the initiation lay with a white extremist and in the melee iron bars were thrown as weapons and some cuts and bruises ensued'.[10] The Greenbanks hostel in Leeds faced trouble on 25 January 1948, where, in the words of the manager: 'The cause appears to be racial prejudice – black men associating with white women.'[11] Disturbances had previously been recorded there in September and December 1947. The Sherburn-in-Elmet hostel in Yorkshire recorded a disturbance on 30 November 1947, as well as a number of other 'outbreaks of one kind or another'.[12] Three months later, problems arose at Pontefract hostel, Yorkshire. In September 1948, Weston-on-Trent hostel, Derbyshire, was the site of disturbances. And, the hostel at Castle Donnington in Nottingham saw a disturbance on 1 August 1948. Again, interracial dances were salient, and '[t]here had previously been trouble at a dance when some of the Irish resented the Jamaicans' advances to white girls (mainly EVWs on the staff)'.[13] Despite the acknowledgement in each of these cases that the Caribbean workers were not the aggressors, the ensuing NSHC correspondence in every instance included the suggestion that they be transferred elsewhere. In a communication about the incident at Castle Donnington, the idea of setting a quota for Caribbean residents, with a maximum of three in any corporation hostel, was proposed. This took place, despite there also being hostilities between different European groups, especially those from the Baltic.[14] The correspondence does not mention a link between these apparently separate incidents, although this is certainly possible. As we shall see at Causeway Green, some of the aggressors travelled from neighbouring hostels.

The Causeway Green 'riot'

In Birmingham after the war, around 100 Caribbeans were similarly accommodated by the Ministry of Labour in overcrowded hostels. These migrants were put up in places such as the Causeway Green hostel, which took fifty, the Salvation Army hostel, Rowton House in Highgate, and the Free Shelter at Winson Green. The largest hostel in the city apparently refused to take black residents, and another imposed a maximum quota of six.[15] Of the approximately 700 men staying at Causeway Green in August 1949, 235 were listed as Poles, 18 as EVWs, 235 Southern Irish, 50 Northern Irish, 65 Jamaicans, and 100 English, Scottish and Welsh.[16]

The breakout of violence at Causeway Green on 8 August was preceded by a number of incidents at the hostel. The report of W. L. Swan, the Regional Welfare Officer, entitled 'Racial Disturbances at Causeway Green Hostel: Jamaicans and Poles', initially describes a 'slight scurry' between Jamaicans and Poles after a dance at the hostel on 3 August 1949. This was followed on 6 August by 'a more serious affair' over the attention of a woman, which would escalate to involve 'a crowd fighting with bottles in the main reception hall'. The report then describes the Jamaicans as withdrawing, only to return 'armed with miscellaneous weapons' and 'throwing bricks etc', before the arrival of the police.[17] Some damage was done to hostel property, including broken chairs, tables, window frames and panes of glass, and eighteen people attended the sick bay for treatment, including a policeman who received a blow to his head that required stitches.

The next day, residents informed the hostel manager that the Poles intended to retaliate in the canteen at midday. The police were called, but apart from a 'skirmish' on the road between three Irishmen and two Jamaicans at 11pm, no incident took place.

The riots began on Monday, 8 August 1949. At 8pm, Polish residents armed with weapons including sticks, stones, razors, factory-made knuckledusters, iron bars, heavy files and lengths of cable commenced an assault on the sleeping block occupied mainly by Jamaicans. Indeed, the Poles had been organising themselves for some time, as some of these weapons had been prepared at their place of work during the day, and there were also reports of their numbers being bolstered by reinforcements from other local hostels. Serious fighting developed, with many missiles – including large lumps of concrete, bottles and whole bricks – being thrown at and into the block. Most of the other occupants in the hostel ran to the air-raid shelters as the fighting continued in and around the building and on the main road, with some of the Jamaicans, who were chased by the Poles, attempting to seek shelter in private homes.

Every policeman in Oldbury had been assembled at the hostel to deal with the trouble. In the eventual round-up, the officers cordoned off all the Jamaicans in the damaged sleeping block. The superintendent of police asked for the immediate removal of all sixty-five Jamaican residents, in part because of his worry that the fifty officers available would not be able to contain the situation. Although in general agreement with the suggestion, the management deemed it impracticable at the time and asked the police to maintain guard all night. Two Jamaicans and two Poles needed hospital treatment, and one policeman was injured.[18]

In the *Birmingham Gazette* story of the events, with the headline 'Jamaicans, told to leave riot hostel, stay put', an NSHC official is quoted as saying: 'We don't want to kick out the Jamaicans, but they are in the minority. There are over 200 Poles in the camp, and only 65 Jamaicans. We couldn't possibly find accommodation for all the Poles.' This article highlights the biased response to the riots, which echoed that at the Castle Donnington hostel in Nottingham a year earlier. Swan's report read: 'on the advice of all parties it seemed most desirable for all of the Jamaicans to be removed before the Poles and British Isles residents returned from work in the evening'. He continued: 'It was known that all of the "white" residents, supported by the residents' committee and, also, the residents in the district in a petition to the Chief Constable and to the Mayor of Oldbury, intended to clamour for the removal of the Jamaicans.' He also added, that '[w]hilst the disturbances with the Jamaicans have mainly affected the Poles, emphasis, by this time, had been given to the wider question of "blacks" versus "whites"'.[19]

Swan's categorical assertion that 'all' of the whites sought the removal of the Jamaicans was not entirely true, as the *Birmingham Gazette* account makes clear: 'Many other hostel residents are incensed that the Jamaicans and not the Poles were told to go.' One resident said, 'It was the same when the Scotch and the Irish lads were in the camp. The Poles always wanted to pick a fight with them.' Ex-artillery sergeant Richard Strauss, until recently a resident in the hostel, added: 'The Jamaicans are, for the most part, a quiet crowd, but the Poles won't leave them alone. Apart from calling them names, and openly insulting them in the camp, they take offence when local girls dance with Jamaicans.'

In the face of the hostility towards them, and the official position that they should leave, the Jamaicans, as the story described it, 'stay[ed] put'. Although they were offered railway warrants to anywhere in England, according to the press article, 'Most of the Jamaicans last night refused to leave the hostel.' Sammy 'Banjo' Walker, a musician, was one of many who decided to stay. He commented:

> I had just returned from Highfield Ballroom, Moseley, where my coloured quintet, the Hot Swing Combo, had been playing, and didn't realise what was happening when I went to my room. I had settled down for the night, and the next thing I knew was that a crowd of Poles had broken into my room. They beat me up and broke the furniture.[20]

Amazingly, as the *Daily Mirror* reported (albeit with the racist opening line 'Chocolate-coloured Sam Walker ...'), Walker went on to perform the following night at the Birmingham Dance Hall.[21]

In the *Gazette* story, Jamaican Horace Halliburton also emerges as an extremely articulate spokesman:

> We are little better than nomads, and consider it very unfair that, though we are British, we are the people to suffer. We have put up with a lot from the Poles, and did not start the recent fights. The Poles brought reinforcements from local hostels, and we were outnumbered by four to one ...

It is not easy for us to find work in England. Even though I hold a London Matriculation Certificate and can speak three languages fluently, I still find it impossible to get a skilled job – because I am a coloured man.[22]

The difficulty of finding work would likely have been compounded by the bad publicity surrounding the event. The Polish presence at the other hostels in the region also worked to influence the Jamaicans' decision to remain. The Regional Welfare Officer's report underlined the Jamaican view that Poles had come from West Bromwich and Wolverhampton to join the rioters on the previous evening, and the West Indians' fear of retaliation, should they be relocated there.[23] The officials recognised this in part, and hoped to transfer them to the Wyken hostel in Coventry, where they thought there would be the least likelihood of reprisal by the Poles. Halliburton, however, was again critical of this idea: 'The authorities have arranged for us to go to Coventry, but there are Poles in the hostel there, and they won't give an undertaking that there will be no trouble.'

There was, however, a mixed response to the attacks among the Jamaicans. Some left that very evening: 'They packed their bags and demanded a police escort. As they walked through the main gates of the camp they were followed by catcalls and jeering from other residents.'[24] The vast majority of Jamaicans who did remain spent the following Tuesday at the hostel, wary of making the journey to work with the tension still simmering. Come the early evening, the other residents had begun to return from work, and they started to congregate in groups, with the whole of Oldbury's police force remaining on guard. By this time, more Jamaicans, in ones and twos, came forward to ask whether they could be led away. The Regional Welfare Officer agreed to issue them with notes to obtain free rail warrants, and said that arrangements would be made with the Ministry of Labour and Colonial Office Welfare to assist those Jamaicans who might wish to go to other towns. A few went further and asked for tickets back to Jamaica. After the issue of the notes (thirty-five in total), most of the Jamaicans wavered in their intention and proposed to leave the hostel the next day after collecting their wages and insurance cards and attending hospital.[25]

Tuesday night also saw the arrival of a coalition representing a number of black groups. These included: the Liverpool and Merseyside Coloured Community Centre, based at Stanley House, Liverpool; journalists from *The Voice*, a newssheet published in Liverpool; the

Association of Africans and People of African Descent; and the League of Coloured People. The report of the Regional Welfare Officer states that the group's general view was that the Jamaicans should be housed together in one hostel. The League had in mind the conversion of a large house it had managed to acquire in Birmingham, which would accommodate twenty or thirty residents. The report also states that they supported the idea of segregating the Jamaicans into one sleeping block; however, this was already the case, despite 'a small number of "coloureds" – the better type' being 'interspersed in other blocks', and despite the objection to the idea among the Jamaican tenants themselves.[26] The latter suggestion was certainly opposed by Horace Halliburton, who wrote a long article in the *Birmingham Gazette* the following Thursday, in which he cited a different reason for the disturbances: 'Fundamentally it boils down to two main factors – accommodation and employment.' Under the headline 'Segregation', he continued: 'The story of Causeway Green riot really started at the beginning of the year when the management suddenly decided to segregate the coloured inhabitants from the Polish and British.' Halliburton argued, 'In my opinion a man has to live with his neighbour before he really gets to know him properly, whereas splitting the races leads to suspicion and estrangement,' and continued by describing his struggles to find work, as well as the saddening tales of everyday racism on the streets of Birmingham. He writes: 'I am heartbroken when I hear mothers point out a coloured man to their children and say: "I'll set the black bogy man on you if you are not well-behaved."'

Local residents, supported by the residents' committee, lost no time in voicing their opposition to the trouble and sent a petition the very next day to the council, Police Superintendent Bache and their local MP, Arthur Moyle. The petition, signed by thirty-six residents in the district drawn from Wolverhampton Road, Brook Road and St Matthew's Road, placed the blame, in no uncertain terms, on the Jamaicans:

> Great distress was caused, to the inhabitants of the private houses, near the huts which were attacked. The coloured men climbed into the gardens and attempted to enter the houses. In one case where a coloured man did enter a house to seek shelter from his pursuers there was a small baby and two aged grandparents.[27]

It ended with a call for the 'coloured' element to be removed, or the 'hostel closed'. This was met with a response directed by the Minister of Labour and National Service, arguing that the suggestion 'would be tantamount to the imposition of a "colour bar" which would be contrary to the policy of His Majesty's Government, and impossible to justify in a commonwealth in which a large proportion of its citizens are coloured'. It also drew attention to the fact that transferring the men to another hostel would create unemployment.[28]

By 10 August it had become clear that '[t]he Jamaicans, as a body, did not want to leave Causeway Green' and '[v]ery few intended to proceed to other towns, notwithstanding earlier requests'. 'The controller had agreed that no coercion should be used for those Jamaicans who were not willing to leave but that we should provide facilities for any who still wished to do so.'[29]

Clearly angry at these developments, the chairman and secretary of the residents' committee met with representatives of the NSHC. They criticised the way in which the hostel administration and police had handled the affair and 'pressed for eviction of all the Jamaicans, and considered that there would be no safety, particularly for the 40 women residents, plus staff until that course was taken'.[30] The Jamaican response was to emphasise the resentment shown to them by most local people. One spokesman argued that:

> They were British subjects, most of them having fought for this country and had been brought here or permitted to come by the British government. When certain types of women were friendly with German POWs there was not much reaction. There was no resentment against foreign workers but as soon as a coloured man was seen in company with a white woman much resentment was in evidence and insults relating to their colour and parentage were shouted around.[31]

It had also become clear that the police did not intend to prosecute any of the offenders, alleging insufficient evidence. They were asked to continue to maintain law and order and warned publicans against supplying too much drink to 'coloured' and 'foreign-speaking' workers. The police did suggest that four Jamaicans who were seen as particularly 'undesirable residents' be evicted from the hostel. A spokesman for the Jamaicans reported that, in the view of the majority of Jamaicans, the four 'undesirables' should face removal. However, in a further show of resistance to the prejudiced response, Swan's report noted that the eviction notices given to two of them '"caused such merriment as to suggest that the recommendation by their coloured representatives was phoney." It was implied that they were selected as it was known they had secured other jobs.' In addition to the four Jamaicans, a Polish resident, described as 'usually present when trouble is afoot', was transferred to another hostel, with similar action proposed for several other Poles.[32]

Between November 1948 and August 1949, there had been several evictions at the hostel by the manager, Mr Flann: nineteen Irish (mainly for drunkenness), eleven British (for disturbances of one kind or another), six EVWs (for various disturbances), ten Jamaicans (mainly for having women in their sleeping quarters) and one Jamaican at the request of other Jamaicans.

It is unlikely that the Irish, British and EVWs were not taking women into their sleeping quarters as well. Indeed, the Jamaicans had noted the absence of any opposition when German ex-POWs were seen with local women. If this was the case, then it would appear that the Jamaicans had been unfairly targeted. In fact, the Jamaicans had complained about discrimination from the manager before, with Flann claiming that he had been threatened by Jamaican residents during the disturbance and had bricks thrown into his bungalow while his wife and child were inside. Despite his claim to have shown 'tolerance and sympathetic understanding' towards the coloured men, Mr Flann seemed to have a particular interest in their removal, and he had been heard to say that 'he will be unable to remain if the Jamaicans are retained'.[33]

Introducing quotas

The idea of a quota, initially raised after the disturbance at Castle Donnington, promptly came back into discussion. The number of three in each hostel, which had been suggested then, was replaced with the equally arbitrary but slightly less restrictive figure of twelve. The policy that sought to impose a limit of 'not more than 12' Jamaicans at any one hostel was set out in a minute from the NSHC's Chief Administrative Officer, Mr Handyside, on 11 August 1949:

> Ultimately after further discussion it was suggested by us as a basis for agreement that a limit should be fixed to the number of West Indians to be accepted as residents at any hostel, and that in any case where that number had already been exceeded action should be taken by the Ministry of Labour as early as possible to bring that figure down. This was accepted in principle and we left the ministry's officers in no doubt that in our view the maximum should be not more than 12.[34]

However, with sixty-five Jamaicans present at Causeway Green prior to the riot, and many refusing to move on afterwards, it was clear that twelve was a particularly ambitious number. Official policy at Causeway Green, therefore, was to reduce the numbers of Jamaicans to thirty.[35] In a letter dated almost two weeks later, an official, who described the atmosphere at the hostel as 'subdued even if smouldering', wrote that 'any attempt to reduce the numbers of Jamaicans at Causeway Green suddenly, other than by gradual running down process, would spread rapidly from hostel to hostel with most unfortunate results'.[36]

On 21 August a special service took place at Birmingham parish church; present was Jamaican activist Horace Halliburton, who was joined by Wledystew Rozycki, a university-trained draughtsmen, now working as a polisher, as a representative of the Poles.[37] The reports of the service reflect the paternalist, unconscious racism of the time: 'In fluent English, Mr Halliburton, an out-of-work machinist said ...'; 'Around them a choir of Englishmen sang "The Church's One Foundation" and the two men forgot their loneliness.' The Reverend Bryan Green, apparently unaware of the cold shoulder so often found in British pews at the time, declared from the pulpit: 'There is a problem here, one of our most crucial problems – the relationship between races. If the church takes a lead she has got a gospel for the age.'[38]

Despite the quota and church service, the council and local residents continued to agitate for a number of months. A meeting was held involving the local mayor, Alderman Good, the local MP, Arthur Moyle (who had obtained special leave of absence from Mr Attlee to be present), Police Superintendent Bache and Swan, the Regional Welfare Officer, in November 1949. Moyle described the residents as 'still scared stiff', although he, and other members of the council, emphasised 'that no racial feeling against the coloured residents remained'. However, and in stark contradiction to this claim, the subcommittee of Oldbury Corporation, which was present, still felt that: 'The hostel generally was a blot on the communal and social life of the district and the health of the community: the sooner the coloured workers and indeed the whole hostel could be removed the better the council would be pleased.' The notes also, sadly, allege that 'in one week six applications had been made for the acceptance [presumably into local authority controlled homes] of illegitimate coloured babies'. It continued, this time shifting the onus on to the white women who engaged in relationships with black men, stating that: 'The August outbreak had been entirely due to the presence of women of an undesirable class.'[39]

The 'rule of twelve' brought in three days after the disturbance soon came in for criticism. It could potentially do 'damage to that good name [of the NSHC] if grounds are given for the accusation of colour prejudice'; it was disapproved of for its 'arithmetic', as the hostels varied in capacity 'from over a thousand places to under a hundred';[40] and it was disparaged on 'policy' grounds, as it frustrated efforts to direct labour to undermanned industries.[41] It came in for additional criticism after a dispute over the placing of a thirteenth 'coloured man' in a hostel.[42] Thus, a call was made for a quota of 10 per cent of the total capacity of a hostel, with a maximum ceiling of thirty.[43] This policy was underscored by a self-assured colonial view of the British capacity to rule, reminiscent of the speeches of imperialist statesmen, such as Birmingham's own Joseph Chamberlain, made half a century earlier.[44] One fairly typical memo, written by NSHC Executive Director R. H. Bindloss, read:

> We should, by this time, know something of handling people of various races and our experience regarding Jamaicans is that, so long as they are in a definite minority of any one nationality, they are fairly easy to handle and we have found that, with certain exceptions, they can live amicably with other white races. Individually, some of the West Indians are decent, well-behaved men but, and this is really important, collectively and when inspired by the presence of sufficient numbers, they can and do become arrogant and insulting. Theoretically, and for those who have not to live amongst them, there should be no reason why all races, white and black, should not live together in complete harmony. But, no amount of wishful thinking will alter the fact that it does not mean a thing to the Poles or the Southern Irishmen that these Jamaicans are British subjects, in respect of whom no colour bar exists. Whether it is acceptable or not, it has to be faced that Poles, together with Southern Irishmen, do not and will not mix with West Indians. It is not in question that we, as a corporation, seek to discriminate against West Indians, but nothing we can do will alter fundamental racial antagonisms.[45]

It was agreed that the numbers of West Indians should be kept as low as possible, and that what the memo would go on to describe as the 'mixing of the unmixables' should not take place. In contrast to the views of Halliburton, segregation was key to maintaining order.

Thus, the 'rule of twelve' was expanded on, and hostels could: (1) accept 'coloured' residents up to 10 per cent of the total capacity of an industrial hostel, subject to a maximum ceiling of thirty; (2) if regarded as potential trouble spots, have a lower ceiling of twelve black people; or (3) not be considered suitable at all. Another letter written by Bindloss on 'The Proportion of Coloured Workers in Industrial Hostels' explained the allocation:

> As regards statement (1), this is where the maximum number of coloured residents are to be housed, following on from your request that we take 10% of the maximum capacity of each hostel, up to a figure of 30. In statement (2), our proposal, to take in only a limited number of coloured residents, is more or less for the following reasons: (a) trouble experienced previously with West Indians, or (b) large number or large proportion of women residents or (c) the British residents (which in this case includes Southern Irishmen) in a minority. In such cases, we think the allocation of 12 beds only reasonable and is in the best interests of the hostels. The reason for statement (3) is that practically all the hostels in this statement are predominantly Polish.[46]

The document still identified Causeway Green as problematic, with a statement that the hostel had seven people over the limit, and a call to reduce the figure to thirty. Therefore, employment became dependent on where black people could be properly housed and looked after, in spite of repeated calls from industry to relax the ceiling.[47]

Conclusion

A critical analysis of what happened at Causeway Green in 1949 certainly disrupts the accepted wisdom that 1958 saw the first post-war 'race riots' in Britain, but it also challenges the dominant narrative that such riots in the first half of the twentieth century were economic in nature and predominantly over access to jobs.[48] The Polish and Jamaican labourers shared an experience of migration, a similar position in many of the least desirable jobs in industry, and a feeling of estrangement. Yet this did not lead to much in the way of class-based comradeship. In fact, it appears that a more primeval sentiment – against interracial relationships – played a vital role in the unrest at Causeway Green.[49]

Racist, patriarchal attitudes seem to have been important causes of the fray. Several Poles admitted that 'they resented Jamaicans taking young girls into the hostel'.[50] This feeling was shared by many locals, who also stereotyped white women who displayed an interest in black men as having loose morals, and black men as criminalised and over-sexed. Local papers were full of quotes such as 'It seems that girls of 14 or 15 who hang about the hostel at night are the cause of most of the fights. It is a pity that something can't be done about them', and 'It is not safe for our wives and children to be out after dark.'[51] Interracial relationships were a festering sore, and three days after this story, there was a report of a stabbing incident involving a mixed union at the Brockworth hostel in Gloucester.[52]

Of course, the 'mixing of the races' did not apply when whites from Eastern Europe were involved. Drawing on parliamentary debates from the time, Kay and Miles point out that the government had a very different view of relationships between displaced persons from the continent and local people, and of those between black people and white Britons, and that the 'replenishment of stock' and 'an infusion of vigorous new blood from overseas' were also important reasons leading to the former's entry.[53] They write: 'They were variously described as "ideal immigrants", as "first-class people, who, if let into this country, would be of great benefit to our stock" and would refresh, enrich, and strengthen "our island population".'[54]

The Causeway Green episode and the agitation around the NSHC hostels highlight the essential contradiction that, for black people, 'it was their labour that was wanted, not their presence'.[55] Throughout the whole discussion about hostels, numbers and quotas runs the tension between the need for labour (of whatever hue) for rebuilding firms, factories and services and the worry about social unrest if concentrations of black people were seen to be too large.

What emerges from this analysis of archival documents is the deep hypocrisy that characterised British 'race' policy from the period when colonial countries gained independence until the late 1960s (when agitation from black organisers and their allies forced anti-discrimination legislation into statute). The natural reaction of government ministers and civil servants was a benevolent paternalism impregnated with a strong dose of 'commonsense' racism born of colonial distrust of colour. They were never to square up to racism. Instead, as in this case, they 'problematised' racism's victims – the Jamaicans. (The Jamaicans were expected to move. There never was an expectation that the Poles, who had started the trouble, would be asked to do so.) But at the same time, with an eye to the New Commonwealth, they were worried that their actions might be attributed to 'colour prejudice', for these were, after all, British citizens.[56] Hence the contortions – attesting to liberal values while discriminating in effect: the dilemma identified by Gunnar Myrdal in his 1944 race study of America.

The reaction of the state, particularly through the NSHC, local council and police, as well as the residents' committee, all united around a wish to remove the Jamaicans and served to legitimise the rioters, and therefore racism itself. The press, too, although slightly more sympathetic (a point highlighted and grumbled about by the NSHC),[57] failed to take an impartial position. Their description of the events as 'racial riots', implying a clash of two equally matched sides, is clearly problematic, as by their own acknowledgement the disturbances largely consisted of Polish residents attacking an outnumbered – by four to one – group of Jamaicans.

What has hitherto not been examined is the way in which early policies, such as those inflicted on black workers using government hostels, may account for the patterns of Caribbean settlement that we take for granted today. In 1948, the Ministry of Labour initially accommodated the *Windrush* immigrants in air-raid shelters in Clapham South. The closest labour exchange to the shelters was on Coldharbour Lane, in Brixton, and this was where many of the Jamaicans went for their documents and permits, and there they were not run out of town.[58] They were to make it their own – with (black) Brixton now a cultural and economic hub of south London.

Notes

1   This chapter would not have been possible without the assistance of Professor Ian Grosvenor and Dr Andy Green. Professor Grosvenor initially told me about the incident, and Dr Green helped me locate some of the primary data on which the study is based. I would also like to thank Jenny Bourne at the Institute of Race Relations, who originally published the paper in *Race and Class* in 2013 and has given permission to republish an edited version of it here. My final thanks go to Professor Hakim Adi for his comments, and the privilege of being included within this collection, as well as to Kesewa John for inviting me to speak on the subject at the 'History Matters' conference in 2017. Any errors or omissions are, however, my own.

2   The major broad-sweep historical studies of the black presence in Britain have not mentioned the incident at Causeway Green. These studies usually describe the events at Nottingham, and then Notting Hill, in 1958 as the first racialised disturbances to take place in the post-war British hinterland, or imply that they were the first incidents of unrest. Cf. Peter Fryer, *Staying Power: The History of Black People in Britain* (London: Pluto, 1984), pp. 376–81; Dilip Hiro, *Black British, White British: A History*

of Race Relations in Britain (London: Paladin, 1992), pp. 38–40; Mike Phillips and Trevor Phillips, *Windrush: The Irresistible Rise of Multi-racial Britain* (London: HarperCollins,1998); Ron Ramdin, *The Making of the Black Working Class in Britain* (Aldershot: Gower, 1987), pp. 204–10; John Solomos, *Race and Racism in Britain* (New York: Palgrave Macmillan, 2003). Studies of public disorder or 'riots' in the twentieth century have also failed to include incidents at Causeway Green and the other NSHC hostels. Cf. Harris Joshua et al., *To Ride the Storm: The 1980 Bristol Riot and the State* (London: Heinemann, 1983), pp. 7–55; Michael Rowe, *The Racialisation of Disorder in Twentieth Century Britain* (Aldershot: Ashgate, 1998); David Waddington, *Contemporary Issues in Public Disorder: A Comparative and Historical Approach* (London: Routledge, 1992), pp. 74–94. Causeway Green has not, however, been entirely absent in the literature; it was briefly noted in Edward Pilkington, *Beyond the Mother Country: West Indians and the Notting Hill White Riots* (London: I. B. Tauris, 1988), pp. 49–51; and in Shirley Joshi and Bob Carter, 'The Role of Labour in the Creation of a Racist Britain', *Race and Class* 15 (3), pp. 53–70, see p. 60. There were also further non-coastal disturbances in Deptford and Camden around the same time that have largely been forgotten and would make interesting areas for future research.

3 See, in particular, 'Disturbances in National Service Hostels Corporation Hostels Due to Incompatibility of Various Nationals', The National Archives (TNA): PRO LAB 26/198.

4 'Cabinet Man-Power Working Party Memo', 30 November 1945, Cab. 134/510, quoted in Joshi and Carter, 'The Role of Labour', p. 55.

5 Dennis Irving, 'The Race Dispute in the Midlands: Polish Workers: Are We Fair to Them?', *Birmingham Gazette*, 12 August 1949.

6 Cf. Fryer, *Staying Power*; Phillips and Phillips, *Windrush*; Ramdin, *The Making of the Black Working Class*.

7 In particular, there was difficulty finding workers for the armaments industries, as they were located in areas with little accommodation. For more information, see, National Archives, *National Service Hostels Corporation: Papers*, 2017, http://discovery.nationalarchives.gov.uk/SearchUI/details/C10137?descriptiontype=Full, accessed 5 December 2017.

8 Ruth Glass observes that although in the early 1950s there were migrants who were initially housed in temporary accommodation, chain migration would become the most common form of migration, where new migrants would travel to the address of a friend or relative. Ruth Glass, *Newcomers: The West Indians in London* (London: Centre for Urban Studies,1960), pp. 45–7.

9 TNA: PRO LAB 26/198, 31 December 1946.

10 TNA: PRO LAB 26/198, 26 February 1947.

11 TNA: PRO LAB 26/198, 26 January 1948.

12 TNA: PRO LAB 26/198, 9 December 1947.

13 TNA: PRO LAB 26/198, 9 August 1948.

14 The NSHC mentions that: 'The nationals of the Baltic States were strongly opposed to each other. This was an antagonism of several centuries and it could not be dissipated merely by bringing them all together for a few weeks in a hostel' (TNA: PRO LAB 26/198, 22 March 1948). The NSHC also voiced concern at 'mixing warring races', such as a number of German former POWs with Poles, Czechs, Yugoslavs and others, in a hostel at Totley Wells, Scotland, in January 1949 (TNA: PRO LAB 26/198, 10 January 1949).

15   Simon Taylor, *A Land of Dreams: A Study of Jewish and Afro-Caribbean Migrant Communities in England* (London: Routledge, 1993), p. 105.

16   TNA: PRO LAB 26/198, 11 August 1949.

17   TNA: PRO LAB 26/198, 'Racial Disturbances at Causeway Green Hostel: Jamaicans and Poles'.

18   TNA: PRO LAB 26/198, 'Racial Disturbances'.

19   TNA: PRO LAB 26/198, 'Racial Disturbances'.

20   'Jamaicans, Told to Leave Riot Hostel, Stay Put', *Birmingham Gazette*, 10 August 1949.

21   'Sam's Heart Was for Once Out of Tune', *Daily Mirror*, 10 August 1949.

22   Horace Halliburton, 'I Protest against the Colour Bar', *Birmingham Gazette*, 11 August 1949.

23   TNA: PRO LAB 26/198, 'Racial Disturbances'.

24   'Police Rushed to Quell a Hostel Riot', *Birmingham Gazette*, 9 August 1949.

25   TNA: PRO LAB 26/198, 'Racial Disturbances'.

26   TNA: PRO LAB 26/198, 'Racial Disturbances'.

27   TNA: PRO LAB 26/198, 9 August 1949.

28   TNA: PRO LAB 26/198, 16 August 1949.

29   TNA: PRO LAB 26/198, 'Racial Disturbances'.

30   TNA: PRO LAB 26/198, 'Racial Disturbances'.

31   TNA: PRO LAB 26/198, 'Racial Disturbances'.

32   TNA: PRO LAB 26/198, 'Racial Disturbances'.

33   TNA: PRO LAB 26/198, 'Racial Disturbances'.

34   TNA: PRO LAB 26/198, 11 August 1949.

35   TNA: PRO LAB 26/198, 22 August 1949.

36   TNA: PRO LAB 26/198, 22 August 1949.

37   'Church Must Lead Against Racial Clash: Rector', *Birmingham Gazette*, 27 August 1949; 'Talk by a Pole and West Indian', *Birmingham Mail*, 22 June 1949.

38   'Church Must Lead Against Racial Clash: Rector', *Birmingham Gazette*, 27 August 1949.

39   TNA: PRO LAB 26/198, 11 November 1949.

40   TNA: PRO LAB 26/198, 3 September 1949.

41   TNA: PRO LAB 26/198, 28 November 1949.

42   TNA: PRO LAB 26/198, 26 October 1949.

43   TNA: PRO LAB 26/198, 28 November 1949.

44   Chamberlain stated: 'I believe that the British race is the greatest of governing races that the world has ever seen … I say this not merely as an empty boast, but as proved and shown by the success which we have had in administering vast dominions' (quoted in Fryer, *Staying Power*, p. 183). See Fryer, *Staying Power*, pp. 165–90 for more on Teutonic and other forms of pseudo-scientific racism.

45   TNA: PRO LAB 26/198, 28 December 1949.

46   TNA: PRO LAB 26/198, 5 January 1950.

47   Much of this opposition came from the regional offices and representatives of business, eager for more cheap labour. See Kevin Searle, '"Mixing of the Unmixables": The 1949 Causeway Green "Riots" in Birmingham', *Race and Class* 54/3 (2013), pp. 44–64, especially pp. 56–9, for a more detailed discussion.

48   Waddington, *Contemporary Issues*, p. 74, argues that the history of twentieth-century urban rioting in Britain occupies two distinct phases: 'a period, from 1900–62, where violence was interracial in form' and 'a period, lasting from the 1970s to the present day, where violence has taken the form of confrontations between black youths

and the police'. Joshua et al. also make a perhaps similar distinction between pre-war and post-war riots, although they highlight that 'neither of these periods nor the categories of violence are discrete' (*To Ride the Storm*, p. 13). The truce between capital and labour forms an important characteristic in explanations of the riots that took place in British port towns during the first part of the twentieth century (cf. Joshua et al., *To Ride the Storm*, p. 36; Ramdin, *The Making of the Black Working Class*, p. 200); Waddington, *Contemporary Issues*, pp. 75–9). Joshua et al. argue that, in order to understand 'the circumstances that shape the concerns of white crowds we must look to the nature of race, class and power in the seaport city ... In the eyes of organised white labour resident colonial seamen not only represented a threat to jobs and wage levels, they were also perceived as an unwitting tool in the hands of capital through which the unions could be contained, even undermined.'

49 The study also raises important questions for further research about racism in Polish and other white migrant communities. Despite the large Jewish contingent, there were certainly instances of antisemitism within the Anders' Army. Cf. Joanna Michlic, Poland's *Threatening Other: The Image of the Jew from 1880 to* *the Present* (Lincoln: University of Nebraska Press, 2008).

50 'Police Rushed to Quell a Hostel Riot', *Birmingham Gazette*, 9 August 1949.

51 Police Rushed to Quell a Hostel Riot', *Birmingham Gazette*, 9 August 1949.

52 'Coloured Man on Stabs Charge', *Birmingham Mail*, 12 August 1949.

53 Diana Kay and Robert Miles, 'Refugees or Migrant Workers: The Case of the European Volunteer Workers in Britain (1946–1951)', *Journal of Refugee Studies* 1 (1988), p. 216.

54 Kay and Miles, 'Refugees or Migrant Workers', pp. 215–16.

55 Ambalavaner Sivanandan, *A Different Hunger: Writings on Black Resistance* (London: Pluto, 1982), p. 4.

56 Cf. Joshi and Carter, 'The Role of Labour'.

57 TNA: PRO LAB, 22 August 1949.

58 Cf. Glass, Newcomers, pp. 46–7; Sheila Patterson, *Dark Strangers: A Sociological Study of the Absorption of a Recent West Indian Migrant Group in Brixton, South London* (London: Tavistock, 1963), p. 55; Phillips and Phillips, *Windrush*, pp. 81–8); South London Press and *The Voice*, *Forty Winters On: Memories of Britain's Post War Caribbean Immigrants* (London: Lambeth Council, 1988).

6 | HISTORY BEYOND BORDERS

Teaching Black Britain and reimagining black liberation

Kennetta Perry

Trinidadian-born artist Horace Ové is perhaps best well-known for becoming the first Black British filmmaker to direct a full-length feature film, following the release of *Pressure* in 1976. In *Pressure*, Ové offers a coming-of-age story about a young black man aiming to forge his own path while negotiating the world of his first-generation migrant parents and the realities of racism in Britain during the 1970s – realities that fuelled forms of radical black activism and resistance among younger generations of Black Britons.[1] But before Horace Ové ever teamed up with writer Sam Selvon to produce *Pressure*, one of his earliest experiences in filmmaking was his work on a short documentary shot in 1968 provocatively titled *Baldwin's Nigger*. This film featured a dialogue between celebrated writer James Baldwin and comedian Dick Gregory as they engaged a largely black audience at the West Indian Student Centre in London in a discussion about what the opening credits described as 'the Black experience in America' and its relationship to 'that of the Caribbean and Great Britain today'.[2]

In the beginning of the film Baldwin is seen addressing a crowded room, recounting a story of an encounter with a West Indian worker at the British Museum who wanted to know where he was from. After explaining that he had been born in Harlem, New York to a mother originally from Maryland and a father born in New Orleans, Baldwin found the man growing exasperated and impatient with his response. Eventually, he began to understand that the man desired an answer about the place where the specific roots of his genealogical tree could be found – information that Baldwin would never be able to provide. He explained to his audience that precisely because his 'entry into America is a bill of sale' he could never truly know where his roots in Africa lay. And because of the ruptured history that brought him to America as enslaved property, he insisted that what he knew of his family's past had been lost. He acknowledged: 'At some point in our history I became Baldwin's nigger. That's how I got my name.'[3]

As the audience remained captivated, Baldwin went on to describe how his exchange with the West Indian worker dramatised some of the tensions and lack of historical understanding between black populations in different parts of the world. He suggested that this divide produced an inability to comprehend shared experiences, appreciate differences, and form meaningful alliances that might upset the social and political order. To illustrate this point, Baldwin suggested that the unfolding of the institution of slavery in the Americas depended on the capture of peoples of varied ethnic backgrounds, with different languages, often unfamiliar to one another. He reasoned:

> [W]hen I became Baldwin's nigger it's also very important to point out I was handcuffed to another man from another tribe whose language I did not speak. We did not know each other. Because if we could have spoken to each other we might have been able to figure out what was happening to us. And if we could have figured out what was happening to us we might have been able to prevent it. We would have had in short a kind of solidarity which is a kind of identity which might have allowed us – which might have made the history of slavery very different ... Well that didn't happen and here we are.[4]

In this instance, the '*here*' where Baldwin saw himself and the largely West Indian audience in London to whom he spoke was in a two-way dialogue that aimed to share their experiences, understand commonalities and differences between them, and mobilise the type of revolutionary consciousness necessary to mount a concerted attack on 'the entire power structure of the Western world'. For Baldwin, this was part of what it meant to actively take hold of freedom. Before concluding his remarks and taking questions from the audience, Baldwin suggested that a key element of working collectively to 'plot against the master' involved unearthing 'our history'. Although he had previously admitted that he had little understanding about 'what it means to be black in London', he told a mainly Afro-Caribbean audience of black Londoners, 'I am part of the history that occurred in the Caribbean, and you are part of the history that occurred in Harlem. And one has got to accept that and find out how to use that.'[5]

Baldwin's comments invite us to consider how and why researching and teaching histories of Black Britain can be viewed as part of a larger potentially transformative and indeed liberatory process of creating much-needed dialogues of political significance across communities of the African diaspora. Since the late 1970s and early 1980s there has been a steady stream of books, articles, academic conferences, grass-roots organising and popular celebrations – including the establishment of nationally recognised commemorations of Black History month beginning in earnest in the late 1980s – documenting the black presence in Britain.[6] Collectively, these developments have laid a critical foundation for the growth of Black British History as both an academic field of inquiry and as a means of understanding how people of African descent have shaped the history of the British Isles and the British Empire more broadly. Understandably, campaigns to represent and incorporate Black British History as part of the national curriculum at all levels of the education system have largely been focused on the importance of these histories in countering negative racial stereotypes, fostering a greater sense of inclusion and centring race and racism within the life of the nation historically.[7] But given that histories of Black Britain are in fact vantage points for exploring the political, social and cultural linkages that have defined the history of African diaspora, it is useful to consider the importance of teaching Black British History as a means of imparting a global understanding of the contours of black history in Britain and beyond.

This essay raises the following questions: what is the value of teaching Black British History as part of a global Black Studies curriculum? How can this be done in such a way as to illuminate James Baldwin's point that we should seek to understand more about the linkages between black histories in different parts of the world while not papering over the specific conditions that have shaped black life across the African diaspora? And how can we begin to think about Black British History as both a means of telling a history of the British nation and empire that incorporates and accounts for the experiences of people of African descent and histories of the African diaspora, but also as a means of developing transnational dialogues about racial politics in both Britain and the United States?

To explore these questions, I would like to reflect on some of the strategies that I have used in the classroom to infuse Black British History into an African and African American Studies curriculum for students in the United States, most of whom typically identify as Black American. Previously, I have constructed these courses under a premise similar to that reflected in James Baldwin's comments offered at the

West Indian Student Centre in 1968. In any Black Studies course, part of my goal is to teach students to understand how and why the study of black history is in fact the study of world history. It is a dynamic story of the African diaspora that traverses geographical boundaries and extends in many directions. It is not a story confined to Britain or the United States – or any one nation, for that matter. It is indeed a history beyond borders. I have found that one of the most effective ways of illustrating this point for the students whom I have taught at US institutions is to challenge them to rethink iconic moments and personalities that they might typically associate with the black freedom struggle in an American context and use them as a type of thoroughfare into black histories and race politics beyond the United States. In doing so my goal is to get students to move beyond national boundaries to understand histories of black activism and visions of freedom as they took shape on a global stage. Britain is key to that story and the political agendas and spaces that have shaped black histories in the UK are essential ingredients.

Here, I would like to offer three examples of such an approach drawn from events of the 1960s and 1970s: the 1963 March on Washington, the travels of Malcolm X and the trial of Angela Y. Davis. In discussing each of these events, I would like highlight what these moments can tell us about Black British History and histories of racial politics in Britain. Essentially, these three events will function as a point of entry, a pathway that provides a means of connecting the threads between African American History, Black British History and the history of the African diaspora. While it can certainly be argued that histories of black America are all too often used to paper over our understanding of the distinct social conditions and political realities that have shaped life for black people in Britain historically, the goal here is not simply to draw a one-way dotted line from the US to Britain.[8] Alternatively, my larger point is to demonstrate how understanding black histories shaped by and within a British context can become a means, or one type of strategy, for disrupting the type of nationally oriented thinking that, as James Baldwin suggested, limits possibilities for revolutionary organising and the formation of transformative solidarities among black populations across borders and boundaries.[9] Making these connections is part the political imperative of black history as a field of inquiry that provides essential reference points and tools for imagining possibilities for black liberation that extends across borders.

London's March on Washington

On 25 August 1963, three days before over a quarter of a million people descended on the National Mall in Washington DC to participate in the historic March on Washington, Claudia Jones wrote to James Baldwin on behalf of a coalition of Africans, Asians and West Indians in Britain expressing a desire to stand in solidarity with the struggles of black people in America for 'democratic rights'.[10] Jones's letter came in response to a plea issued by Baldwin and several other American expatriates living in Paris at the time to show demonstrations of solidarity all around the world with the upcoming March on Washington for Jobs and Freedom.[11] In her letter, Jones noted that the group that she spoke for, the London-based Committee of Afro-Asian Caribbean Organisations, had formed in the aftermath of the assassination of civil rights campaigner Medgar Evers and the ongoing news of violence against black protesters in places such as Birmingham, Alabama during the spring of 1963. She explained that the support of black communities in Britain for the March on Washington and the broader cause of 'Negro equality' in America stemmed from their belief that this movement was one that was shared and linked to anti-colonial struggles for liberation, independence and human dignity being waged by Africans, Asians, West Indians and other colonised people around the world, including in the United Kingdom. As a demonstration of solidarity, Jones shared with Baldwin her Committee's plans to make representations of support at the US Embassy in London on 28 August 1963, the same day as the March on Washington. Additionally, she solicited a statement of support from him that could be read at a separate solidarity march in London to be held three days after the Washington march to bring attention to the importance of anti-racist struggle and coalition building in Britain.[12]

Claudia Jones certainly needed no invitation from James Baldwin to consider why developments taking place in the United States were only one front in a wider movement for black liberation. Before arriving in Britain in 1955 following her deportation from the United States, Jones had acquired an extensive amount of political experience as a journalist, editor, organiser and speaker. She began her political career working in defence of the Scottsboro Boys during the mid-1930s. She held national positions in the Communist Party USA, served as editor of *Negro Affairs* and penned essays that laid the groundwork for modern black feminist thought with her ideas about the super-exploitation of black women workers. Once she arrived in London in 1955 she hit the ground running. Although she became involved in a number of social and political organisations, one of Jones's most enduring legacies in Britain came from the establishment of the *West Indian Gazette* newspaper. The pages of the *West Indian Gazette* provided a type of gathering place for black people in Britain to create a sense of community and plug in to world affairs. And it was in the pages of the *Gazette* that she helped black communities in Britain understand that black struggle anywhere should be of concern to black people everywhere.[13]

As organisers including Claudia Jones made plans for London's solidarity march, they developed a list of slogans meant to capture their intent to show support for the March on Washington. As expected, many of the slogans spoke directly to their desire to offer an open display of unity and comradeship between Black Americans and black communities in Britain. Expressions including 'Support Negro Peoples Struggles in the USA', 'US Negroes, Your Fight is Our Fight' and 'End Racialism Now' spoke directly to the plight of Black Americans and championed the urgency with which activists framed their demands for civil rights and social justice. But alongside their rallying cries of solidarity, Black British activists and organisers also developed protest slogans that captured some of the specific issues that defined how they made connections between the struggles for citizenship and equal justice being waged by Black Americans and those of black communities in Britain. Just as organisers envisioned a march that demonstrated solidarity with Black Americans, they also aimed to create a platform to publicise and draw greater attention to particular concerns facing black people in Britain. Slogans including 'End Colour Bar in Britain' and 'Repeal the Immigration Act' reminded audiences in Britain that their message of solidarity in struggle was just as much a local one as it was a transatlantic one.[14] And, in fact, as organisers prepared to trek from Ladbroke Grove to the US Embassy, it was precisely the racially charged issue of 'immigration' that symbolised one of the major battlegrounds where the struggle against racism, or what was often described as the 'colour bar', was being fought in Britain during the early 1960s.

By August 1963 it had been little more than a year since the Commonwealth Immigration Act of 1962 had gone into effect. While the British Nationality Act of 1948 formally ensured the continuity of a long tradition of migration to Britain from parts of the empire, including British colonies in Africa and the Caribbean, the Commonwealth Immigration Act did the reverse. It effectively rescinded the automatic right of migration for British subjects arriving from the Commonwealth and created different categories of British citizens from the Commonwealth based on their potential relationship to the labour market. From its inception, the racial overtones of the bill were unmistakable. Throughout the 1950s, a number of British cities including London, Manchester and Birmingham experienced an increase in black settlement and the formation of black communities largely populated by newcomers. And at the time of the bill's passage the overwhelming majority of Commonwealth citizens arriving in Britain represented non-white migrants coming from parts of the Caribbean and the Indian subcontinent.

Although the black presence in Britain is well documented before the twentieth century, much of the demographic transformation happening in British cities during this period, which resulted in greater racial and ethnic diversity, was associated with Commonwealth migration trends occurring following World War Two. And policymakers certainly took notice. For over a decade before parliament ever considered what became the Commonwealth Immigration Act, British officials in the Home Office and the Colonial Office actively debated in private about how to design a scheme for regulating Commonwealth migration in such a manner that did not explicitly deny entry on the grounds of race or place of birth, but could produce a result that accomplished such a goal.[15] Given that Britain touted the ideals of multiracialism, universal rights and flexible borders as part of the post-war Commonwealth ideal, officials knew that they could expect a backlash if it appeared that any decision to regulate Commonwealth migration had racial motivations. But in the wake of widely reported incidents of racial violence, including the infamous Nottingham and Notting Hill 'white riots' in 1958, coupled with the circulation of popular stereotypes about the sexual and economic threat that West Indian men in particular posed, they were able to leverage a type of media fiction about the problem that the growing presence of black newcomers posed for the white working classes to justify the need for implementing migration controls.

Early reaction to the Commonwealth Immigration Act among Black British activists and political organisers came swiftly and with biting criticism. A brilliant strategist and political analyst, Claudia Jones encouraged a view of the bill that considered its implications for those Commonwealth citizens contemplating moving to Britain from places such as Jamaica, Barbados, Pakistan and Nigeria, as well as those who had already made the journey and were working to become fully incorporated into British society. Describing the bill as a form of 'legalised apartheid', Jones suggested that its impact carried a double edge.[16] Invoking the well-known racial practices of South Africa, a regime that had become internationally synonymous with the preservation of white power through the disenfranchisement of a black majority, Jones suggested that the underlying premise of migration restrictions aligned with the same mantra adopted by racists – 'Keep Britain white' – by creating barriers of exclusion that, by design, disproportionately affected people of colour. To be sure, not only did the bill send a message about who the nation valued as potential migrants by creating barriers for black working-class newcomers seeking employment opportunities in Britain, but in Jones's opinion it also advanced the same logic of second-class citizenship that black people in Britain experienced on a day-to-day basis as they encountered such things including housing ads that barred their application, job prospects that disappeared when employers discovered their race, and acts of violence. So, then, just as migration restrictions literally closed the border for large numbers of Commonwealth migrants, they also reinforced and gave additional credence to the notion that black people did not belong as British citizens, nor were they welcome. This, in fact, is the message that Black British activists took to the streets of London in solidarity with the March on Washington in August 1963. Like Black Americans, they too saw themselves as second-class citizens in a nation that promised them equal rights irrespective of race even if the specific conditions that sought to cheapen the value of their status as citizens took shape in different ways.

Malcolm X in Smethwick

Nearly a year after the Committee of Afro-Asian Caribbean Organisations galvanised marchers in a show of solidarity with the March on Washington for Jobs and Freedom, as the general election of 1964 approached, the issue of immigration controls remained central to the anti-racist political agendas adopted by black activists and organisations. Moreover, with the racially charged campaign of Conservative candidate Peter Griffiths, who managed to unseat the Shadow Foreign Secretary Patrick Gordon Walker to become MP for the West Midlands town of Smethwick, immigration became a crucial wedge issue that dominated political debate throughout the election season and beyond. Since immigration restrictions had come under Harold Macmillan's Conservative government in the wake of opposition from Labour MPs including Patrick Gordon Walker, the Conservative Party stood as defenders of their efforts to limit what remained a largely non-white Commonwealth migration. By default, this meant standing behind a law designed to exclude those migrants from enjoying the full rights and entitlement associated with British citizenship. Griffiths staked his campaign on this premise and actively campaigned to a local base of supporters who were hostile to black and Asian newcomers.

While it is unclear exactly which group began to paper the town of Smethwick with flyers emblazoned with the incendiary slogan 'If you want a nigger for a neighbour, vote for Labour', the local popularity of the sentiment brought national attention to Griffith's campaign and to the town of Smethwick. Although Griffiths did not take credit for openly adopting the slogan, which ultimately became synonymous with his campaign, as white constituents in his district embraced the underlying idea of the openly racist message captured in the slogan, Griffiths did little to distance himself from the sentiments. In fact, in an interview with *The Times*, he suggested that those who adopted such views did not deserve a rebuke since the slogan represented what he described as 'a manifestation of popular feeling'.[17]

Even though Peter Griffiths entered the halls of parliament as an outcast because of the racist anti-immigrant views that he championed as a candidate for Smethwick in the general election of 1964, when Malcolm X came to Britain in February 1965, Griffiths was one of the people that he desired to meet.[18] This meeting never happened. However, accompanied by a team from the BBC, Malcolm X made a point of documenting his face-to-face confrontation with the place that had brought Griffiths to political infamy. More specifically, during his visit, Malcolm X journeyed to Marshall Street in Smethwick, a place that flagrantly displayed an open hostility towards what was described at the time as the presence of 'coloured immigrants'. Smartly dressed, wearing his signature browline glasses, BBC cameras captured footage of Malcolm X as he strolled down Marshall Street. Two of the most iconic frames from this footage depict him standing before a sign indicating his location on Marshall Street and another as he stood peering through a window at a for-sale sign posted on a property in the street. These images were not accidental. They functioned as part of a larger critique that Malcolm X intended to make about the state of race relations and the political economy of racism affecting black and Asian communities in Britain during the mid-1960s. As Malcolm X took questions from reporters who followed his short trek down Marshall Street, he explained that he had taken a detour from a speaking tour, which included stops at the London School of Economics and Birmingham University, to visit Smethwick because he had been disturbed by 'reports that the coloured people in Smethwick are being treated badly'. He explained, 'I have heard they are being treated as Jews were under Hitler,' and suggested to reporters that people of colour in the area should work proactively to combat such treatment and not 'wait for the fascist elements in Smethwick to erect gas ovens'.[19] In doing so, he issued a call for direct resistance and strategic organising in the face of white supremacy, racial exclusion and discrimination.[20]

Even after the election of Peter Griffiths, developments in the town of Smethwick remained national news. This was in large part due to the decision of the Conservative faction of the local council to pursue a controversial plan to use public funds to buy vacant properties on Marshall Street in an effort to block black and Asian families from purchasing or renting property on the street. According to Conservative councillors, the goal of buying properties on Marshall Street to limit people of colour from occupying homes was meant to avoid seeing the area evolve into a 'ghetto' – a term that carried racial connotations and signalled a type of urban decline marked in part by concentrations of black settlement.[21] To accomplish this, Conservatives aimed to maintain a white majority residential population on Marshall Street. Defending the Conservative position, one of the local councillors insisted that 'colour prejudice' or racial discrimination did not drive their agenda. Instead, he imprudently suggested that keeping the number of black and Asian families residing on the street at less than half would provide a means for more successfully integrating black and Asian newcomers.[22]

Malcolm X's decision to walk along Marshall Street challenged the very premise of local Conservatives' restrictive housing plans. Whereas white residents, including a local coalition of white housewives, pursued an agenda to keep black residents out of their neighbourhoods, Malcolm X made a different claim about life on Marshall Street for black people. With BBC cameras in tow, he claimed it as a place where black people could leisurely stroll, contemplate occupying property, and where they should have an expectation to rightfully belong. Moreover, as a figure known globally for his commitment to black liberation and his unflinching message to oppose all forms of white supremacy 'by any means necessary', his presence in Smethwick sent a powerful message that highlighted the ways in which local communities – and more specifically the everyday life in individual neighbourhoods – were some of the very places where black people in Britain found their rights to settle and become fully incorporated into British society on their own terms tested and under siege.[23]

In 2012, the Nubian Jak Community Trust issued a blue plaque commemorating Malcolm X's visit to Smethwick. The marker recognised him as an 'international civil rights campaigner' who had advocated for 'desegregated housing in Smethwick with his visit to Marshall Street in 1965'.[24] But well before Marshall Street in Smethwick ever captured the type of national headlines that ultimately placed it on Malcolm X's itinerary during his visit to Britain in the weeks before his death, housing had long proven to be a key arena where black people in Britain experienced the day-to-day impact of racism and second-class citizenship. The testimonies of first-generation black migrants settling in Britain following World War Two consistently highlight the difficulties of securing affordable, quality housing in large measure due to de facto racial practices that made it socially acceptable to discriminate on the basis of race in considering housing applicants or in determining fees for renting or purchasing property. As the British population as a whole faced post-war housing shortages, black migrants typically found the process of securing accommodation even more daunting as they entered the bottom of waiting lists for public housing and had to negotiate with landlords charging exorbitant rental fees for overcrowded spaces with subpar amenities. According to May Cambridge, who migrated from Kingston, Jamaica to England during the 1950s, the search for decent housing often involved preparing oneself for rejection. She explained:

> The 'no Irish, Black or Dogs' signs are no myth – sometimes you would knock on the door with a vacant sign in the window, some would say the room had just gone, others would just slam the door in your face while the less forthright wouldn't bother opening the door but you could see the curtains twitching.[25]

It was precisely stories like that of May Cambridge which prompted grassroots organisations, including the London-based Coloured People's Progressive Association (CPPA), to make housing a key focal point of their work in local black communities during the late 1950s. Formed in the aftermath of the Notting Hill violence, which primarily targeted black residents in West London during the summer of 1958, under the leadership of Frances and Don Ezzrecco, not only did the CPPA concern itself with advocating on behalf of the safety and security of black residents, but it also provided assistance for black newcomers who wanted to seek relief from racketeering landlords who violated rental agreements and tenancy laws.[26]

In the months following Malcolm X's visit to Smethwick, the newly elected Labour government introduced Britain's first national anti-discrimination policy – the Race Relations Act of 1965. This act vaguely prohibited racial discrimination in 'places of public resort' and made 'incitement to racial hatred' a criminal offence. However, with the glaring omission of any provisions addressing racial discrimination in the areas where black people encountered the sting of second-class citizenship on a day-to-day basis – in housing and the employment sector – it was obvious that the Act provided little more than a sticking plaster for an open wound. Moreover, when the Labour government coupled the passage of anti-discrimination policies with the extension of what many Black Britons regarded as racially motivated immigration controls, it provided yet another example of the state's active role in maintaining a system that would not fully honour or safeguard the rights of back people as British citizens.

Lobbying for a more effective anti-discrimination policy became the main agenda of an organisation known as the Campaign Against Racial Discrimination (CARD). CARD was formed in the aftermath of Martin Luther King Junior's visit to London during a stopover on his way to claim the Nobel Peace Prize in Oslo in 1964. Although factions within the organisation debated the extent to which CARD should focus its energies on influencing the legislative agenda of a new Labour government, under the leadership of David Pitt CARD became a leading advocate for expanding the scope of the first Race Relations Act. Part of the strategies that CARD adopted to make a case to officials and the larger public about the problem of racial discrimination and the ineffectiveness of the Race Relations Act of 1965 came from the playbook of American civil rights organisations, including the Student Non-Violent Coordinating Committee (SNCC) and the Congress of Racial Equality (CORE). Just as the Freedom Riders had aimed to expose the lack of federal enforcement of civil rights law throughout the American South, in making a case for stronger anti-discrimination policies, CARD activists also desired to qualify and quantify the forms of discrimination in a variety of areas that defined black life in Britain during the 1960s, including housing, the consumer marketplace, interactions with the police and the employment sector. In doing so, despite the internal tensions that threatened its survival during the late 1960s against the backdrop of the rising tide of Black Power politics, CARD proved essential in laying a blueprint for provoking a national conversation about the existence of racial discrimination in British public life – a conversation that still remains as relevant and necessary in the twenty-first century.[27]

Defending Angela Davis and resisting the power of the state

When federal authorities arrested Angela Y. Davis in connection with an armed raid on a local courtroom in California in October 1970, her case garnered the attention of supporters sympathetic to her cause around the world. Jonathan Jackson, the younger brother of George Jackson, one of three men charged with the murder of a white prison guard at Soledad prison, led the raid that resulted in the escape of two black inmates and the shooting dead of the presiding judge. Yet according to authorities, Davis, a college professor and outspoken radical activist, had purchased the guns used in the raid just two days earlier. Before the police killed Jonathan Jackson during his attempt to flee, he allegedly demanded the release of his brother and the two other men, who had become known as the Soledad Brothers, as a type of ransom for the five hostages that he had kidnapped. And it was the link between Davis and the guns used in the raid, coupled with her connection to a larger campaign to seek justice on behalf of the Soledad Brothers, that police used as evidence to charge her as part of a conspiracy of kidnapping and murder.[28]

During the nearly sixteen-month period that Angela Davis remained incarcerated without bail, her case became an international cause célèbre as supporters from around the globe raised funds, protested and petitioned US officials on her behalf. On 4 December 1971, the London-based West Indian Standing Conference sponsored a 'Free Angela Davis Dance' held at Finsbury Town Hall. Proceeds from the event went to the Islington branch of the Angela Davis Defence Committee in London.[29] In addition to the Islington branch, a separate branch worked under the same name in Harrow. Just days after

Davis finally made bail in February 1972, supporters from the Harrow branch of the Angela Davis Defence Committee issued a resolution expressing support for efforts in parliament to seek a repeal of the most recent legal attack on the rights of black people in Britain, the Immigration Act of 1971, and resolved to 'oppose racialism and racialist legislation' in their own country as an extension of their support for Davis.[30]

As previously discussed, before Angela Davis's case became a rallying cause for British supporters, the issue of immigration control had become one of the most important legislative flashpoints of British race politics during the 1960s and early 1970s. Whereas previous acts had included provisions to limit a largely non-white Commonwealth migration stream, the conditions set forth in the 1971 act essentially closed the border for migrants coming from parts of the Commonwealth in Africa, the Caribbean and Asia to enter Britain on a permanent basis. Moreover, this act implicitly sanctioned a heightened level of surveillance and suspicion of black and Asian communities in Britain as immigration law became the pretext used to revoke citizenship rights and create so-called 'illegal' immigrants who could be detained and deported. Just as immigration control officers held the power to enforce what these provisions would mean for those seeking to enter Britain, for those already residing in the country, police were on the front lines of enforcing the meaning of the devalued citizenship status that immigration law had created for black people. And as surely as members of the Harrow committee who supported Angela Davis witnessed the unfolding of the trial of nine grassroots organisers charged in the aftermath of a demonstration against racial profiling, harassment and violence by the Metropolitan Police in the autumn of 1971, they also saw the parallels between the abuses of state power that delivered unjust outcomes in the legal system for black defendants in both the US and Britain.

The trial of the 'Mangrove Nine' shed light on the long-standing issues that shaped relationships between black people in Britain, the police and the criminal justice system. After nearly two years of police raids on the Mangrove Restaurant, operated by Frank Critchlow, a place that had become a hub of black social and political life in London during the late 1960s and early 1970s, local organisers including Darcus Howe and Althea Jones-Lecointe arranged a march to protest what had become nothing short of a targeted campaign by the

Metropolitan Police to disrupt a black business, stifle black political activity and intimidate black people from forming a community. As marchers encountered a heavy police presence, tensions rose, conflict ensued and violence erupted. In the aftermath, police arrested nine individuals on a host of charges including inciting a riot, affray, causing bodily harm and possessing offensive weapons in connection with the clash between protestors and police. And just as Angela Davis would place the US criminal justice system on trial as the state of California brought a set of politically motivated charges against her based on perceptions of her radical politics and her embrace of the Black Power movement, many comparisons can be made with the Mangrove Nine as defendants, who employed a similar strategy to defend themselves before the state.[31]

Even before Angela Davis would get to place a request before the court to have her trial moved to a venue with a more racially and ethnically diverse jury pool, the defendants in the Mangrove Nine trial had already brought national attention to their case by making a request for an all-black jury of their peers as a legal right of citizenship under British law.[32] Although the judge in the case denied the request, the Mangrove defendants, including Darcus Howe and Althea Jones-Lecointe, a key leader in the British Black Panther organisation, helped transform the dynamics of the courtroom into a platform for highlighting some of the biases and inequities embedded in the legal process that shaped their fate in the criminal justice system and their relationship to the state. By defending themselves, interrogating potential jurors about their views on the meaning of Black Power, resisting what they deemed to be unfavourable judicial procedures in the courtroom and raising questions and offering commentary, Mangrove defendants became architects of their own defence and prosecutors of the state. Arguably, in many ways this strategy yielded dividends. Not only did it produce a jury that included two black people, but, perhaps more importantly, it resulted in the dismissal of some of the most serious charges against the Mangrove Nine, full acquittals for five of the defendants, and suspended sentences for four who were found guilty of lesser charges.[33] Moreover, similar to the trial of Angela Davis, the Mangrove Nine case represented an important media event that black activists leveraged to bring greater public visibility to the everyday indignities and denials of justice that black people in different parts of the world routinely faced in their encounters with the police and the wider legal system. It is in the process of broadening our approach in such a way that allows students to see these types of links between people, experiences, places and times that we as educators and scholars can begin to shape a more robust historical consciousness that may in turn have an impact on how current generations diagnose key issues and devise political solutions needed to address issues shaping the conditions of black life in the present. This, too, requires conversations that transcend the borders of individual nations and the way we frame black history in pursuit of those strategies.

When most students taking Black Studies courses encounter the literary work of James Baldwin, the fierce oratory of Malcolm X, or the rhetoric and imagery associated with iconic figures from the Black Power Movement including Angela Davis in a frame that does not take a global and diasporic approach, they are less likely to gain a sense of how these individuals shaped and were shaped by Black Britain. But in my own classroom, what I have found is that Black British History provides an instructive context and counterpoint that challenges students to reconsider events, personalities and agendas that have shaped the meaning of black freedom within the US and throughout the African diaspora. By exploring the linkages and particularities between histories of Black America and those of Black Britain, the classroom becomes a space where students are invited to rethink their assumptions about the exceptionality of US civil rights campaigns, movement strategies and visions of anti-racism. Moreover, in reckoning with black histories through a diasporic perspective, they are also encouraged to re-evaluate how they understand what it means to be black in historical terms. In this sense, blackness and the conditions shaping anti-blackness become more than simply markers of identity. Instead, students are able to see these categories as they are structured differently in time and space and in relation to state power and economic realities. But just as the differences between historical experiences in different geographical spaces have to be accounted for, as James Baldwin suggested fifty years ago in his dialogue at the West Indian Student Centre, connecting the dots is critical and holds the potential for transforming the course of history. Therefore, in threading these ties, the study of black history is a necessary tool of empowerment for students on both sides of the Atlantic to collectively imagine radical possibilities for seizing a type of freedom without borders in our current moment.

Notes

1 Horace Ové, *Pressure* (British Film Institute, 1976).

2 Horace Ové, *Baldwin's Nigger* (British Film Institute, 1969). For more on Baldwin's engagement with the racial politics of postcolonial Britain, see Rob Waters, '"Britain is No Longer White": James Baldwin as Witness to Postcolonial Britain', *African American Review* 46 (2013), pp. 715–30.

3 Ové, *Baldwin's Nigger*.

4 Ové, *Baldwin's Nigger*.

5 Ové, *Baldwin's Nigger*.

6 Selected titles include Folarin Shyllon, *Black People in Britain, 1555–1833* (London: Oxford University Press, 1977); Peter Fryer, *Staying Power* (London: Pluto Press, 1984); Paul Gilroy, *Ain't No Black in the Union Jack* (Chicago: University of Chicago Press, 1987); Ron Ramdin, *The Making of the Black Working Class in Britain* (London: Gower, 1987); Gretchin Gerzina, *Black London: Life Before Emancipation* (New Brunswick: Rutgers University Press, 1995); Norma Myers, *Reconstructing the Black Past: Blacks in Britain, 1780–1830* (London: Frank Cass, 1996); Jeffrey Green, *Black Edwardians: Black People in Britain, 1901–1914* (London: Routledge, 1998); Hakim Adi, *West Africans in Britain, 1900–1960* (London: Lawrence and Wishart, 1998); Marc Matera, *Black London* (Berkeley: University of California Press, 2015); David Olusoga, *Black and British* (London: Macmillan, 2016); Miranda Kaufmann, *Black Tudors* (Oneworld, 2017).

7 The Black and Asian Studies Association has been one of the leading organisations in this work since the early 1990s. Their work is foundational for understanding more contemporary campaigns advocating for a decolonised curriculum at UK universities.

8 For an excellent discussion of this dynamic, see Jacqueline Nassy Brown, 'Black Liverpool, Black America and the Gendering of Diasporic Space', *Cultural Anthropology* 13/3 (1998), pp. 291–325.

9 Although his approach is not necessarily historically grounded, this point is also implicit in Paul Gilroy's *The Black Atlantic: Modernity and Double Conscious* (London: Verso, 1993).

10 Claudia Jones to James Baldwin, 25 August 1963, Claudia Jones Papers, Donald Hinds Private Collection.

11 Mary Dudziak, 'The 1963 March on Washington: At Home and Abroad', *Revue Française d'Études Americaines* 107 (2006), pp. 64–7.

12 Claudia Jones to James Baldwin, 25 August 1963.

13 For more on Jones, see Marika Sherwood, *Claudia Jones* (London: Lawrence and Wishart, 2000); Bill Schwarz, 'Claudia Jones and the *West Indian Gazette*: Reflections on the Emergence of Post-colonial Britain', *Twentieth Century British History* (2003), pp. 264–85; Carole Boyce Davies, *Left of Karl Marx* (Durham: Duke University Press, 2008).

14 'List of March Slogans', n.d., Claudia Jones Papers, Donald Hinds Private Collection. See also Kennetta Hammond Perry, 'US Negroes, Your Fight is Our Fight: Black Britons and the 1963 March on Washington' in Robin D. G. Kelley and Stephen Tuck (eds), *The Other Special Relationship* (London: Palgrave, 2015).

15 Bob Carter, Clive Harris and Shirley Joshi, 'The 1951–1955 Conservative Government and the Racialization of Black Immigration' in Winston James and Clive Harris (eds), *Inside Babylon* (London: Verso, 1993).

16 Memo, Claudia Jones on behalf of the Afro-Asian-Caribbean Conference, 31 January 1962, Claudia Jones Research Collection, Schomburg, New York.

17 'Candidate Seeks Apology', *Guardian*, 11 March 1964.

18 Grame Abernathy, '"Not Just an American Problem": Malcolm X in Britain', *Atlantic Studies* 7/3 (2010), p. 290.

19 'Britain's Most Racist Election: The Story of Smethwick, 50 Years On', *Guardian*, 15 October 2014.

20 For more on Malcolm X's visit, see Stephen Tuck, *The Night Malcolm X Spoke at Oxford Union* (Berkeley: University of California Press, 2014), Chapter 5.

21 'Housing Move at Smethwick', *Guardian*, 7 December 1964.

22 'Housing Move at Smethwick', *Guardian*.

23 For the most detailed discussion of Marshall Street and race politics in Smethwick, see Alice Ritcherle, 'Opting Out of Utopia: Race and Working Class Political Culture in Britain During the Age of Decolonization, 1948–1968' (PhD thesis, University of Michigan, 2005), Chapter 5.

24 'Plaque to Honour Malcolm X Visit to Smethwick in 1965', BBC News, 21 February 2012.

25 'May Cambridge', *Forty Winters On: Memories of Britain's Postwar Caribbean Immigrants* (London: *The Voice* newspaper, 1988), p. 32.

26 'Many Voices on Notting Hill', *Kensington News and West London Times*, 29 May 1959.

27 For more on the history of CARD, see Kennetta Hammond Perry, *London Is the Place for Me* (New York: Oxford, 2016), Chapter 6; Benjamin W. Heinemann, Jr., *The Politics of the Powerless: A Study of the Campaign Against Racial Discrimination* (London: Oxford University, 1972).

28 Angela Davis, *Angela Davis: An Autobiography* (New York: Random House, 1974).

29 'Free Angela Davis Dance' flyer, n.d., Movement for Colonial Freedom Papers, Box 75, SOAS.

30 Harrow branch of Angela Davis Defence Committee resolution, 27 February 1972, Movement for Colonial Freedom Papers, Box 72, SOAS.

31 Anne-Marie Angelo, 'The Black Panthers in London, 1967–1972: A Diasporic Struggle Navigates the Black Atlantic', *Radical History Review* (2009), pp. 17–35; Robin Bunce and Paul Field, *Darcus Howe: A Political Biography* (London: Bloomsbury, 2013), Chapters 7–11.

32 'Defence Demands All Black Jury', *Guardian*, 6 October 1971.

33 'Mangrove Four Sentenced', *Guardian*, 17 December 1971; Robin Bunce and Paul Field, 'Mangrove Nine: The Court Challenge Against Police Racism in Notting Hill', *Guardian*, 29 November 2010.

7 | 'THE SPIRIT OF BANDUNG' IN 1970s BRITAIN

The Black Liberation Front's revolutionary transnationalism

W. Chris Johnson

This chapter charts the origins and early years of the Black Liberation Front (BLF), a revolutionary socialist organisation founded in North London in 1971. Part of a broad constellation of Black Power groups in Britain at the time, the BLF was a small, clandestine collective of first- and second-generation immigrants from Africa, Asia and the Caribbean. For various reasons, including protecting their own personal and collective security, BLF members were secretive. They did not seek fame or publicity. Opposed to hierarchy and authoritarian leadership, they practised democratic and collective decision making. 'In the cause of survival for Black people all over the world,' BLF members devoted themselves to the unglamorous work of unifying, empowering and safeguarding disparate black populations – 'peoples of African, Asian, Caribbean and Latin American origin who share the common enemy, the common oppressor'. Organising at the intersection of diasporas, members of the BLF described themselves as embattled 'Third World minorities' lacking the numbers, and therefore the power, to activate a revolution within Britain. Locally, they institutionalised a politics of 'survival' through social welfare programmes for vulnerable and abused black populations, particularly youth, prisoners and the formerly incarcerated, and people with mental illness. Globally, they leveraged their position 'inside the belly of the monster' to support movements for independence and self-determination in their 'home countries'. Theirs was a vision of total liberation for the world that required complete political, cultural, economic and territorial decolonisation.[1]

Black Power for the Third World

In mission as well as membership, the BLF was heir to the Universal Coloured People's Association (UCPA), a multiracial 'anti-racist, anti-fascist, anti-imperialist' organisation that operated in chapters across

Britain from June 1967 to July 1970. The UCPA promoted a 'Third World ideology' of Black Power that would unite 'revolutionary movements in the Caribbean, Latin America, Asia, Africa and elsewhere, to secure human rights, dignity and justice for oppressed people'.[2] Grounding the organisation in the tradition of the 1955 Asian-African Conference, the UCPA called for a revival of 'the Spirit of Bandung' locally and internationally. 'We Asian, African and Latin-American countries and peoples need to co-operate in the economical and cultural fields,' the organisation argued, to overturn 'the prolonged period of colonial and semicolonial exploitation and oppression'.[3]

During the summers of 1967 and 1968, the Home Office exploited provisions in the 1965 Race Relations Act to arrest UCPA speakers, writers, and spokespersons – including founding chair Obi Egbuna – on charges of 'incitement to racial hatred'. Accusing the police of trying 'to silence all critics of white racist oppression', the UCPA appealed to 'all Black People in Britain', as well as 'kith and kin' in their 'home countries', to plan collective, coordinated, cross-border campaigns against instruments of British imperialism. 'Any time you hear of racist attacks against Black people in Britain,' the organisation urged, 'take immediate reprisals against British Companies, British Interests and British subjects in African, Asian and Caribbean countries.'[4]

In the autumn of 1968, the Home Office targeted Tony Soares, the presumed new 'leader of the UCPA'.[5] Praised by comrades as 'a militant defender of black people's rights', Soares was born to a Goan family in East Africa and came of age in Tanzania, Mozambique, India and Portugal before arriving in Britain in the early 1960s. A veteran of anti-colonial student movements in Mozambique and Portugal, and a student of liberation movements worldwide, Soares worked to build relationships, connections and alliances among freedom fighters inside and outside UK borders.[6] On 9 October 1968, an undercover detective attended a weekly public meeting of the Notting Hill Vietnam Solidarity Campaign at Essex church. There, the detective claimed, a man she knew as 'Tony Sinaris' distributed a leaflet that encouraged protestors to form 'small commando units' to attack US infrastructure in London. The leaflet, assembled by members of the UCPA and the Working People's Party of England, repurposed language from an essay in Robert F. Williams's *The Crusader* newsletter, published the previous year. *The Crusader* was freely available in London's radical bookshops. On 27 October, the demonstration proceeded without incident of 'urban guerrilla warfare'. Four days later, on the evening of 31 October, three detectives detained Soares outside the Baker Street post office as he left work.[7] Instead of plagiarism, Soares was indicted on three charges of incitement to violence. On 24 February 1969, Soares was convicted of two of the charges and sentenced to two years in prison.[8]

Ideological and interpersonal conflicts had fractured the UCPA into a number of collectives scattered about London's black enclaves. Harold Moore, editor of the organisation's *Black Power Newsletter*, had been expelled from the London branch. In May 1970, the Manchester branch expelled spokesperson Ron Phillips.[9] At the end of July 1970, the Trinidad-born Trotskyist George Joseph and the Jamaica-born scholar Alrick Cambridge transformed the UCPA into the Black Unity and Freedom Party (BUFP). Based in Lewisham, the BUFP fore-grounded interracial working-class solidarity within Britain, and revived the Trotskyist anthem 'Black and White, Unite and Fight'. In Brixton, the Trinidad-born medical student Althea Jones-Lecointe oversaw the Black Panther Movement, founded by a group of former UCPA members in the spring of 1968. Although the Black Panther Movement had adopted the emblem and name of the Oakland, California-based Black Panther Party for Self-Defense, the organisation had no formal ties to its muse across the Atlantic.[10] Divided more by borough than beliefs, the BUFP and the Black Panther Movement lobbied for political reforms within the UK to combat state and vigilante violence, and to bolster the citizenship rights of Black British people. While both organisations carried the banner of Afro-Asian solidarity, they were led by Caribbean-born university students, with a rank-and-file membership largely of Afro-Caribbean youth. 'The Spirit of Bandung' seemed to be slipping away.[11]

While he was in prison, Soares had been invited to join the North London Collective of the Black Panther Movement in Haringey by four of its organisers: Farid Cama, Harold Moore, Valentino Jones and Anselm Samuel. Composed of about twenty regular members, the North London Collective operated out of Samuel's house at 99 Crouch Hill Road in Haringey. At that time, Samuel and the other three men were embroiled in a conflict with the Panther's Brixton-based central committee. Soon after Soares joined the collective, the central committee suspended the four men and the North London Collective elected to form its own organisation. After two meetings of discussion and debate, they decided on a name: the Black Liberation Front.[12]

Survival and liberation

During weekly Sunday meetings, the freedom dreamers defined and refined their purpose, platform and ideology. The BLF retained the UCPA's definition of black as 'all non-white peoples of African, Asian, Caribbean and Latin American origin' and foregrounded that identity in its ever-evolving manifesto: *Revolutionary Black Nationalism.* The problem, they agreed, was an ongoing global 'genocide' of non-white peoples. Across 'the Americas, Southern Africa, Australia, and New Zealand', the BLF argued, white-settler colonial regimes had devastated indigenous peoples and their lands. Debt, extractive industries and imperialist wars increased suffering inaugurated by slavery and colonialism. Within Britain, they observed, 'Black people are denied human rights and are socially and cultural dehumanised.' As a minority population, the BLF feared that an attempt at armed revolution would be 'suicidal'. Instead, they planned to develop a range of 'survival' programmes to improve the lives of black people and build strong, united, self-reliant black communities in Britain. The next stage of struggle would harness the resources of those communities to support liberation movements at 'home', and the creation of unified socialist states in Africa, South Asia, the Caribbean, Latin America and the Middle East.[13]

The BLF's revival of 'the Spirit of Bandung' made it uniquely comfortable for activists situated at the conjuncture of diasporas. 'There was a natural fit and synergy, both in terms of the politics and in the human relationships between people,' recalls the activist Ansel Wong, a Trinidad-born artist of African, Carib, Chinese and Portuguese descent. Before meeting Tony Soares and joining the BLF, Wong had built close relationships with various Black Power movements and black arts collectives in the Caribbean and North America. A university-educated teacher and artist, Wong was 'an acceptable face' for the organisation, a respectable front for subversive activities. Bridging borders of class and race and natal nation, the relationship between Wong and Soares – the artist and the insurgent – was representative of the solidarities the BLF demanded, personified and struggled to build.[14]

The BLF quickly established a base – the Grassroots Storefront – where they sold radical and revolutionary literature, African crafts, posters, clothing and music. They also started a newspaper: *Grassroots.* Sold by members, writers and supporters outside Tube stations in Brixton, Notting Hill and Finsbury Park, *Grassroots* circulated throughout the black enclaves of London, within prisons, and – by its third issue – across the United Kingdom. A collective work of revolutionary collage, *Grassroots* assembled news, dispatches, letters, analysis and artwork from freedom fighters throughout Britain and around the world.[15] Alongside critiques of racism, imperialism and state violence, *Grassroots* condemned sexism and gender oppression and upheld models of black women's 'aggressive revolutionary fervour' across the world.[16]

The August 1971 issue of *Grassroots*, for instance, featured an analysis of black women as the 'most exploited section of the working class'. The column was an abridged mash-up of essays published in the May 1971 pamphlet *Black Women Speak Out*, an anthology of writings by the Black Women's Action Committee of the Black Unity and Freedom Party. In a broadside dedicated to the memory of the Trinidad-born Communist revolutionary Claudia Jones, the Black Women's Action Committee distilled the concept of triple exploitation – advanced by Jones and Louise Thompson Patterson in New York during the 1930s and 1940s – to a grassroots audience in 1970s London: 'Black women suffer in three ways, 1. we are poor 2. we are black 3. we are women ... being all three in western/capitalist society means that all the shit from whitemen, whitewomen and Black men fall on our head.'[17]

While resurrecting a key part of the UCPA constitution, the BLF's demand for 'an end to the oppression of Black women from all quarters' emerged from more recent theorising by friends and comrades in the Black Women's Movement in Britain, particularly BLF member Gerlin Bean. Brought up in a rural village in Hanover, Jamaica, where she was nurtured by traditions of communal living and mutual aid, Bean migrated to England in 1960 to train to become a nurse. In 1970, Bean dedicated her life to community empowerment and revolutionary politics, centring her advocacy on the defence and empowerment of black women, children and youth. Bean's political wanderlust led her to the front lines of a range of freedom movements against racism, sexism, militarism, homophobia, poverty, unemployment, economic exploitation, child abuse and ableism in Britain, Zimbabwe and the Caribbean. For Bean, like her comrades, these campaigns were inseparable, interwoven stages of a global struggle for Total Liberation.[18]

Repression breeds resistance

Through travel and correspondence, both Tony Soares and Ansel Wong had established contact with chapters of the Black Panther Party in the United States. During the summer of 1971, the International Section of the Black Panther Party, headquartered in Algiers, arranged for the BLF to publish seven essays written by Eldridge Cleaver about a recent trip to the Congo. The BLF printed excepts in *Grassroots* and published the pamphlet, *Revolution in the Congo*, in August.[19] Later that month, Kathleen Neal Cleaver, Secretary of Communication for the International Section, invited the BLF to become the UK chapter of the Revolutionary Peoples Communication Network, a transnational system to exchange information and coordinate action among 'oppressed peoples all over the world'.[20]

In August 1971, *Grassroots* announced the BLF's alliance with the International Section. The same issue featured a page from *The Black Panther Community News Service* on 'Organizing Self-Defense Groups'. The article, written by Panther Field Marshall DC (Donald Lee Cox), featured illustrated instructions on how to safely shoot and clean a rifle, as well as recipes for homemade explosives. Cox later issued a correction because the recipes for a 'Self-igniting Molotov Cocktail' and 'People's Handgrenade' did not work. *Grassroots* cited its source, informing readers that the article was from the Panther newspaper, which was legally available in UK bookshops. Two months later, following the complaint of a community relations officer in Hackney, Special Branch officers detained Soares for questioning. As distribution manager for *Grassroots*, Soares denied that he had anything to do with editorial content for the issue. He was working long hours as a clerk at the North Kensington Law Centre, he said, and did not have time to contribute to *Grassroots*.[21]

Later that month, Soares took an extended working holiday. Wong and Soares travelled together from London to Paris and then Soares flew alone to Dar es Salaam. In Tanzania, Soares spent time with family and met with representatives from the People's Movement for the Liberation of Angola (MPLA) and the Mozambique Liberation Front (FRELIMO) at their offices. Soares travelled on to Algiers, where he liaised with revolutionary movements there, including the Panthers. At the headquarters of the International Section, Soares and Eldridge Cleaver discussed Cleaver's recent essay 'On Lumpen Ideology'. The BLF published the essay in pamphlet form following Soares's return to London.[22]

While Soares was in Africa, *Grassroots* reported that warrants had been issued for the arrest of the newspaper's editor and distribution manager. Several months later, on 9 March 1972, Inspector Hovell and Detective Sergeant Peter Westcott arrested Soares as he signed on at the Hammersmith Labour Exchange. In a replay of events from October 1968, Soares was indicted on four charges of incitement to violence for distributing previously published material. The police raided Soares's flat, confiscating his papers and notebooks from Algiers. Special Branch ransacked the Storefront, seizing the supplementary school textbooks and supplies, organisation files, merchandise, and £250 in cash. 'The offices were stripped bare,' *Freedom News* reported.[23] At the committal hearing on 15 March, Hovell and Westcott revealed that they belonged to a Special Branch espionage unit organised in July 1971 to spy on black activists.[24]

The month-long trial opened on 20 February 1973. The Special Branch detectives presented detailed dossiers on each defence witnesses, many of them BLF members or affiliates who had collaborated on issues of *Grassroots*. During cross-examination, Hovell threatened to arrest defence witnesses for information revealed in their testimony. After an eight-hour deliberation, the jury found Soares guilty of attempting to incite arson and incite readers to make explosives. In a ruling that shook the Old Bailey, King-Hamilton sentenced Soares to 200 hours of community service. He was also bound over for seven years to keep the peace. The judge threatened a prison sentence to 'exceed double figures in years' were Soares to confront similar charges in the future. The judgment was a clear warning to Soares, said solicitor Benedict Birnberg, 'to keep out of political activity'.[25]

The threat extended far beyond Soares and *Grassroots*. Observers argued that the ruling invited the suppression of any and all dissent against racism, fascism and economic exploitation. Since the mid-1960s, the Home Office had systematically targeted black organisations for promoting self-reliance and strategies for self-defence. Meanwhile, individuals such as Enoch Powell and white supremacist groups including the National Front not only promoted violence against black communities with impunity, but their appeals were answered with organised campaigns of bloodshed and fire.[26] The government's assault on *Grassroots* for printing plans of a bomb coincided with a series of actual bombings of black homes and businesses. Within one hour on 15 March, five explosives ignited across South London. One destroyed the Black Panther Movement's bookshop in Brixton.[27] 'Will the same efficient detective work which brought Soares to the Old Bailey result in a successful prosecution of the fascist groups who are now terrorizing black shopkeepers and have burned down their property in some parts of the country?' asked the *West Indian World*.[28]

Rather than crush the BLF, the assault on *Grassroots* replenished visions of collective action. Special Branch had seized much-needed community donations. Perennially in debt to printers, *Grassroots* went on hiatus for nine months. After being evicted from 54 Wightman Road, the BLF's base of operations shifted to Ladbroke Grove in December 1972. With £10, donated books and the help of community members, BLF operatives squatted an empty shop at 61 Golborne Road and set up a new Grassroots Storefront. The support of a broad network of members, allies, friends and volunteers also made it possible for *Grassroots* to return to print in August 1973.[29]

Following his conviction, Soares noted that the prosecution had surely 'intimidated' some black activists, but the movement for his defence had 'also served to radicalize others'.[30] Following Soares's arrest, a Grassroots Defence Committee organised benefit concerts, dances, poetry readings, film screenings, teach-ins and publicity to rally community members and organisations.[31] After an early planning meeting at 54 Wightman Road, four young members of the Fasimbas, a South London radical black arts and self-help community organisation, were attacked by a group of plainclothes transit police as they left the Oval Tube station, arrested on fabricated charges of mugging, and later sentenced to two years in prison.[32] 'The prisons of Britain are overcrowded with Black Men,' Defence Committee member Sister Dara reflected after a visit to Pentonville. Justice did not exist for black people in Britain or in 'any part of the world', Sister Merle lamented after a benefit dance in June 1972. Both revolutionaries called for armed revolution and world war.[33]

In order to contribute to 'the struggles of kith and kin overseas', black communities in Britain first had to build a base of strength.[34] 'Blacks born and bred in Britain cannot be called Black British because they will never be accepted as such by the white society,' the BLF argued in *Revolutionary Black Nationalism*. Discrimination in housing and jobs, police repression, judicial persecution, and the state's refusal to combat 'the flames of fascism' supported the organisation's long-standing claim that inclusion within the British nation state was impossible. But endemic poverty, unemployment and a burgeoning homeless crisis revealed the necessity for immediate coordinated action. Inviting black organisations nationwide to unite and strategise and mobilise together, the BLF called for the formation of 'an organisation that is powerful enough to exist as a parallel government in the Black community, and effective enough to virtually replace the national government'.[35]

Serve the people

In the spring of 1971, the BLF announced the Grassroots Project, a panoramic programme designed to entertain, educate and protect black youth in North London. The project started out with a youth club – the Black Berets – which offered arts, games and sports activities every Tuesday and Thursday night, and courses in black history on Fridays at the Grassroots Storefront. Although the club started out with a few games and a table-tennis table, it recruited 200 members in its first month and had to expand into the West Green Community Centre.[36] The launch of the Grassroots Project coincided with the May 1971 publication of Bernard Coard's landmark study, exposé and manifesto: *How the West Indian Child Is Made Educationally Sub-normal in the British School System*.[37] Like many community organisations across the UK, the BLF answered Coard's call to counteract the abuse, humiliation and miseducation of black children by opening a supplementary school. Supported by donations of books, paper, furniture and volunteer labour, the Headstart Education and Leisure Programme opened on 26 September 1971, offering classes in English, art and maths, as well as African and Asian history, on Sunday mornings and homework tutorials each evening. By the end of the year, the BLF had opened a legal advice service and organised a Prisoners Welfare Committee to coordinate book donations, visits and correspondence to incarcerated people, support their families, and assist with their transition upon release. The BLF also planned to stretch its community development work across borders. During the summer of 1971, the organisation started raising funds for a volunteer expedition to Tanzania.[38]

Special Branch's raid on the Grassroots Storefront in March 1972 stalled some of these projects, but BLF members continued incubating new cooperatives inside and outside the organisation.[39] Following the move to 61 Golborne Road in December 1972, members discovered that the neighbourhood was already nourished by 'a large number of community organisations providing various services'. Rather than replicate existing programmes, Ansel Wong, Gerlin Bean, Tony Soares and fellow BLF member Lu Garvey devised a non-profit self-help scheme 'to put the skills of the community at the service of the community'. With the aid of expert technicians and other volunteers, the BLF set up cooperative workshops in the basement of 61 Golborne Road to train unemployed youth in printing and typesetting, barbering and electrical repair.[40]

In Brixton, Gerlin Bean and Ansel Wong collaborated on a vision-ary transformation of the Gresham youth centre into twin initiatives: the AHFIWE supplementary school and ABENG, 'a youth club with facilities for counselling, advice and vocational training'. Through his involvement in revolutionary politics, supplementary schools and black arts collectives around the Atlantic, Wong had formulated an interdisciplinary, decolonial black studies curriculum. A youth and family counsellor sensitive to the traumas of exile, Bean helped black children and their parents cope with the impact migration, poverty and structural racism had on their lives, relationships and mental health. According to homeless youth themselves, intergenerational conflicts between parents and children were partially responsible for the grow-ing number of youth living on the street.[41] Anchored in empathy, respect and compassionate listening, Bean and Wong's radical men-torship encouraged 'reluctant learners, under-achievers and those with behavioural problems' to recognise themselves as artists, entrepre-neurs, intellectuals and freedom dreamers.[42]

As the Grassroots Self-Help Project expanded in Ladbroke Grove and Notting Hill, B. B. Hannibal and N. N. A. Pepukayi led an effort to resurrect a BLF base in Haringey. Equipped with church and gov-ernment grants, and plenty of volunteer labour, Operation Headstart leased and renovated a building on West Green Road in May 1975. The ground floor featured a books, crafts and record shop. The Headstart Supplementary School occupied the top floor. 'Soon faced with the fact that housing and homelessness are the major problems among Black youths in North London', Operation Headstart secured a few short-term properties from a housing trust and placed them under the management of its subsidiary – the Ujima Housing Association. At the same time, the BLF assembled a portfolio of houses, flats and hostels in West London for the use of homeless youth, visitors and volunteers, and formerly incarcerated people.[43]

Ujima emerged alongside 'a strong black squatting movement' in Britain. In Brixton and Notting Hill, BLF operatives such as Ansel Wong and Zainab Abbas occupied empty houses and mobilised the talents of community volunteers to make the squats suitable for temporary accom-modation.[44] An African Arab born in Middlesbrough, Zainab Abbas was the child of Nubian-Egyptian immigrants. In the late 1960s, Abbas made her way south from Middlesbrough to Birmingham. In Handsworth, she was embraced by a community of Pan-Africanist revolutionar-ies centred at the Afro-Caribbean Self-Help Organisation (ACSHO).

Founded by the Jamaica-born activist Bini Brown in 1964, the ACSHO established the country's first Saturday supplementary school in 1967. Abbas taught maths.[45] The group from Handsworth travelled regularly to London, strategising and socialising with allies in the Black Panther Movement at Rhodan Gordon's Backayard centre on Portobello Road.[46] Panther activist Olive Morris, by then an icon of the squatters' movement, invited Abbas to move into an empty room at 64 Railton Road, a squat she shared with fellow activist Liz Turnbull. Morris and Turnbull took Abbas around Lambeth, and trained her in methods of breaking into empty houses and squatting black families. Through Morris, Abbas met Gerlin Bean. As she had for many young women, Gerlin Bean mentored Abbas, and introduced her to various organisations in London, including the BLF.[47]

Pan-Africanism and the Third World

In June 1974, Zainab Abbas, Gerlin Bean and Ansel Wong travelled to Dar es Salaam as members of the British delegation to the Sixth Pan-African Congress.[48] Addressing the congress on behalf of his comrades, the Manchester-based activist and former UCPA member Ron Phillips declared that 'the black minority' in Britain had 'a deep, historic, and permanent membership in the Third World anti-imperialist front'.[49] For Abbas, the highlight of the week was the 'Resolution on the Palestine Question'. In support of the self-determination of the Palestinian people, the congress recognised 'the struggle of the Palestinian people to be an integral part of the struggle of liberation movements in Africa and the entire Third World'. The moment was a thrilling affirmation of Abbas's personal and political investments in Afro-Arab unity, Pan-Africanism and the Third World. Before moving to Northern England after World War Two, Abbas's mother worked as a nurse in the British Mandate for Palestine, where she witnessed atrocities committed by the Zionist Irgun gang and volunteered for the Arab Liberation Army. Her mother's lessons on Egyptian African history, Palestinian resistance and the Pan-Africanism of Gamal Abdel Nasser politicised Abbas as a child.[50]

While drafting the address to the congress, the British delegates collaborated on a definition of Pan-Africanism: 'the unity of all the people of Africa, and of Africa descent throughout the world, in revolutionary struggle for the total liberation of this continent from colonialism, from neo-colonialism, from racism, from imperialism, and Zionism'.[51] Formulated after the 1973 October War, the definition of African-Arab unity echoed the UCPA's declarations of support for the liberation of 'the Arab lands' after the June 1967 Arab-Israeli war.[52] But it also reflected the unique interventions that anti-Zionist activists such as Abbas brought to the BLF at that time. 'The struggle of the Palestinians for the restoration of their homeland is an important lesson for all oppressed people,' *Grassroots* proclaimed later that year. 'For Black People seeking the liberation of Africa and the Caribbean, the parallels are only too clear.' The article was the first *Grassroots* published on Palestine and Palestinians. Four years later, in the 1977 revision to *Revolutionary Black Nationalism*, the BLF added Palestine to the list of 'once Black Lands' occupied by 'white minority settler regimes'.[53]

At the Sixth Pan-African Congress, Abbas helped strengthen the BLF's links with various liberation movements across Africa and the Middle East, and helped establish new relationships. She was aided by personal introductions from journalist and exiled SWAPO leader Emil Appolus, who worked at the Gresham Project. When they returned to London, delegates briefed the community on the congress and the state of freedom movements in Southern Africa.[54] *Grassroots* did the same. Sharing 'intercepted' information on Rhodesia and South Africa's plans to invade Mozambique, the July issue of *Grassroots* urged readers to send material support and medical supplies to the movements. 'Join an organisation here to prepare yourself psychologically for the day when we may all have to go fight in South Africa,' the BLF pleaded, 'for the apartheid system is so vicious and it is backed by all the white Western nations.'[55] In the subsequent issue, Abbas published three essays on the status of freedom struggles in Namibia, Zimbabwe and Angola.[56] By the end of the year, Abbas and Appolus had set up a publishing firm, Kalahari Press, as a clearing house for the movements.[57]

Following the Sixth Pan-African Congress, the BLF gradually centred Africa and Pan-Africanism in its platforms and programmes. Working with other organisations nationwide, the BLF helped launch Africa Liberation Day in 1975.[58] That same year, the BLF revived a programme, dreamed up and deferred in 1971, to export its self-help community development to Africa. The Grassroots West Africa Project sent volunteers to West Africa to work on construction, school and agricultural projects during the summer.[59] In 1977, the organisation partnered with Harambee House in Birmingham and the George Jackson Trust in Manchester to expand the project. The collaborative

Pan-African Exchange Scheme sent youth from Britain to Senegal, Nigeria, Ghana, Tanzania and Sierra Leone 'to develop lasting links at the grassroots level between the people living in Africa and their descendants in Britain'.[60] At the Annual General Meeting of 1977, the BLF voted to 'give full priority' to the programme.[61] That same year, the BLF also instituted 'SALSA & SALT', a voluntary tax and donation programme to provide material assistance to freedom fighters in Southern Africa.[62]

By the end of the decade, the BLF had abandoned the concept of Revolutionary Black Nationalism. 'African' had come to define and replace 'black' for many members. Inspired by the triumph of the anti-colonial struggle in Mozambique, and by FRELIMO's ongoing efforts to build a socialist government, the BLF advanced an ideology of Revolutionary Pan-Africanism that was 'against capitalism and imperialism and for socialism'.[63] Amidst global resistance to apartheid in the 1980s, the BLF officially rebranded as a revolutionary Pan-Africanist organisation. 'We believe,' *Grassroots* declared, 'that the African people in Britain must break out of the idea of being an isolated community in Britain, and build strong political, cultural and social links with other Africans throughout the world.'[64]

Freedom dreamers in the BLF struggled continuously to define their political philosophy. Through discussion and debate, they offered visions of a democratic social future for Africa and the Third World that were irresistible to their communities and threats to powerful enemies. The BLF may not have achieved its goal of eradicating white supremacy, patriarchy, colonialism and empire as part of a global socialist revolution, but the organisation did realise many of its aims. More than 'survival', the organisation and its allies provided shelter, security, education and community for untold numbers of black people in the UK. Within the borders of their collective and communities, BLF members practised the revolution they wanted to activate worldwide, and created new modes of solidarity through kinship, cooperation and care.

Notes

1 Universal Coloured People's Association (UCPA), 'Black Power: A Definition By the UCPA', *Black Power Newsletter*, c. July 1969, JOU 30/2, George Padmore Institute (GPI); Black Liberation Front, 'Revolutionary Black Nationalism: An Ideology for Survival and Liberation', c. 1971, unpublished manuscript, Papers of Tony Soares, private collection (hereafter Soares Papers; some materials now held by the Black Cultural Archives in Brixton); revised and published as

Revolutionary Black Nationalism: A Paper for Discussion (London: Black Liberation Front, 1973), WONG/6/40, Papers of Ansel Wong (hereafter Wong Papers), Black Cultural Archives (BCA), 1–3; Ali Bey Hassan, *Revolutionary Black Nationalism: Unity and Struggle Against Domination* (London: Black Liberation Front, 1977), Soares Papers, 3, 7; Luam Kidane and Hawa Y. Mire (eds), 'Constellations of Black Radical Imagining: Black Arts and Popular Education', *Our Schools/Ourselves* 24/3 (Spring 2015), pp. 1–8; Leanne Betasamosake Simpson's formulation of 'Constellations of Coresistance' in *As We Have Always Done: Indigenous Freedom Through Radical Resistance* (Minneapolis: University of Minnesota Press, 2017), especially pp. 211–31.

2   UCPA, 'UCPA Constitution', 22 June 1968, 2; UCPA, 'Black Power: A Definition by the UCPA', p. 4.

3   Farid Cama, 'Concerning "The Spirit of Bandung"' and Afric Asilam, 'Middle East Notes', *Black Power Speaks* 2 (June 1968), pp. 17–18; UCPA, 'Black People Unite!', UCPA file, 01/04/04/01/04/01/17, Black History Collection, Institute of Race Relations (IRR), London.

4   UCPA, 'A Special Statement by the UCPA Concerning the Arrest of Three Black Brothers', c. July 1968, Soares Papers.

5   J. T. A. Howard-Drake, 'Anti-Semitism Among Black Power Groups', 2 January 1969, HO 376/154, National Archives of the United Kingdom (TNA).

6   'Tony Sinaris Jailed for Political Reasons', *Black Power Newsletter*, c. July 1969, p. 5.

7   Metropolitan Police, 'Antecedents of Antonio Moushino Leo De Sousa Soares', 19 November 1968, *Regina v. Soares*, Autumn Session 1968, CRIM 1/5034, TNA; Peter Shipley, *Revolutionaries in Modern Britain* (London: Bodley Head, 1976), pp. 167–8.

8   Robert C. Toth, 'London Quiet, Braces for Vietnam Protestors', *Los Angeles Times*, 27 October 1968, E4; *Regina v. Soares*; Robert F. Williams, 'USA: The Potential of a Minority Revolution, Part III', *The Crusader*, September–October 1967, p. 6; 'Alleged Incitement in Pamphlets', *The Times*, 22 February 1969, p. 3; '2 Years for Riot Instigator', *Guardian*, 25 February 1969, p. 6; UCPA, 'Tony Sinaris Soares Jailed for Political Reasons', p. 5; 'Britain Releases Political Prisoner', *Black Dwarf*, 7 July 1970, p. 6; Special Branch, New Scotland Yard, 'Black Power in the United Kingdom', 11 August 1970, HO 325/143, TNA; 'The Case Against Tony Soares and Grass Roots Black Community Newspaper', BLF file, 01-04-04-01-04-01-04, Black History Collection, IRR.

9   UCPA Manchester Branch, 'The Exposure & Expulsion of a Con (Ron Phillips) by UCPA', 01/04/04/01/04/01/17, IRR; Special Branch, 'Black Power in the United Kingdom'.

10   Interview with Neil Kenlock, 'The Amazing Lost Legacy of the British Black Panthers', *Vice*, 8 October 2013, https://www.vice.com/en_uk/article/9bz5ee/neil-kenlocks-photos-give-the-british-black-panthers-the-legacy-they-deserve, accessed 26 September 2018.

11   Special Branch, 'Black Power in the United Kingdom', Appendix B; 'The Black Unity and Freedom Party Manifesto', *Black Voice* 2/1 (c. December 1970), p. 2; Joan Anim-Addo, *Longest Journey: A History of Black Lewisham* (London: Deptford Forum, 1995), p. 116; Harry Goulbourne, 'Africa and the Caribbean in Caribbean Consciousness and Action in Britain', *David Nicholls Memorial Lectures*, no. 2 (Oxford: David Nicholls Memorial Trust, 2000), pp. 123–7; Winston N. Trew, *Black for a Cause … Not Just Because: The Case of the 'Oval 4' and the Story of Black Power in 1970s Britain* (Peterborough, NH: TaoFish, 2012), p. 223; Anne-Marie Angelo, 'The

Black Panthers in London, 1967–1972: A Diasporic Struggle Navigates the Black Atlantic', *Radical History Review* 103 (2009), pp. 17–35; W. Chris Johnson, 'Guerrilla Ganja Gun Girls: Policing Black Revolutionaries from Notting Hill to Laventille', *Gender and History* 26/3 (November 2014), pp. 661–787; Rosalind Eleanor Wild, 'Black was the Colour of Our Fight: Black Power in Britain, 1955–1976' (PhD thesis, University of Sheffield, 2008), pp. 90, 93–109; Tony Soares, in discussion with author, 24 September 2012, London.

12   Bro. Sam (Anslem Samuel), 'Letter from North London', *Black People's News Service*, May 1970, NEW/17/3, GPI; Black Workers Coordinating Committee, 'Black Nurses Unite!', UCPA file, 01/04/04/01/04/01/17, IRR; London Metropolitan Archives; Peter Marshall to G. L. Angel, 26 November 1975, HO 376/222, TNA; Valentino A. Jones, *We Are Our Own Educators! Josina Machel: From Supplementary to Black Complementary School* (London: Karia Press, 1986); Tony Soares, discussions with author, 24 September 2012 and 18 March 2018, London; Wild, 'Black was the Colour of Our Fight', pp. 103–4; see also R. E. R. Bunce and Paul Field, 'Obi B. Egbuna, C. L. R. James and the Birth of Black Power in Britain: Black Radicalism in Britain 1967–72', *Twentieth Century British History* 22/3 (2001), pp. 391–414.

13   'Constitution and Structure of the Black Liberation Front', n.d., Soares Papers; 'What is the BLF', *Grassroots* 4/3 (c. October 1975), p. 3; Ali Bey Hassan, *Revolutionary Black Nationalism: Unity and Struggle Against Domination* (London: Black Liberation Front, 1977); JoNina M. Abron, 'Serving the People: The Survival Programs of the Black Panther Party' in Charles Earl Jones (ed.), *The Black Panther Party (Reconsidered)* (Baltimore: Black Classic Press, 1998), pp. 177–92; David Hilliard (ed.), *The Black Panther Party: Service to the People Programs* (Albuquerque: University of New Mexico Press, 2008).

14   'Revolutionary Black Nationalism: A Paper for Discussion', 1971, Soares Papers, 8; Zainab Abbas and Ansel Wong, in discussion with author, 1 November 2015, London; Ansel Wong, interview by Anne Walmsley, 16 June 1987, CAM/6/85, GPI; Rob Waters, 'Student Politics, Teaching Politics, Black Politics: An Interview with Ansel Wong', *Race and Class* 58/1 (2016), p. 21.

15   'A Spark in Grass Roots Can Start a Prairie Fire', *Grassroots* 1/3 (c. June 1971), p. 6.

16   'Afro-Asian Women's Organisation', *Grassroots* 4/7 (c. June 1975), pp. 5, 7.

17   BWAC, BUFP, *Black Women Speak Out* (c. May 1971), WONG/6/39, Wong Papers; 'Some Thoughts on Black Women's Liberation', *Grassroots* 1/4 (August 1971), p. 8; Gail Lewis, interviews, 15 and 18 April 2011, C1420/14, 'Sisterhood and After: The Women's Liberation Oral History Project', British Library, transcript, pp. 103–4; Abbas and Wong, in discussion with author, 1 November 2015, London. On triple exploitation, see Charisse Burden-Stelly, 'Constructing Deportable Subjectivity: Antiforeignness, Antiradicalism, and Antiblackness during the McCarthyist Structure of Feeling', *Souls* 19/3 (2017), pp. 347–8.

18   UCPA, *Black Power: A Special Statement* (c. July 1967), p. 14; 'Constitution and Structure of the Black Liberation Front'; Gerlin Bean, interview by Kwame Phillips, 20 February 2009, ORAL/1/3, 'The Heart of the Race: Oral Histories of the Black Women's Movement', BCA; Gerlin Bean, interview by Ashley Whitfield, 9 September 2009, IV/279/2/20/1a-b, 'Do You Remember Olive Morris?: Oral History Project', Lambeth Archives; Abbas and Wong, in discussion with author, 1 November 2015,

London; Abbas and Bean, in discussion with author, 5 December 2016. On discrimination against black nurses such as Bean, see Black Women's Action Committee, 'Black Nurses Are Ruthlessly Exploited to Prop-Up Health Service', *Black Women Speak Out, c.* May 1971, WONG/6/39, Wong Papers. On Gerlin Bean, see also Nathalie Thomlinson, *Race, Ethnicity and the Women's Movement in England, 1968–1993* (London: Palgrave Macmillan, 2016), pp. 66–9; Tanisha C. Ford, *Liberated Threads: Black Women, Style, and the Global Politics of Soul* (Chapel Hill: University of North Carolina Press, 2015), pp. 151–4.

19 'The Split in the Black Panther Party', *Grassroots* 1/1 (*c.* April–May 1971), pp. 1, 3, 6; Betty Carter to supporters of the Black Panther Party, *c.* July 1969, Soares Papers; Kathleen Neal Cleaver to Tony Soares, 21 October 1970, Soares Papers; Bill Stephens to Soares, 22 July 1971, Soares Papers; Kathleen Neal Cleaver to Soares, 28 August 1971, Soares Papers; Eldridge Cleaver, *Revolution in the Congo* (London: RPCN/Black Liberation Front, 1971). The articles 'Black GI Released to Panthers', 'Revolutionary Peoples Communications Network' and 'Organizing Self-Defense Groups', *Grassroots* 1/4 (August 1971), pp. 3, 5, 10; 'Revolutionary Peoples Communication Network', *Grassroots* 1/5 (*c.* October 1971), p. 5; see also Kathleen Neal Cleaver, 'Back to Africa: The Evolution of the International Section of the Black Panther Party (1969–1972) in Jones *The Black Panther Party (Reconsidered)*, pp. 211–51.

20 Stephens to Soares, 22 July 1971, Soares Papers; Kathleen Neal Cleaver to Soares, 28 August 1971, Soares Papers; Kathleen Cleaver, 'Call for Justice', Black GI Rally, Heidelberg University, 4 July 1971, Soares Papers.

21 'Revolutionary Peoples Communications Network' and 'Organizing Self-Defense Groups', *Grassroots* 1/4 (*c.* August 1971), pp. 3, 5, 10; Field Marshall DC (Don Cox), 'Organizing Self-Defense Groups', *Black Panther Community News Service* IV/20 (18 April 1970), p. 7; 'Correction', *Black Panther Community News Service* IV/22 (2 May 1970), p. 17; 'Black Are "Good Money"', *Grassroots* 1/5 (*c.* October 1971), p. 2; Black Peoples Information Centre, 'Grass Roots Harassed', *National and International News Bulletin* 1/16 (20 November 1971), p. 2; 'Editorial' and 'C. R. O. Traitor', *Grassroots* 1/6 (*c.* November 1971), p. 2; 'Grass-Roots Editor Sacks Lawyer', *West Indian World*, 16 March 1973, p. 2; 'Dock Brief', *Race Today* 5/4 (April 1973), p. 102; 'CRC Danger to Black Community', *West Indian World*, 2–8 April 1973, p. 1.

22 'Dock Brief', p. 102; 'Mozambique Massacres', *Grassroots* 3/2 (*c.* August 1973), p. 2; Monique A. Bedasse, *Jah Kingdom: Rastafarians, Tanzania, and Pan-Africanism in the Age of Decolonization* (Chapel Hill: University of North Carolina Press, 2017), pp. 74–7; Soares, in discussion with author, 24 September 2012 and 18 March 2018, London.

23 'Free Tony Soares', *Black Voice* 3/2 (1972), p. 8; 'Bro. Tony Charged/Bail Refused', *Freedom News*, 18 March 1972, p. 2; 'The Case Against Tony Soares and Grass Roots Black Community Newspaper', *c.* July 1972, BLF file, 01-04-04-01-04-01-04, IRR; Andrew Cockburn, 'Soares vs. The Vampires', *IT* 150 (22 March 1973), pp. 9–10.

24 'Grass Roots Trial', *Race Today*, February 1973, p. 37; 'The Case Against Tony Soares and Grass Roots Black Community Newspaper'.

25 Grassroots Defence Committee to Comrades, *c.* March 1972, Soares Papers; 'Tony Gets Bail', *Time Out*, 14–20 July 1972, p. 4; 'Grass Roots Editor for Trial', *West Indian World*, 8 December 1972, p. 2; 'Grass Roots Trial', p. 37; Peter Cole, 'Protests Over Mental

Check on Militant', *Guardian*, 24 March 1973, p. 6; Peter Cole, 'The Non-Inciting Agitator', *Guardian*, 3 April 1973, p. 6; 'Dock Brief', p. 102; Henry Louis Gates Jr., 'Black London', *Antioch Review* 34/3 (Spring 1976), p. 308; Wild, 'Black was the Colour of Our Fight', pp. 107–8, 155, 188; Wong, in discussion with author, 19 September 2012; Soares, in discussion with author, 24 September 2012.

26 'It's All Happening', *Grassroots* 3/1 (*c.* November 1972), p. 4.

27 Statement of the Black Panther Movement, 19 March 1973, WONG/5/2, Wong Papers.

28 'Grass Roots Editor for Trial', p. 2; A. Sivanandan, 'Justice For Whom?', *Race Today* 5/4 (April 1973), p. 99; Cockburn, 'Soares vs. The Vampires', pp. 9–10; Robert Govender, 'Soares Sentenced to Work', *West Indian World*, 2–8 April 1973, p. 1; Don Atyeo, 'Blacks Bombed', *IT* 154 (17 May 1973), p. 1.

29 'BLF Statement', *Grassroots* 3/1 (*c.* November 1972), p. 11; Advertisement, *Grassroots* 3/1 (*c.* November 1972), p. 10; 'Grassroots Appeal', *Grassroots* 3/2 (*c.* August 1973), p. 7; 'Grass Roots Storefront', *West Indian World*, 29 March–4 April 1973, p. 5; Black Workers Movement, *Freedom Fighter*, *c.* 1974, WONG/7/12; Soares, in discussion with author, 24 September 2012; Waters, 'Student Politics, Teaching Politics, Black Politics', p. 23.

30 Atyeo, 'Blacks Bombed', p. 1.

31 Grassroots Defence Committee to Comrades, *c.* March 1972, Soares Papers; Poster, 'Grassroots Defence Concert', 16 April 1972, WONG6/35, Wong Papers; Advertisement, '"Grass Roots" Benefit Late Night Movie', *Red Mole*, 16 October 1972; 'Black Words: A Benefit for Tony Soares and Grass Roots', October 1972, WONG/6/81, Wong Papers; 'BLF Statement', p. 11.

32 'The Oval Four', *Grassroots* 3/1 (*c.* November 1972), pp. 2–3; 'Oval Four: Cause for Concern', *West Indian World*,

3 August 1973, p. 7; Desrie Thomson-George, 'Interview with the Oval Four', *Grassroots* 3/2 (*c.* August 1973), p. 4; Winston Trew, letter to the editor, *Grassroots* 3/6 (*c.* November 1974), p. 1; Trew, *Black for a Cause*.

33 Sister Dara to Soares, 4 May 1972, Soares Papers; Sister Merle to Soares, 21 June 1972, Soares Papers.

34 'Paper on Unity and Black Organisations: Toward a Black United Front', *c.* 1973, Soares Papers; 'Unity', *Grassroots* 3/2 (*c.* August 1973), p. 5.

35 BLF, Revolutionary Black Nationalism: A Paper for Discussion (BLF: London, 1973), p. 6.

36 'Black Berets', *Grassroots* 1/1 (*c.* April 1971), p. 6; 'BLF News' and 'Black Berets', *Grassroots* 1/2 (*c.* May 1971), p. 6; 'Grassroots Project' and 'Black Berets Youth League', *Grassroots* 1/3 (*c.* June 1971), p. 6.

37 Bernard Coard, *How the West Indian Child is Made Educationally Sub-Normal in the British School System* (London: New Beacon Books, 1971), p. 39; 'Genocide Through Schools', *Grassroots* 1/2 (*c.* May 1971), p. 1; Ansel Wong, 'Foreword', *AHFIWE: Journal of the AHFIWE School and ABENG* 1 (*c.* 1974), WONG/2/1, Wong Papers; see also Hazel V. Carby, 'Schooling in Babylon' in Centre for Contemporary Cultural Studies, *The Empire Strikes Back: Race and Racism in 1970s Britain* (London: Hutchinson, 1982), pp. 181–210; Kehinde Andrews, *Resisting Racism: Race, Inequality and the Black Supplementary School Movement* (London: Institute of Education Press, 2013).

38 'Headstart Education and Leisure Programme', *Grassroots* 1/4 (August 1971), p. 10; 'Headstart' and 'Legal Advice', *Grassroots* 1/5 (*c.* October 1971), p. 10; 'Prisoner's Com.', *Grassroots* 1/6 (*c.* November 1971), p. 10; 'BLF News: BBYL', *Grassroots* 2/7 (*c.* January 1972), p. 10; 'BLF Projects', *Grassroots* 3/2 (*c.* August 1973), p. 7; 'Books Behind Bars', *Grassroots* 3/3 (*c.* April 1974), p. 2; 'Trip to

Africa', *Grassroots* 1/3 (*c.* June 1971),
p. 6; 'Africa Trip', *Grassroots* 1/4 (*c.*
August 1971), p. 10.

39 'What is the BLF', p. 3.

40 Author's emphasis. 'Grass
Roots Self Help Community Project',
c. 1973–74), BLF file, 01-04-04-01-04-01-04,
IRR; 'Community Services', *Grassroots*
3/4 (*c.* July 1974), p. 11; 'Grass Roots Self
Help Project Report for the period 1.1.75
to 30.6.76', Soares Papers.

41 'Do Black Parents Even Care?',
Grassroots 3/4 (*c.* July 1974), p. 4; 'Do
Black Parents Care?', *Grassroots* 3/5 (*c.*
October 1974), p. 5; *Operation Headstart
Annual Report: 1976–1977*, Soares Papers;
Wong, interview by Zahra Dalilah.

42 Gerlin Bean, *Shrew* 3/8
(September 1971), p. 10; Gerlin Bean,
'Letter to the Editor', *Race Today* (August
1973), p. 226; 'Report on the Gresham
Summer Project (1–30 August 1973)',
WONG/2/6, Wong Papers; 'Gresham
Project's Supplementary Education
Scheme: "AHFIWE School"', *c.* January
1974, WONG/2/3; 'AHFIWE School
Coordinator's Report and Financial
Report', 10 May 1974, WONG/2/3; David
Lloyd, 'AFIWE Head Sacked', *Grassroots*
4/7 (July–August 1976) p. 6; 'Council
for Community Relations in Lambeth
Supplementary Education Scheme:
Ahfiwe School', *c.* 1978, WONG/2/4,
BCA; Bean, interview by Whitfield;
Bean, interview by Phillips; Ansel Wong,
interview by Anne Walmsley, 16 June
1987, CAM/6/85, GPI; Waters, 'Student
Politics, Teaching Politics, Black Politics',
pp. 23, 31 n14; Wong, interview by Zahra
Dalilah, 16 February 2017, 'The GLC
Story Oral History Project', transcript
at http://glcstory.co.uk/wp-content/
uploads/2017/09/End-of-project-
report-GLC-Story.pdf; Bean and Wong,
discussion with author, 6 December
2016, London.

43 'Grass Roots Storefront', p. 5;
'Operation Headstart', *Grassroots* 4/5
(April 1976), p. 2; *Operation Headstart
Annual Report: 1976–1977*, Soares
Papers; L. J. Ross, *How Many Storeys:
Celebrating 25 Years of Ujima Housing
Group* (London: Ujima Housing Group,
2002), p. 2.

44 'BLF Projects', *Grassroots* 3/4
(*c.* July 1974) p. 11; 'How to Squat' and
Black Women's Group letter to the
editor, *Grassroots* 3/5 (*c.* October 1974),
pp. 5, 10; Wong, interview by Dalilah;
'Ujima Housing Association', *Grassroots*
3/6 (*c.* November 1974), p. 11.

45 Afro-Caribbean Self-Help
Organisation, *Harambee: Black
Unity*, April 1970, JLR/3/1/25, GPI; Jim
Bergman and Bernard Coard, 'Trials
and Tribulations of a Self-Help Group',
Race Today (April 1972), pp. 112–14;
'Birmingham's Harambee', *West Indian
World*, 8 May 1974, p. 13; Poppy Brady,
'Community Organisation Celebrates
50 Years of Activism', 14 August 2014,
http://www.voice-online.co.uk/article/
community-organisation-celebrates-
50-years-activism; African Caribbean
Self-Help Organisation, '!Resurrection!',
informational leaflet, n.d., in author's
possession.

46 Louis A. Chase, 'Curry Politics –
Backayard', *West Indian World*, 31
December 1971, p. 9; 'Backayard
Attacked', *BackAyard News Sheet*, *c.*
June 1973, WONG/7/33; 'Black Peoples
Information Centre', *Freedom News*, 30
June 1973, NEW/17/2, GPI.

47 'Rooftop Defiance', *West Indian
World*, 5–11 February 1973, p. 1; Beverley
Bryan, Stella Dadzie and Suzanne
Scafe, *The Heart of the Race: Black
Women's Lives in Britain* (London:
Virago Press, 1985), pp. 151–5; Gerlin
Bean, interview with Ashley Whitfield
of the Remembering Olive Collective,
9 September 2009, 'Do You Remember
Olive Morris? Oral History Project',
Olive Morris Collection, Lambeth
Archives; Ford, *Liberated Threads*,
pp. 138–58; Tanisha Ford, 'Finding Olive
Morris in the Archive: Reflections on

the Remembering Olive Collective and Community History', *Black Scholar* 46/2 (2016), pp. 5–18. On Bean's mentorship, see Gail Lewis, 'Visions of Legacy: Legacies of Vision' in Kathy Davis and Mary Evans (eds), *Transatlantic Conversations: Feminism as Travelling Theory* (London: Routledge, 2016), p. 172.

48 'The Sixth Pan African Congress', *Grassroots* 3/3 (*c.* April 1974), p. 6.

49 'Six Pan-African Congress Declares Total War on Imperialism, Neo-Colonialism', *Moss Side News* 1/2 (*c.* July 1974), p. 3.

50 Abbas, in discussion with author, 19 September 2012.

51 *Resolutions and Selected Speeches from the Sixth Pan African Congress* (Dar es Salaam: Tanzania Publishing House, 1976), pp. 56–66, 86, 88, 132-133; ephemera from the Sixth Pan-African Congress, WONG/8/2, Wong Papers; Zainab Abbas, 'Preface' in Emil Appolus (ed.), *The Resurgence of Pan-Africanism* (London: Kalahari Publications, 1974), pp. 5–6; Abbas, in discussion with author, 19 September 2012; Abbas and Wong, in discussion with author, 1 November 2015; Abbas and Bean, in discussion with author, 5 December 2016.

52 Afric Asilam, 'Middle East Notes', *Black Power Speaks* 2 (June 1968), p. 17.

53 Brother Kimathi (Ansel Wong), 'The Palestinians', *Grassroots* 3/6 (November 1974), p. 8; Leila Khaled, 'A Palestinian Lament', *Grassroots* 3/3 (*c.* April 1974), p. 6; S. Kadifa, 'Afro-Arab Unity', *Grassroots* (April–May 1977), p. 3; Hassan, *Revolutionary Black Nationalism*, pp. 1, 10, 11.

54 'Pan African Committee', *Grassroots* 3/5 (October 1974).

55 'South Africa, Rhodesia to Invade Mozambique', *Grassroots* 3/4 (*c.* July 1974), p. 3.

56 Zainab Abbas, 'Black Africans Fight Three Major Wars of Liberation', *Grassroots* 3/5 (*c.* October 1974), pp. 4, 9.

57 *Resolutions and Selected Speeches from the Sixth Pan African Congress*, pp. 56–66, 86, 88, 132–3; ephemera from the Sixth Pan-African Congress, WONG/8/2, Wong Papers; Abbas, 'Preface', pp. 5–6; Abbas, in discussion with author, 19 September 2012; Abbas and Wong, in discussion with author, 1 November 2015; Abbas and Bean, in discussion with author, 5 December 2016.

58 'BLF Projects', *Grassroots* 4/2 (*c.* July 1975), p. 11; 'What is the BLF', p. 3; 'Africa Liberation Committee Statement', *Black Voice* 9/1 (1975), p. 6; 'Africa Liberation Day A Success', *Grassroots* (August 1977), p. 14.

59 'Trip to West Africa', *Grassroots* 4/1 (May 1975), p. 15.

60 'African Exchange Scheme', *Grassroots* (January 1977), p. 12; 'Volunteers Return from Africa', *Grassroots* (October–November 1977), p. 12.

61 'Programme for 1977', Soares Papers.

62 'An Appeal for SALSA & SALT', *Grassroots* (January 1977), p. 16; 'Grassroots Sends Cheque to ZANU', *Grassroots* (August–September 1977), p. 20.

63 BLF, *Pan-Africanism*, Black Liberation Series No. 4 (London: Black Liberation Front, *c.* 1986), LIBFRONT, BCA.

64 'The Black Liberation Front: What We Believe', *Grassroots* (May–June 1984), p. 15.

8 | THE EVOLUTION OF IDEAS AND PRACTICES AMONG AFRICAN-CENTRED ORGANISATIONS IN THE UK, 1975–2015

Claudius Adisa Steven

Introduction

Black people's struggle for civil and human rights has been shaped by the social and political environment in England at any given time. Yet, whereas in the United States black organisations and the struggle for civil rights have undergone much research and analysis, very little work has been done regarding the modern history and practices of African-centred organisations in England, and their impact on the wider Black British community. This chapter aims to remedy this by examining the changing nature of African-centred organisations in England from 1975 to 2015. Furthermore, it aims to explore how African-centred organisations have been influenced by African-centred trends in the United States and the extent to which they have been shaped by circumstances in Britain.

From as early as the eighteenth century, 'black' activism in England has been represented in many forms. The use of the term 'black' in England has been applied in several ways, from racial categorisation to political association. Racially, 'black' has generally been identified with black African ancestry, which is seen in physical appearance, colour and other visible characteristics. Politically, in England from the 1960s to the 1980s, 'black' was used as a unifying term by African, Caribbean and South Asian people in their struggle against racism, marginalisation and exclusion.[1] For the purposes of this chapter, 'Black' written with a capital 'B' will refer to people of African descent and those of dual heritage.

Relevance and purpose

African-centred organisations in Britain have served as self-appointed custodians and advocates of 'African' cultural practices for Black populations in England, although membership is generally drawn from the Caribbean community. Although small in number, they have had a significant influence on framing the cultural identity of what is some-times referred to as the second-generation Black population in England.[2] This second generation was the generation of Black British citizens who were born or raised in Britain after their parents' migration from the Caribbean in the period from the 1940s to 1960s, commonly known as the 'Windrush Era'. This led to the construction of new transnational cultural identities distinct from the host nation and resonating with the Pan-African experience of oppression and a need to unite around a common struggle. The ideals of Pan-Africanism have manifested in different forms in relation to socio-political environment, location and time; as such, there is no single definition. However, Pan-Africanism can be broadly described as a social and political movement for the 'emancipation of African peoples and those of the African diaspora'.[3]

The focus of this chapter is thus to explore the relevance and purpose of African-centred organisations in England (those that sup-posedly have precolonial African concepts and values as their cultural foundation), such as the Pan-African Congress Movement (PACM), Alkebu-Lan Revivalist Movement (ARM), Ausar Auset Society (AAS) and the Nation of Islam (NOI). They have all been prominent in importing a brand of Black cultural nationalism from organisations such as the Nation of Islam (NOI) in the United States. Although varying in the scope of its definition, 'cultural nationalism' has been described as 'a belief system and set of practices rooted in the idea that a people's distinctiveness is based on cultural elements like shared values, ways of life, and aesthetics'.[4] As such, Black cultural national-ism is rooted in the idea of the recovery and restoration of traditional African cultural systems. These include morals, values and political and economic traditions, underpinned with the ideal of nationhood.

The impact of the Sixth Pan-African Congress

There were several key political influences on the Black community in England during the 1960s, including the movements for civil rights and Black Power in the United States, the visits to England by Malcolm X (formerly of the NOI) in 1964 and 1965 and of Stokely Carmichael (formerly of the Black Panther Party) in 1967. Another key influ-ence was Pan-Africanism and the series of six Pan-African congresses held in Europe, America and Africa from 1919 to 1974. The first four Pan-African congresses were organised by African American activ-ist W. E. B. Du Bois. The most important Pan-African congress, for its uncompromising and radical stance, was the fifth in Manchester in 1945, led by black activists residing in Britain, primarily by the Trinidadian former Communist George Padmore and Kwame Nkrumah, later to become the leader of Ghana's struggle for independence.[5] Yet, with regard to the present discussion, it was the Sixth Pan-African Congress in Tanzania, in 1974, which had a profound impact on members of Black organisations such as the Black Liberation Front (BLF) in England.[6]

The BLF was formed in 1971 by former members of the British-based Black Panther Movement, originally established in 1968.[7] The BLF stood for similar demands as its predecessor, although 'its tone was more urgent, confrontational and occasionally even apocalyptic'.[8] However, after delegates from the BLF and others attended the Sixth Pan-African Congress, in Dar es Salaam, there was a move by some towards representing the Black struggle through the expression of indigenous African culture. This development was a culmination of an ongoing debate during the 1960s in Africa and the diaspora, including Britain, which identified racism as the main cause of African oppression.

The demand for an African expression rooted in African cultural values and traditions also called for a concerted effort for the annual observance of African Liberation Day (ALD). ALD is an annual event held on 25 May to celebrate the struggles for the total liberation of Africa and Africans, especially the continent's liberation from all forms of colonial and neo-colonial rule. It marks the first historic meeting of thirty-two independent African states and the founding of the Organisation of African Unity in Ethiopia in 1963.[9] Following the delegates' return from Dar es Salaam, some members of the BLF and others went on to form the Pan-African Committee (PAC), led by activist and campaigner Ron Phillips.[10] The PAC operated as a coalition of Pan-African organisations, out of which, in 1977, 'it evolved into the Pan-African Congress Movement which was an organisation in its own right'.[11]

Strictly an African family occasion

The Pan-African Congress Movement (PACM) has been a leading organisation in Pan-African affairs in England since its founding. Founding members included Ron Phillips of the Universal Coloured Peoples Association's Manchester branch, Lu Garvey of the BLF, Nkrumah Pepukayi, former member of the BLF and founder of

Pepukayi Books Distribution Services in London (1994), Fritz (Tenny) Louis, Berrenga Bandele and Adasa (Dorothy) Bandele of the Black People's Freedom Movement in Nottingham, Bini Butuakwa (formerly Bini Brown) and Marcel Sculley of the African Caribbean Self-Help Organisation (ACSHO) (1964) in Birmingham, and Cecil Gutzmore, author, lecturer and member of the Pan-African Society Community Forum.[12] After establishing the PAC, Phillips took the post of London Director of FESTAC 77 (Festival of African Culture), also known as the Second World Black and African Festival of Arts and Culture, which was co-organised by the government of Nigeria and UNESCO and held in Lagos, Nigeria in 1977.[13] However, as Gutzmore states:

> when he [Phillips] left or was dismissed from the FESTAC ... he came back and ... he proposed that we become the PACM and I along with Colin Prescott, who didn't stay within the group, wrote the PACM's first two page ... theoretical paper.[14]

The PACM also operated as an umbrella organisation for its various branches in London, Nottingham, Wolverhampton, Bristol, Birmingham and Manchester. The political mandate of the PACM was to promote and maintain Pan-Africanism and in particular to provide a forum where Black people could be informed of what was happening in the Pan-African world.[15] This was done in meetings to raise consciousness, transmit information and instil Pan-Africanism as the core ideological framework for thinking and action.[16] These sessions were publicised as 'Strictly an African Family Occasion', a phrase coined by the PACM that came into popular use by other African-centred groups, to enable the Black community to come together to discuss their issues and decide on a course of action for themselves.[17]

The PACM was also instrumental in the promotion of the seasonal celebration of Kwanzaa and the annual observance of Ancestors' Day on 1 August to commemorate the ancestors who endured and fought under the system of enslavement. The main national focus of the PACM was to put on events and seminars to celebrate ALD. The first such ALD was held in Nottingham in 1975. Over the years it has been held in different locations throughout England, with the largest and most spectacular being held in Handsworth Park, Birmingham, in 1977. This event pulled in an estimated crowd of up to 30,000 Black people in solidarity and support of the global African liberation struggle.[18] The PACM's ALD has included solidarity messages from activists from Africa and the Caribbean, as well as keynote speeches from African-centred scholars based in the United States, such as John Henrik Clarke, Yosef Ben-Jochannon, James Small, Charles Finch, Jewel Pookrum, Oba T'Shaka and his wife Sister Anasa T'Shaka, and Leonard Jeffries and his wife Rosalind Jeffries.[19] The African-centred perspective became conceptualised in the 1980s by Molefi Kete Asante in the ideological framework called Afrocentricity, 'which means, literally, placing African ideals at the centre of any analysis that involves African culture and behaviour'.[20]

Beyond ALD, the work of the PACM is marked more specifically by the activities of its local branches in supporting workers' rights, providing access to housing and providing supplementary education, as well as monitoring the activities of the police.[21] For example, in the 1970s and 1980s, the PACM in London had its headquarters above Headstart Books and Crafts in West Green Road, Tottenham, delivering Sunday workshops that taught Black history and culture and related African-centred topics. Presently, the PACM in London organises a weekly Community Information Workshop at the Maa Maat Cultural Centre in Tottenham, North London. The PACM also run a YouTube channel, PACMTV, where lectures and events are uploaded, 'reaching out to the Pan-African World'.[22]

In Birmingham, the PACM operates through its affiliated member the ACSHO at 104 Heathfield Road, Handsworth (aka 104). As well as the local grassroots programmes, the ACSHO had an international arm and was instrumental in raising funds to provide material support in the form of food, clothes, medicine and money to liberation movements in Southern and South Africa.[23] Support was distributed to liberation groups such as the South West African People's Organisation (SWAPO) of Namibia, FRELIMO in Mozambique, the People's Movement for the Liberation of Angola (MPLA) and the African National Congress (ANC) of South Africa. The ACSHO also set up the Marcus Garvey Foundation, a registered charity that raised funds to provide famine relief during the crises in Ethiopia from 1983 to 1985.[24]

Another arm of the ACSHO's practices is the establishment of African spiritual ceremonies and rituals to underpin its political and cultural activities. Spiritual disciplines, such as pouring libations in honour of the ancestors, building community shrines and enacting nature rituals, are informed by traditional African cultural systems. In particular, the ACSHO works with VU.VA.MU – which translates into English as 'return only to the place where you lost' – a belief system which states that, in order for Africans to reach their true potential, they must return to the point where they were lost or gave up their power and take the right path to their destination.[25] For VU.VA. MU, this point was on 3 May 1491, when King Nzinga Nkuwu of the Kongo kingdom abandoned the god of his ancestors and converted to Christianity.[26] VU.VA.MU follows the teachings of Mfumu Kimbangu,[27] a spiritual leader and prophet (1887–1951), and Yaya Kimpa Vita,[28] a revolutionary leader and prophet (1684–1706), from the Kongo (present-day northern Angola).[29] The ACSHO building is an official African spiritual centre of VU.VA.MU, and some members attend retreats in Angola and other parts of Africa.[30]

However, other members of the PACM have acknowledged that initially the movement was politically and culturally motivated and did not see spirituality as a tool for liberation. Nevertheless, the PACM community workshops have provided a platform for African spiritual practitioners to present their concepts. One group of attendees of the 1980s workshops were particularly influenced by the spiritual teachings and in 1987 went on to found the Alkebu-Lan Revivalist Movement, an 'African-nationalist, Pan-Africanist' organisation grounded in the traditions of African spirituality.[31]

The 'Turbulent 80s'

The 'Turbulent 80s', so-called by political commentators for the decade's industrial, political and cultural unrest, was a vibrant time of Black uprising.[32] March 1981 saw the 'Black Peoples Day of Action', and in April of the same year riots broke out on the streets of Brixton.[33] In September 1985, Brixton became the centre for demonstrations,[34] and in October 1985 there was the Broadwater Farm uprising in Tottenham, North London.[35] Black youth in England sought refuge among their own kind, creating a distinct 'Black-British' cultural expression fused with Caribbean, America and African influences in distinction to the host culture.[36] Amidst the backdrop of social unrest, several black organisations were formed by the second-generation black community in England.

One such organisation was the Alkebu-Lan Revivalist Movement (ARM), a group of like-minded activists who came together to found a 'Pan-Africanist nationalist organisation' that was underpinned by authentic African spirituality and culture. The ARM adheres to the

Pan-Africanist nationalist ideologies of Marcus Garvey and Malcolm X. Its nationalism is premised on the concept of 'Race First and seven essential principles of: Land Ownership, Proud Heritage, Self-Governance, Self-Reliance, Self-Defence, Separatism and Repatriation'.[37] The movement was started in January 1987, pioneered by its spiritual leader Brother Leader Mbandaka, and it operates out of Mama Afrika Kulcha Shap, in Leyton, East London. The ARM has had a prominent presence in African-centred events, with its unique representation of an African-centred expression. The ARM, primarily represented by Brother Leader Mbandaka, is often scheduled to speak at Pan-African forums and is present at public meetings.

The ARM has several 'cultural imperatives', such as a monthly 'Nommo Session', where members of the ARM, or guest speakers, present and interact with the African community on various African-centred topics, books and films.[38] Public gatherings also include the annual 'Month of Mosiah Opening Ceremony', a thirty-one-day celebration that aims to 're-ignite the spirit, mission and vision' of the life, teaching and legacy of Marcus Garvey. This celebration takes place in the month of August, referred to as 'Mosiah', in honour of the month Garvey was born.[39] Garvey is also bestowed with the title 'The Most Eminent Prophet and King His Excellency Marcus Mosiah Garvey', which, in the view of the organisation, is befitting of his status in Pan-Africanism.[40] Similar recognition and homage is given to Malcolm X; during the month of February there is an annual commemoration of the life and lessons of Omowale Malcolm X. Omowale is a name common among the Yoruba people of Nigeria and is translated into English as 'The child has come home'.

Seasonal cultural events such as Kwanzaa have also been organised by the ARM as part of its community programme. Moreover, in reaching out to a broader audience, the ARM has a Monday evening radio show called 'Afrika Speaks with Alkebu-Lan' on the internet-based community radio station 'Galaxy: Afi We Station' (102.5 FM). Galaxy Radio – 'The only de-brainwashing station' – is renowned in the African-centred and wider black community in London and has a history of note in its own right.[41] Another aspect of the ARM's public arm is the publication of *The Whirlwind: The Voice of the Nation* newspaper, which is also available online on the ARM's official website. The ARM also has a Saturday school and a Home School Collective programme for home-schooled students and those seeking an alternative educational setting.[42]

The ARM was born out of what members felt was a void in the spiritual dimension to the liberation struggle. As Brother Leader Mbandaka explains: 'There was an absence in the community, at the time, of a nationalist Pan-Africanist liberationist movement that was underpinned by a strong spiritual cultural philosophy, a strong identifiable spiritual cultural philosophy and we felt that it was desperately needed within the community.'[43] The ARM is a liberation movement that is based on an African-centred spiritual, cultural philosophy called Alkebu-Lan Livity. Brother Leader Mbandaka continues:

> Alkebu-Lan is one of the oldest names on historical records for the African continent and therefore represents our motherland and our people and our culture pre the Maafa – pre enslavement, [pre] colonization of African people. Livity is a Rastafari word that we have adopted which incorporates the words live and divinity so it means divine living and so combined ... Alkebu-Lan Livity means living according to the divine teachings and traditions of our mother culture.[44]

Although not practising a specific African spiritual system, such as the Ifa divination system from the Yoruba people in West Africa, but rather a synthesis of African spiritual systems common throughout Africa, and taking into account the journey from the Caribbean to Britain, Mbandaka explains:

> It's a synthesis of authentic spiritual traditions, spiritual systems, as we understand them on the African continent and the spiritual retention that we manifest in parts of the Caribbean [and] South America. We understand that we carry those traditions with us and they give specific expression according to the social and political, even, context in which we find ourselves as a people.[45]

In their lifestyle and customs the members of the ARM strive to represent an authentic African nationalist organisation, underpinned with a spiritual dimension that reflects authentic African spiritual values and concepts. Therefore, the ARM carries out various traditional African ritual practices on behalf of its members and the community, such as 'rites of passage' ceremonies to mark the four stages of the growth cycle: birth, adulthood, marriage and passing over. The ARM uses the Shona language to say prayers and blessings to Mwari (the Divine Creator), to open and close its presentations and ceremonies. The term 'Tendai Mwari', meaning 'be thankful unto the creator', is injected throughout their utterances.[46]

The use of such terms to give reverence to the creator for one's good speech is comparable to the gospel pastors' use of the phrase 'All glory be unto God' and the NOI leaders who commonly say 'All praises due unto Allah'. The use of a traditional African language reaffirms the connection to authentic traditional African culture. Some groups refer to even earlier linguistic forms, such as that found in Ancient Egypt or Khemet (the ancient name for modern-day Egypt) to establish authenticity. For example, members of the Ausar Auset Society greet and depart with the word 'Hetepu', meaning 'peace', which is similar to the Catholic greeting 'Peace be with you'.

The Nile Valley civilisation and the reawakening of Black consciousness

> The Ausar Auset Society (AAS) is an international Pan African Spiritual organisation committed to the upliftment of traditional African culture and values, providing Afro centric based spiritual training to the descendants of Africans in the diaspora.[47]

Although recorded as beginning in 1990, the AAS in England was founded over a period of 'progression through inspiration to initiation' from 1981 to 1990 by Ur Aua Khem Men Sih Napata, Paramount King of the Ausar Auset Society in Europe. 'Ur Aua', which is translated from the 'Kamitic' (an alternative to Kemetic as spelled and phrased by the AAS), equates to 'Paramount King', a title reflecting his role and position in the AAS in Europe. The AAS was originally founded by Shekhem Ur Shekhem (King of Kings) Ra Un Nefer Amen I in Harlem, New York in 1973.[48] Prior to joining the AAS, Ur Aua Khem Men Sih was an avid Pan-Africanist who was accused of atheism for his views regarding the three major religions of Judaism, Christianity and Islam. As Ur Aua Khem Men Sih notes:

> I was termed ... 'an atheist' because on looking at the religious teachings that was [sic] offered to my people and what it had done for my people I didn't see that there was any juice in it. So as a Pan-Africanist, Africa was home so it was about returning home.

Ur Aua Khem Men Sih had studied the teachings of tai chi, qigong and the martial arts and was a reader of philosophy, psychology and health. In or around 1981 he was in Ghana, where, he explains,

'I got this inspiration that I needed to reconnect with god.'[49] On returning to London he found himself at Headstart Books and Crafts, run
by Nkrumah Pepukayi at the time, and was drawn to a book entitled
*Ageless Wisdom Guide to Healing: Health Teachings of the Ageless Wisdom
Book 1* by Ra Un Nefer Amen (1983). He read the preface and there,
he explains, 'I found my teacher.' In a matter of days, he had flown to
New York to make contact with Ra Un Nefer Amen.[50]

In 1985, Ur Aua Khem Men Sih and a group of eleven people
in London 'coalesced around the ideas' of Ra Un Nefer Amen and
maintained contact with Shekhem Ur Shekhem. Following a period of
training and consultation, the group was eventually given permission
to be called the Ausar Auset Study Group in Europe. Then, in 1990,
the book *Metu Neter Volume 1* was published, and, as Ur Aua Khem
Men Sih states, 'I said every single Black person in England had to
have access to this book, so I began to give lectures from the Metu
Neter.'[51] The teachings of the *Metu Neter Volume 1* are presented as 'a
practical syncretism of the best of what the kametic (Ancient Egypt),
the Dravidian (Black India), and the Canaanite (true Kabala) religions
have to offer'.[52] As Ra Un Nefer Amen teaches:

> *The solution to our problem is the restitution of the science of life that
> actually gave birth to civilization.* The only way that this can be done
> is by correlating the spiritual doctrines, and religious practices of the
> founding civilisations with those of the Black civilization of today.[53]

Ra Un Nefer Amen presents the 'Divine Plan' in the *Metu Neter Volume
1* as 'not museum pieces that are the delight and folly of historians, but
as a lived system'.[54] As such, the AAS claims to offer a practical way
of living a balanced life of 'spirituality, health and wealth', as Ur Aua
Khem Men Sih explains regarding the aims of the AAS:

> Our aim and our goal is to assist our people to reclaim their true
> identity. We take it seriously that the restoration of the African
> consciousness is of paramount importance to our liberation but that
> consciousness cannot be predicated on information alone. You have
> to take the information and apply it. So the Ausar Auset way is a
> doing way ...[55]

As a result, membership of the AAS is not sought on a wide scale
but consists of an estimated 150 dedicated members who have

applied the teachings of the AAS in their lives and an unquantified number of study group attendees. Study groups are held throughout England – in Bristol, Birmingham, Manchester, Sheffield, Bradford, Ipswich and different locations in London, including the central base in Kensal Green, North-west London. The teachings of the AAS are disseminated via public classes, workshops and major events and by inviting visiting priests and priestesses from the Ausar Auset Nation to make their teachings available.[56] Classes include African-centred spiritual teachings in Kamitic philosophy, cosmology, ritual, oracle consultation, meditation, the power of yoga and yogic breathing, nutrition, herbalism, qigong, African history and culture.[57]

The AAS's philosophical teaching is a syncretism of 'Kamitic Nile Valley teachings', including 'the Pyramid Texts (2350 BC) ... the Coffin Text (2200 BC) ... The transformation of Ra and of overthrowing Apep (1950 BC) and most notably the so-called Book of the Dead (1500 BC)'.[58] While it could be argued that some of the practices employed by the AAS emanate from Eastern traditions, such as the Hebrew Kabala in correlation to the Tree of Life meditation system, Buddhist chants in guided meditation and Chinese yoga for balancing body and mind, Ra Un Nefer Amen argues that 'in reality it is a modification of the Light taken by Blacks from Nubia into Tigris, and Indus Valley in prehistoric times'.[59] Furthermore, it is argued that the traditional Nile Valley spiritual systems of antiquity were systematically destroyed by foreign invaders and the teachers went into hiding, maintaining their traditions to 'varying degrees'.[60] Therefore, in reclaiming these practices as authentic to Africa, Ur Aua Khem Men Sih explains:

> the teachings spread. So now, we go back into those ancient teachings and we take that which is true ... wherever truth is found it must be used ...
>
> [W]hy shouldn't we go back and fetch that which is ours, isn't that what Sankofa is ...[61]

The Sankofa bird of the Akan people of West Africa is a symbolic representation of claiming back your history as you move forward to your future.[62] As such, without 'disavowing anybody's religion', in examining the differences between belief, faith and conviction, Ur Aua Khem Men Sih concludes:

The African religion is a means in which you become convinced that you are made in the image and likeness of God and therefore you are a god. You may be a god infant or god in potential, but you can find your way back to your divinity through a process of initiation, through a way of living ...[63]

The three-pronged approach of spirituality, health and wealth that underpins the transforming philosophy of the AAS is comparable to the triad of spiritual, political and economic informing the practices of the NOI in England.

POWER

There is some indication of an early influence of the Nation of Islam (NOI) in England, since, following a speech in London by Malcolm X in 1965, audience member Michael de Freitas was inspired to change his name to Michael X and set up the Racial Awareness Action Society (RAAS).[64] However, the organisation in its current form reputedly began in October 1985 in a domestic front room in Walthamstow, East London, when a BBC TV news report broadcast an excerpt of a speech made by the Honourable Minister Louis Farrakhan in Madison Square Garden, New York, on 7 October. The news report had the effect of stirring the consciences of brothers Michael and Andrew. As former assistant minister of Mosque 1B in West London, Brother Andrew Muhammad explains:

I didn't realise that it [NOI] was still here, I thought this was a bygone organisation and then we started to get one or two tapes passed around in the community, audio tapes, and I used to listen to these audio tapes and they were like blowing our minds ... we would take these tapes back to my mother's house, sit down and devour ... the knowledge, wisdom and understanding coming from this man [Farrakhan] and it was from there we started to invite friends ... to come into my mother's house, sit down and listen to the tapes together ... that is how the Nation of Islam started, literally, just by us listening to tapes ... and it started to flourish from there ... we just realised we wanted to take it a bit more serious now than just listening to tape.[65]

The circulation of audio cassettes of Minister Farrakhan's speeches, in particular the address entitled 'Power at Last, Forever!: The Overwhelming Event' given on 'Saviours' Day' in Chicago in February 1985, is commonly cited by early NOI members for awakening the minds of members of the Black community in London.[66] Following the media exposure of Farrakhan, in January 1986 the Hackney Black People's Association (HBPA), founded by St Vincent-born Pan-African activist Lester Lewis, invited him to London to address the Black community.[67] This invitation was met with opposition by the British-Israeli parliamentary group, which convinced the then Home Secretary, Douglas Hurd, to issue a ban preventing Farrakhan from entering Britain based on his alleged anti-Semitic views.[68] This sparked the 'Lift the Ban on Farrakhan' campaign. Inspired by the teachings of Farrakhan, a small contingent of six enthusiasts led by Brother Michael left London to attend 'Saviours' Day' in Chicago in 1989. The group met with Farrakhan, who bestowed the title of Muhammad on Brother Michael and sent him 'back to do the work of building a Nation'.[69]

Over time, the NOI established study groups in Brixton, South London, under Hilary Muhammad (in 1989) (now European Regional Representative Minister Abdul Hakeem Muhammad); Shepherds Bush, West London, under Michael Muhammad (in 1991); Hackney, East London, under Wayne Muhammad (in 1994); and Tottenham, North London, under Bertram Muhammad (in 1997).[70] In February 1997, 300 NOI members travelled from London to Chicago to observe 'Saviours' Day', when Minister Farrakhan appointed the East London group as the first NOI mosque in Europe, responsible for administering study groups in Paris, Switzerland and Birmingham.[71]

At its conception, the goal of the NOI in London was to implement the political, economic and spiritual strategy called POWER, an acronym for 'People Organised and Working for Economic Rebirth', set out in Farrakhan's keynote speech on 'Saviours' Day' in 1985.[72] For example, the West London contingent based in Mosque 1B, Goldhawk Road, Shepherds Bush, went on to establish economic programmes, such as Elijah's Garden Restaurant, two Yours Produce grocery stores in Shepherds Bush and Harlesden, two Respect for Life bookshops in Dalston and Harlesden, and a catering company called Cuisine for Life, which provided vegetarian and wholesome food for NOI members and public events. The NOI also ran a supplementary school, called Star Chamber Academy, in Hammersmith, West London.[73] Furthermore, in order to bring the message of Farrakhan to the wider community, in the summer of 1998 live concerts were held in various popular venues, including the renowned Hammersmith Palais in West London. Dubbed the 'Hip Hop Day of Atonement' and the 'Reggae Day of Atonement', these concerts were also aimed at addressing the derogatory tone of music at the time. Various progressive artists and musicians were invited to write and produce music to be sold and performed live on stage.[74] In recognition of the Million Man March, organised by the NOI in Washington DC in 1995, the West London branch organised the '10,000 Man March', a rally held in Trafalgar Square in October 1998. Observing the event was the then Supreme Captain Sharif Abdul Muhammad of the NOI in the US.

The NOI also produced two bi-monthly newspapers, *Sign of the Times* and *POWER*, highlighting issues relating to the Black community in England, which were to be sold along with the official NOI publication *The Final Call*. At its height in the 1990s, the NOI in London had a membership of around 600, with the West London contingent averaging 300.[75] Women played a fundamental role in the day-to-day running of the organisation – 'they were the rock', outnumbering the men three to one in the membership.[76]

Members of the NOI have a distinct appearance: the men (the Fruit of Islam or FOI) in their crescent moon and star bow ties and blue suits, or formal suits; the women (Muslim Girl Training (MGT) and General Civilisation Class (GCC)) in their stylish but modest garments and head coverings. As such, the NOI came into the spotlight of the British media when members appeared outside Hannibal House in Elephant and Castle, South London, at the Stephen Lawrence inquiry in 1998 at the behest of Stephen's father, Neville Lawrence.[77]

Since 1998, the leadership and administration of the NOI have gone through some changes comparable to those of its parent organisation in the US, but these are beyond the scope of this chapter.[78] At present, the NOI England continues under the sole leadership of the official spokesman for Farrakhan, the European Regional Representative Minister Abdul Hakeem Muhammad, operating from Muhammad Mosque no. 1 in Brixton, South London. Regular Sunday study groups and public forums are held to address issues in the Black community. The members of the NOI are active participants in providing support to political and cultural rallies; for example, they work in collaboration with the Rastafari Movement UK to host the annual Africa International Day of Action community family fun day in Kennington Park in London. In this regard, the long legal battle against the ban on Farrakhan continued when, in August 2017, Lambeth County Council issued a permit prohibiting a live stream or pre-recorded address by Minister Farrakhan, or any public address by NOI members at the Kennington Park event.[79]

Although often misunderstood for its pro-Black stance, the spiritual dimension of the NOI is the foundation of its philosophy. As Brother Andrew explains: '[W]hen we look at the teachings it is a healing for all people ... regardless of their age, colour, creed or class.'[80] Brother Andrew continues:

> What the Honourable Elijah Muhammad done [sic], and I bow to his wisdom, he applied Islam to us in a way that we as a people, based on our history and what we have been through, could identify with it and absolutely apply it too.[81]

In regard to its authenticity as an African spiritual system, NOI argues that Africa is not restricted to the geographical location designated by 'Western imperialists' but extends into the so-called Middle East, which is an extension of the African continent, as Brother Andrew explains:

> The Middle East is only a term devised in 1948 by politicians to separate ... Northern Africa from the rest of Africa. They built a man-made canal [Suez Canal] so when you talk about Islam it is an African-based spiritual faith.[82]

Brother Andrew concludes: 'I say this all the time: Africa is our throne, but the world is our home.'[83] The geographical inclusion of the 'Middle East' as North-east Africa opens up the question of African authenticity beyond the land mass of the African continent and beyond the scope of this chapter.

Conclusion

In conclusion, this chapter has introduced four British-based African-centred organisations, describing their early development and influences. It has mentioned some key individuals as well as aspects of their ideologies and practices, which stem from several traditions found in Africa and the diaspora. These individuals and organisations can be seen as custodians of a sense of African-ness, one that also incorporates the experiences of their historical journey from the Caribbean to England.

The second-generation Black British community, who, out of alienation from the host society, moved in search of community, identity and an understanding of their place in the world, would have undoubtedly come into contact with one or more of these organisations, via workshops, public meetings or the dissemination of books, newsletters and mixed media. Their relevance and importance are such that these organisations to some extent represent the bastions of an African-centred approach to the socio-political condition of the Black population in England. They stand as the pioneers who plough on, sometimes to the disdain of the community they seek to uplift, and although their purpose may seem futile. They plough on through the darkness, handing the light of resistance to the next generation till the dawn of African liberation is at hand.

Notes

1 Sarita Malik, *Representing Black Britain: Black and Asian Images on Television* (London: SAGE Publications, 2002), p. 19.

2 Eddie Chambers, *Roots and Culture: Cultural Politics in the Making of Black Britain* (London: I. B. Tauris, 2017), pp. 51–77.

3 Hakim Adi and Marika Sherwood, *Pan-African History: Political Figures from Africa and the Diaspora since 1787* (London: Routledge, 2003), p. vii.

4 K. McCray, 'Cultural Nationalism' (unpublished manuscript, Atlanta Metropolitan State College, 2016), p. 1.

5 Hakim Adi and Marika Sherwood, *The 1945 Manchester Pan-African Congress Revisited: With Colonial and ... Coloured Unity (The Report of the 5th Pan-African Congress)* (London: New Beacon Books, 1995).

6 Rosalind Eleanor Wild, '"Black Was the Colour of Our Fight": Black Power in Britain 1955–1976' (PhD thesis, University of Sheffield, 2008), p. 98.

7 Wild, '"Black Was the Colour of Our Fight"', p. 104.

8 Wild, '"Black Was the Colour of Our Fight".', p. 105.

9 Molefi Kete Asante and Ama Mazama (eds), *Encyclopaedia of Black Studies* (London: SAGE Publications, 2005), p. 45.

10 Cecil Gutzmore, personal communication, 19 November 2017.

11 Nkrumah Pepukayi, personal communication, 13 June 2017.

12 Cecil Gutzmore, personal communication, 19 November 2017.

13 UNESCO, 'Festac 77: Lagos Festival', http://ww.unesco.org/archives/multimedia/?pg=33&s=films_details&id=29, accessed 9 January 2018.

14 Cecil Gutzmore, personal communication, 19 November 2017.

15 Nkrumah Pepukayi, personal communication, 13 June 2017.

16 Nkrumah Pepukayi, personal communication, 13 June 2017.

17 Nkrumah Pepukayi, personal communication, 13 June 2017.

18 Bini Butuwaka, personal communication, 15 February 2016.

19 Bini Butuwaka, personal communication, 15 February 2016.

20 Molefi Kete Asante, *The Afrocentric Idea* (Philadelphia: Temple University Press, 1987), p. 6.

21 Cecil Gutzmore, personal communication, 19 November 2017.

22 PACMTV, https://www.youtube.com/channel/UCGkQmMgShGFgoiJWxoQ8oug, accessed 15 February 2018.

23 Nkrumah Pepukayi, personal communication, 13 June 2017.

24 Bini Butuwaka, personal communication, 15 February 2016.

25 Ne Kunda Niaba, personal communication, 9 July 2017.

26 VU.VA.MU, *Pour la Rehabilitation de l'Homme Noir/For the Black Rehabilitation/Pona Lisiko Ya Bayindo*, http://bayindo-bolamuka.skyrock. com/2219813605-VU-VA-MU-POUR-LA-REHABILITATION-DE-L-HOMME-NOIR-FOR-THE-BLACK.html, accessed 14 February 2018.

27 Bundu Dia Kongo, 'Mfumu Kimbangu', http://bundu-dia-kongo.org/ history/messangers-prophets/mfumu-kimbangu.html, accessed 13 February 2018.

28 John K. Thornton, *The Kongolese Saint Anthony: Dona Beartriz Kimpa Vita and the Antonian Movement, 1684–1706* (Cambridge: Cambridge University Press, 1998).

29 Bini Butuwaka, personal communication, 15 February 2016.

30 Bini Butuwaka, personal communication, 15 February 2016.

31 Brother Leader Mbandaka, 'The Origin of Alkebu-Lan', https://www. youtube.com/watch?v=BTf3aCx_v3o, accessed 12 January 2018.

32 Brother Leader Mbandaka, 'The Origin of Alkebu-Lan'.

33 Horace Campbell, *Rasta and Resistance: From Marcus Garvey to Walter Rodney* (London: Hansib, 2007), pp. 202–6.

34 'From the Archives: Riots in Brixton after Police Shooting', *Guardian*, 30 September 2009, https://www. theguardian.com/theguardian/2009/ sep/30/brixton-riots-1985-archive, accessed 15 February 2018.

35 'What Caused the 1985 Tottenham Broadwater Farm Riots?', BBC News, 3 March 2014, http://www.bbc. co.uk/news/uk-england-london-26362633, accessed 15 February 2018.

36 Chambers, *Roots and Culture*, pp. 51–77.

37 Brother Leader Mbandaka, personal communication, 6 April 2016.

38 Alkebu-Lan Revivalist Movement, 'Category: Nommo Sessions', http:// www.alkebulan.org/category/nommo-sessions/, accessed 20 January 2018.

39 Alkebu-Lan Revivalist Movement and UNIA-ACL Mosiah Division #304, 'Presents the Month of Mosiah Opening Ceremony', https:// alkebulanrevivalistmovement.wordpress. com/2016/06/10/mosiah-opening-ceremony/, accessed 20 January 2017.

40 Alkebu-Lan Revivalist Movement and UNIA-ACL Mosiah Division, 'Presents the Month of Mosiah Opening Ceremony'.

41 Galaxy Radio, 'A Fi We Station', http://galaxyafiwe.com/about/, access 15 February 2018.

42 Amitiye Lumumba, personal communication, 18 February 2018.

43 Brother Leader Mbandaka, personal communication, 6 April 2016.

44 Brother Leader Mbandaka, personal communication, 6 April 2016.

45 Brother Leader Mbandaka, personal communication, 6 April 2016.

46 Alkebu-Lan, 'What is Alkebu-Lan', https://alkebulanrevivalistmovement. wordpress.com/2014/09/29/post/, accessed 20 January 2018.

47 Ausar Auset Society Europe, 'Welcome', http://www. ausarausetsocietyeurope.com/, accessed 17 January 2018.

48 Ur Aua Khem Men Sih, personal communication, 6 March 2018.

49 Ur Aua Khem Men Sih, personal communication, 6 March 2018.

50 Ur Aua Khem Men Sih, personal communication, 6 March 2018.

51 Ur Aua Khem Men Sih, personal communication, 6 March 2018.

52 Ra Un Nefer Amen, *Metu Neter Volume 1: The Great Oracle of Tehuti and the Egyptian System of Spiritual Cultivation* (Brooklyn: Khamit Corp., 1990), p. 2.

53   Ra Un Nefer Amen, *Metu Neter Volume 1*, p. 21, emphasis in the original.

54   Ra Un Nefer Amen, *Metu Neter Volume 1*, p. 2.

55   Ur Aua Khem Men Sih, personal communication, 6 March 2018.

56   Ur Aua Khem Men Sih, personal communication, 6 March 2018.

57   Ausar Auset Society Europe, 'Taui Network Europe', http://www.ausarausetsocietyeurope.com/Classes.html, accessed 1 January 2018.

58   Ur Aua Khem Men Sih, personal communication, 6 March 2018.

59   Ra Un Nefer Amen, *Metu Neter Volume 1*, p. 44.

60   Ra Un Nefer Amen, *Metu Neter Volume 1*, pp. 35–45.

61   Ur Aua Khem Men Sih, personal communication, 6 March 2018.

62   African Heritage, 'Adinkra Symbols and the Rich Akan Culture', https://afrolegends.com/2014/08/27/adinkra-symbols-and-the-rich-akan-culture/, accessed 1 February 2018.

63   Ur Aua Khem Men Sih, personal communication, 6 March 2018.

64   Wild, '"Black Was the Colour of our Fight"', pp. 32–3.

65   Andrew Muhammad, personal communication, 5 March 2016.

66   'Saviours' Day 1985', https://www.youtube.com/watch?v=dotpt48NA8U, accessed 1 March 2018.

67   Rosalind Muhammad, 'The Rise of the Nation of Islam in London. Part 1', *The Final Call: On-Line Edition*, http://www.finalcall.com/perspectives/noi-london5-6-97.html, accessed 1 March 2018.

68   Dawn-Marie Gibson, *A History of the Nation of Islam: Race, Islam and the Quest for Freedom* (Santa Barbara: Praeger, 2012), pp. 99–100.

69   Critical Analysis, 'Leo Muhammad: Joining the Nation of Islam UK', https://www.youtube.com/watch?v=9Xxn5ztv1V4, accessed 1 March 2018.

70   Muhammad, 'The Rise of the Nation of Islam in London'.

71   Muhammad, 'The Rise of the Nation of Islam in London'.

72   Andrew Muhammad, personal communication, 27 February 2018.

73   Andrew Muhammad, personal communication, 27 February 2018.

74   Anonymous (former NOI member), personal communication, 27 February 2018.

75   Anonymous (former NOI member), personal communication, 27 February 2018.

76   Andrew Muhammad, personal communication, 5 March 2016.

77   Anonymous (former NOI member), personal communication, 27 February 2018.

78   Critical Analysis, 'Leo Muhammad: "Bloodless Coup in the West"', https://www.youtube.com/watch?v=bbY34D29rMY, accessed 1 February 2018.

79   'Sign the Petition: The Black Community Has Been Denied Leadership for Over 30 Outrageous Years', https://www.change.org/p/lift-the-ban-on-minister-farrakhan-from-entering-the-uk-freespeechforall2015, accessed 2 February 2018.

80   Andrew Muhammad, personal communication, 5 March 2016.

81   Andrew Muhammad, personal communication, 5 March 2016.

82   Andrew Muhammad, personal communication, 5 March 2016.

83   Andrew Muhammad, personal communication, 5 March 2016.

9 | THE NEW CROSS FIRE OF 1981 AND ITS AFTERMATH

Carol Pierre

Introduction

The New Cross Fire of 1981 is a decisive moment in Black British History. Number 439 New Cross Road was the scene of a devastating fire in the early hours of 18 January 1981. Thirteen black teenagers, who were celebrating two of their friends' sixteenth birthdays, lost their lives,[1] a further twenty-seven victims suffered serious injuries and a fourteenth young person, traumatised, plunged to his death eighteen months later.[2] The cause of the fire remains unknown, yet the possibility of a racist arson attack continues to be discussed. Arguably, the aftermath of the fire is as important as its cause, exposing institutional and local racism on the one hand, and, on the other, inciting people to unite in protest and support of the victims.

Enoch Powell's aggressive 'Rivers of Blood' speech in 1968, inciting anti-immigration sentiment, galvanised the National Front (NF) and fascist organisations to actively provoke and harass immigrants who were considered intruders among settled white communities.[3]

By 1971, the black population of Britain had reached 200,000;[4] however, the Immigration Act, passed in 1971, restricted settlement rights for all Commonwealth immigrants.[5]

In 1978, Margaret Thatcher MP, on national television, voiced the opinion that 'people [were] really rather afraid that [the] country might be rather swamped by people of different culture'.[6] Thatcher claimed that such fears were reflected in growing NF allegiance. In 1979 Thatcher became prime minister and within two years had proposed a new Nationality Act (1981), limiting citizenship rights. This act was supported by Home Secretary William Whitelaw, who, in a parliamentary debate, claimed that Britons should be separated into 'insiders' and 'outsiders'.[7] Through economic decline and increased class polarisation under Thatcher, authoritarianism and police powers intensified.[8] Violent conflicts between black people and the police informed Thatcher's discussions on black criminality,[9] nurturing aggressive and abusive stop and search (SUS) arrests.[10]

The New Cross Fire should be viewed within this national context, and more specifically within the local context. In January 1971, a West Indian party in Sunderland Road, Forest Hill was firebombed, leaving twenty-two injured, only two of four suspects were belatedly sentenced, and the incident received minimal press coverage.[11] As a result, 150 black people descended on Ladywell police station demanding action.[12] Tempers escalated again in April 1975 when police violently stormed a party in Brockley, arresting sixteen and banning Jah Shaka's sound system from playing locally. Jamaican-born Shaka was, and remains, South-east London's pioneering reggae sound system legend. Three hundred local residents met at the Moonshot Community Centre in New Cross in protest against the ban.[13] The Lewisham 24 Affair, in May 1977, saw police raid sixty black households without legitimate premise, arresting twenty-four people and trying nineteen for conspiracy.[14]

A significant moment in the history of race relations in South London was the Battle of Lewisham, when, in August 1977, 5,000 NF supporters marched with racist banners through Lewisham. Anti-racists confronted them, a battle ensued, and police protected the NF, leading to anti-NF demonstrators clashing directly with the police.[15] Three months later the Moonshot was firebombed.[16] Deptford's Albany Empire community theatre burned down in July 1978, from unknown causes. A racist attack was suspected as a response to the theatre's support of cultural diversity and Rock Against Racism (RAR): a socialist movement using live music events to unite black and white people in the struggle against fascism and racism.[17] Racism, at both a political and more rudimentary level, and resolute community reactions against it provide the backdrop to the New Cross Fire and the events that followed.

The New Cross Massacre Action Committee

Two days after the fire, the New Cross Massacre Action Committee (NCMAC) was founded by John La Rose, Darcus Howe, Roxy Harris and Alex Pascall. Trinidadian-born La Rose had come to the UK in 1961 and established New Beacon Books, the first UK Caribbean publishing house, bookshop and international book service, and in the same year he co-founded the Caribbean Artists Movement. During the 1960s he was involved with the Black Education movement, founded the George Padmore Supplementary School, and continued his activism for black supplementary education initiatives.

From 1972 to 1973, La Rose chaired the Institute of Race Relations and, in 1975, he set up the Black Parents Movement, which together with the Black Youth Movement and the *Race Today* Collective formed 'the Alliance'. Darcus Howe, a political activist, founded the *Race Today* Collective 1973, whose publication *Race Today* was a mouthpiece for UK and worldwide grassroots struggles and campaigns. Roxy Harris, of West African descent, was a founding member of the Black Parents Movement and a coordinator of the George Padmore Supplementary School. Alex Pascall, born in Grenada, developed *Black Londoners* in 1974 for BBC Radio London; by 1978 it had become Britain's first black daily radio show.

The NCMAC was a coalition of organisations: 'the Alliance', the Pan-African Congress Movement (PACM) and the left-wing Black Unity and Freedom Party (BUFP). These organisations all fought against racial injustice, within the political and social domain, while the PACM worked towards the decolonisation of Africa through international conferences and negotiations, and the *Race Today* Collective, as well as the BUFP, were publishing houses for journals focusing on race relations, education, politics and racist violence.

In a rapid response to the tragedy, the NCMAC interviewed the police and Mrs Ruddock, who had lost her house and two children, broadcasting interviews on Pascall's *Black Londoners* BBC radio show. The NCMAC later observed the first inquest and, dissatisfied with an inconclusive decision, appealed for a second inquest.[18] Hundreds gathered outside the burnt shell of the house at a mass meeting organised by the NCMAC held on Sunday 25 January 1981. From the beginning, the NCMAC maintained the belief that the fire was a racially motivated attack and was part of a trajectory of racist violence in the local area during the proceeding decade.[19]

Within the NCMAC, the Black People's Assembly was restricted to black people, to preserve from within the integrity of black people affected by the fire, which was largely believed to have been perpetrated by a white racist. The General Assembly, formed as an offshoot of the Black People's Assembly, was accessible to all who backed the objectives of the campaign;[20] it held weekly conferences to discuss ideas and guide the action committee led by La Rose. A fire fund was established to assist the bereaved, help with funeral costs and care for the injured. The New Cross Fire's importance is reflected in the rapid and professional organisation of campaigns, uniting local residents with London's black communities, seeking justice for the victims of

New Cross, and challenging government neglect, the police investigation and media misreporting.

The government

Institutional responses to the New Cross Fire are emblematic of the institutional racism of the period. No words of sympathy were sent to any of the families by the Queen or the prime minister. However, only weeks later, Thatcher's condolences were sent when a club in Dublin, Ireland, caught fire.[21] The local MP, John Silken, whose office was a few doors away from the scene of the fire, raised no concern for his Deptford constituents. His silence was condemned by many, including *Fight Racism! Fight Imperialism!* (FRFI), the newspaper of the Revolutionary Communist Group,[22] who quoted an anonymous resident as lamenting: 'If the fire had taken place in a kennel and killed 12 dogs there would have been more response.'[23]

A letter to parliament from the NCMAC, dated 23 February 1981, demonstrated the anger of the black community at 'the failure of both Parliament and the media to focus the attention of the public on the appalling tragedy in New Cross'.[24] A further letter to Prime Minister Thatcher protested against 'the failure of ... Government to reflect the outrage ... of the black community'.[25] Thatcher eventually wrote to Sybil Phoenix, founder of the Moonshot and leading community worker, who was one of the first people at the scene of the fire, and who was engaged in counselling families and liaising with the police in search of answers.[26] Thatcher's letter of acknowledgement five weeks after the tragedy, addressed to Phoenix and not to the bereaved families themselves, was seen by many as a 'serious and calculated insult'.[27] In addition, the letter to Phoenix requested that the prime minister's condolences should be passed on to '[her] people'. Phoenix later declared: 'Who gave me people? They're your people.'[28] Thatcher's response can be considered the affirmation that black people could live, work and vote in Britain but were still not considered an integral part of the British population.

Ross Howells, a Moonshot community worker in 1981, later becoming Baroness Howells MP, stated that the lack of institutional acknowledgement 'showed the country had no respect for the black community', which fuelled anger.[29] If the government had provided moral and material support for all those involved, the aftermath of the fire could have been made less painful. The New Cross Fire and the 'establishment's' casual dismissal of it would prove to be an awakening moment for the local and black community and a catalyst for citywide social action.

The police

Days after the fire, when police detained partygoers for questioning,[30] Howells claimed that it would not be believed that black youths could just have been enjoying themselves with no trouble.[31] The NCMAC was also adamant that 'no black scapegoat' should be charged with murder.[32] Anecdotes from the night of the fire and reports from the first police officers at the scene concurred that a man was seen speeding away after throwing a projectile against the house. Police soon dropped this line of inquiry. Howe claimed that, 'as the anger rose, the incendiary devices disappeared'.[33] In the fire's aftermath, Howe received a letter stating that 'party-[youts] ... defied instructions to tone-down ... earsplitting – monkey – music ... until flames suddenly silenced them',[34] a sinister reminder of the campaign being conducted by Conservative MP Jill Knight against 'noisy' black house parties.[35] Whether or not the New Cross Fire was arson, considering the history of racist attacks in the local vicinity, this proposition deserved to be taken seriously.

A letter from the NCMAC to the commissioner of the Metropolitan Police deplored the failure of the police 'to understand the outrage ... of the black community',[36] and the fact that after six weeks the police had dismissed a racial motive and had brought no one to justice for the thirteen deaths. David Michael, Lewisham's first black police officer, described the Lewisham police force throughout the 1970s as behaving less like a community service and more like an 'occupying army', since it was dismissive of locals, especially black people. Michael claims that, in 1981, the police were 'inherently racist', and that many were NF sympathisers. Although he has never believed in the firebomb theory, he admits that police spent disproportionate amounts of time 'plaguing' black house parties and believes that contemporary policing and criminal justice were 'cultures' no one would be proud to have been a part of.[37]

The NCMAC's Fact-finding Commission (FFC) was created in response to police investigations, to independently amass testimonies from those involved. The police investigation was led by Lewisham Borough Commander Stockwell, whose integrity had been disputed at the coroner's inquest.[38] Howells testified that the police acted 'like vigilantes looking for a black culprit' and were 'very agile in arresting young black people'.[39] Linton Kwesi Johnson, born in Jamaica and educated in South London, was a political activist from an early age, a member of the Black Panthers and later of the Black Parents Movement, the *Race Today* Collective and the NCMAC. With regard to the New Cross Fire, he spoke of a police campaign of 'disinformation', framing black youths and forcing them to make false confessions, hoping that people would forget the firebomb theory. Interviews with survivors and victims' families confirmed that young black party attendees were subject to intense interrogation in which they were pressured into signing statements that a fight had taken place before the fire took hold.[40]

The press

Newspaper reports similarly underplayed the possibility of a racist attack. Partygoers were reported as having criminal records and 'typically disorderly West Indian behaviour' was suggested as a cause of the fire.[41] However, the 22 January edition of the *Lewisham Mercury*, headlined 'Death of the Innocents', reported on the fire extensively, with initial investigation results, witness statements[42] and condolences from Asquith Gibbes, Lewisham's black community liaison officer, who urged witnesses to come forward, offering Lewisham Council community relations offices as a safe place to meet with the police.[43]

Subsequent editions of the *Lewisham Mercury* highlighted the police failure to reassure the black community. Commander Stockwell, alarmed at the high levels of emotion running through black community groups, stated that the investigation should be 'kept at a reasonable level'.[44]

Two years prior to the fire, there had been an uproar from anti-racist groups over the racist shooting of Carl Foster in Lewisham. His brother Chris, in the aftermath of the fire, at a gathering at the Moonshot, exhorted the crowd to 'go back to your communities ... organise ... the police are hiding things ... it's up to us to find out what's going on.'[45]

The Black People's Day of Action

The Black People's Day of Action (BPDA) was conceived in an NCMAC general meeting shortly after the fire; the demonstration on 2 March 1981 would follow a prearranged route agreed with the police, departing from New Cross, proceeding through South London to Fleet Street, home of the British press, then on to Westminster and ending at Speakers' Corner, Hyde Park. It was the biggest black protest to date in Britain,[46] with up to 20,000 people attending.[47] A month earlier, at a fire fund benefit gig in Deptford, Jah Shaka had exhorted crowds to: 'March against ... Tory Government ... the racist nationality bill ... British Police ... fascists and racist organisations ... murders of black people.'[48]

The march brought New Cross to a standstill, a protester reported:

> We swept out ... like a mighty host ... [a] pulsating rippling serpent ... demand[ing] ... bus drivers leave their vehicles and join the march, bang[ing] on car windows and harang[uing] amazed commuters, as traffic jammed to let the march pass.[49]

Schoolchildren in Peckham jumped over railings to join the march.[50] The *Lewisham Mercury* reported this as a 'Day of Dignity'[51] and criticised the national press, such as *The Sun*, which focused on the small-scale looting carried out by a breakaway group at Blackfriars, naming the march 'The Day the Blacks Ran Riot in London'.[52] The march was an undeniably visible display of grief among the black community, hitherto unseen. One speaker exclaimed:

> The first time in ... history this has happened in this country ... It was believed black people did not exist – we have shown they do.[53]

Some banners read '13 Dead and Nothing Said' and 'New Cross Massacre Mass Murder'; others had 'Come What May We Are Here to Stay', 'Down with Colonial Mentality' and 'NF in Police Uniform'.[54] The march was pivotal not only in showing solidarity for the victims of the fire but in encouraging a greater discussion about overcoming institutional oppression.

The NCMAC's *Declaration of New Cross* was written in the fire's early aftermath and officially delivered at the BPDA:

1   On Sunday, 18th January, 1981, in an unparalleled act of savagery, 13 young people, aged from 14 to 22, were murdered at 439 New Cross Road, in the heart of London, capital city of Britain. They were attending a birthday party. They were black.

2   The national authorities in Parliament and Government, in a further act of barbarianism, ignored the tragedy of the families of the dead and injured. But they sent messages of condolence to the fire victims in Ireland, for cynical reasons of state.

3   The authorities have ignored for three decades the pain, the rage and the outrage of the black communities around the country at the racial murders, injuries and threats to our existence. Threats have come even from the highest authorities in the land.

4 The New Cross Massacre Black People's Day of Action is another stage in the response of the black people and of allies in the country to their savagery and this barbarianism.

5 We warn the country and the world that there will be no social peace while blacks are attacked, killed, injured and maimed with impunity on the streets or in our homes.[55]

The declaration outlined the handling of the fire as part of a trajectory of racism in Britain. Brixton Black Women's Group issued a statement: '[O]nce again black people are under attack ... this is not an isolated incident ... we must defend our sisters and brothers.'[56] *Fight Racism! Fight Imperialism!* situated the fire within a series of assaults, ranging from threats to the burning of black people's cars.[57]

Community responses

Fi know seh dem kine a ting deh couda happn to wi
Inna disya Great Britn
Inna Landan tiddey
...
It couda be mi it couda be yu
Linton Kwesi Johnson, 'New Craas Massakah'[58]

Kwesi Johnson acknowledged that racist aggression had escalated since Powell's speech, which 'empowered' the extreme right wing, and he considered the New Cross Fire to be a peak in the 'spate of racist and fascist attacks' since the 1950s. After the Sunderland Road firebombing, he claimed that hostility was fuelled by politicians publicly voicing their concerns over 'loud' black house parties. Kwesi Johnson believed that racism was most prolific within institutions; he considered that the white working class, alongside the black working class, was battling against racism as well as '[Thatcher's] radical government ... with a plan to dismantle the welfare state'.[59]

In March 1981, a local resident wrote to *Grassroots*, the monthly newspaper of the Black Liberation Front, to explain that the Southeast London community had been subject to multiple racist attacks by fascists, who he believed were responsible for the fire. For this resident, the evidence was visible through a strong Deptford NF following,[60] when the NF won over 3 per cent of the constituency vote in the 1979 general election.[61] He found further evidence in the racist letters sent to the victims' families: '[It] was a great day ... all those niggers going up in flames ... I will see the day that all the black filth is sent back to Africa ...'[62]

Sociologist Les Back remembers the NF's 'effective grip' in 1970s South London, the political energy of racist nationalism, and consequently the everyday racial tensions and difficulties. He states: 'Linton Kwesi Johnson wrote "1981 was the defining year in the black presence in London". I think he's right ... 1981 began with the inferno.'[63]

The fire had a profound effect on the local community: 'everyone who lived in the area seemed to know somebody who was connected in some way'. Back's understanding of the fire's aftermath was that it 'revealed much about political positions on multiracial London'. While some people around him considered the fire an exemplification of anti-black hostility, others, mainly middle-aged, felt it was a 'dubious' party gone wrong. The nature of the response was 'a political education' for Back: what being anti-racist meant, why it was important as a white person to have a sense of humility towards the situation, and for people to understand where the 'line between affiliation and violation is drawn, not claiming to know more than you did or to be one to speak about it'. London, was a 'chequerboard of black and white spaces'; it was difficult to live a colour-coded life when the struggle was much more complex than just white against black. For years, the memory of the fire has touched members of both the black and white community, with its proximity and the damage caused. These lives mattered to people who every day saw 'the burnt-out shell ... this wound scorched into the streets ... loom[ing] as a powerful symbol'.[64]

John Turner, then Albany Theatre's artistic director, ran local community cultural development programmes and supported both Rock Against Racism and the All Lewisham Campaign Against Racism and Fascism. Having worked so closely with Deptford's multicultural community, the death of the children felt like a communal loss. To pay homage he composed the song 'The Flowers Are Dying at the Door', alluding to the 'flowers of youth' but also the prolonged investigation process. The song was performed by his band Rubber Johnny for a short period of time after the tragedy: 'it was there, it was heartfelt and then we took it out', not wanting it to be 'construed as an exploitation of grief'.[65]

Other individuals and organisations honoured the victims of the fire, sending condolences and donations. A message from the Moonshot read:

Their deaths have touched us all. They are our sons and daughters, brothers and sisters, school friends and neighbours ... we have ... [given] support ... along with other Lewisham people ... to begin to build something good on the ashes of grief and sadness ... We must not despair.[66]

Thirty-five years later, the fire continues to shock and outrage those who were present at the time and the younger generations. As local resident William (Lez) Henry, formally known on the local sound system scene as Lezlee Lyrix, declared, the New Cross Fire was a 'generational tragedy'.[67]

Conclusion

The New Cross Fire and its aftermath contributed to the growing consciousness of black oppression, institutional racism and the need to engage in organised struggle against these. The Black People's Day of Action was precipitated by the fire, with racial discrimination, unemployment and the lack of opportunities faced by Black Britons adding further impetus.[68] The fire would not only affect the local community; arguably, it would go on to disrupt the rest of London, motivating the explosive Brixton riots in April 1981.[69] One may speculate whether these riots would have erupted when they did had the establishment treated the New Cross Fire victims differently. Furthermore, the strength and momentum shown in the BPDA demonstrated that black communities were united and powerful. Similarly, had reactions to the fire been more efficiently and sensitively handled, this may have set a precedent for the police handling of suspect black deaths – significantly the murder of Stephen Lawrence in 1993. Arguably, the blatant racism proven in the Macpherson Report (1999) mirrors the way in which the New Cross Fire case was handled. In 1997, four years after the Lawrence case, the fire investigation was reopened. In 2001, two years after publication of the report acknowledging 'institutional racism',[70] the police announced grounds for a new inquiry into the New Cross Fire.[71] The second New Cross Fire inquest in 2004 again returned an open verdict, and so the families and the community remain in limbo. Upon reflection, one sees how those in the highest positions of command, senior politicians and police officers, to this day continue to ignore or to underplay the suffering of black people in the UK and fail to bring justice to affected families. It is only when action taken by individuals and community groups is too difficult to ignore that institutions are forced to react, albeit with limited impact.

On a national level, and even London-wide, the New Cross Fire and its aftermath remain largely unrecorded and unknown. However, on a local level, the fire, like the death of Stephen Lawrence, has left an indelible imprint on the community. The Stephen Lawrence Centre in Deptford is a constant reminder of the racism and injustice faced by Lawrence and his family. Memorials to commemorate and honour the victims of the New Cross Fire have been erected in the local area. A blue commemorative plaque at 439 New Cross Road was commissioned by the Nubian Jak Community Trust, a charity that honours the histories and contributions of black people in Britain. A commemorative plaque can also be found outside the Catford Civic Suite; a boulder engraved with the names of the victims stands as a memorial in Fordham Park, New Cross; and a striking stained-glass triptych was created for St Andrew's Church in Brockley, where many of the victims and their friends attended the youth club. The Goldsmiths College New Cross Award is an ongoing homage to the victims of the fire, allowing Lewisham-educated young people to fulfil ambitions those victims were so tragically deprived of.[72] The legacy of the New Cross Fire has become part of the social fabric of the streets of Southeast London.

Dedicated to all those still suffering from the scars of the New Cross Fire and to the fourteen victims who will not be forgotten.

Humphrey Geoffrey Brown	Born 4 July 1962	Died 18 January 1981, age 18
Peter Campbell	Born 23 February 1962	Died 18 January 1981, age 18
Gerry Paul Francis	Born 21 August 1963	Died 18 January 1981, age 17
Andrew Gooding	Born 18 February 1962	Died 18 January 1981, age 18
Roseline Henry	Born 23 September 1964	Died 18 January 1981, age 16
Patricia Johnson	Born 16 May 1965	Died 18 January 1981, age 15
Patrick Cummings	Born 21 September 1964	Died 18 January 1981, age 16

Owen Thompson	Born 11 September 1964	Died 18 January 1981, age 16
Steve Collins	Born 2 May 1963	Died 18 January 1981, age 17
Lloyd Hall	Born 28 November 1960	Died 18 January 1981, age 20
Glenton Powell	Born 18 January 1966	Died 25 January 1981, age 15
Yvonne Ruddock	Born 17 January 1965	Died 24 January 1981, age 16
Paul Ruddock	Born 19 November 1960	Died 9 February 1981, age 20
Anthony Berbeck	Born 17 August 1962	Died 9 July 1983, age 20

Notes

1 Clive Bloom, *Violent London: 2000 Years of Riots, Rebels and Revolts* (New York: Palgrave Macmillan, 2010), p. 394.

2 John La Rose, Linton Kwesi Johnson and Gus John, *The New Cross Massacre Story: Interviews with John La Rose* (London: New Beacon Books, 2011), p. 56.

3 Bloom, *Violent London*, p. 360.

4 Jerry White, *London in the Twentieth Century: A City and its People* (London: Vintage, 2008), pp. 133–9.

5 Ian R. G. Spencer, *British Immigration Policy since 1939: The Making of Multi-racial Britain* (New York: Taylor and Francis, 1997), p. 144.

6 '1978: Le Swamped de Margaret Thatcher', *Daily Motion*, http://www.dailymotion.com/video/x28votz, accessed 26 April 2018.

7 *Parliamentary Debates* (Commons), 5th ser. [1981], v. 997, c. 935. As cited in Kathleen Paul, *Whitewashing Britain: Race and Citizenship in the Postwar Era* (Ithaca: Cornell University Press, 1997), p. 183.

8 Stuart Hall, *Drifting into a Law and Order Society: The Cobden Trust Human Rights Day Lecture 1979* (London: Cobden Trust, 1980), p. 3.

9 Paul Gilroy, *There Ain't No Black in the Union Jack: The Cultural Politics of Race and Nation* (London: Routledge, 2002), p. 88.

10 Paul Gilroy, *There Ain't No Black in the Union Jack*, pp. 13–14.

11 Joan Anim-Addo, *The Longest Journey: History of Black Lewisham* (London: Deptford Forum Publishing, 1995), pp. 125–6.

12 Elizabeth M. Williams, *The Politics of Race in Britain and South Africa: Black British Solidarity and the Anti-Apartheid Struggle* (London: I. B. Tauris, 2015), p. 132.

13 Race Today 1975, 'Mek' it Blow: Police Raid New Cross Jah Shaka Blues Dance' in *Transpontine: South East London Blogzine*, http://transport.blogspot.co.uk/2015/10/mek-it-blow-police-raid-new-cross-jah.html, accessed 19 July 2016.

14 Anim-Addo, *The Longest Journey*, p. 131.

15 Anim-Addo, *The Longest Journey*, pp. 132–5.

16 Anim-Addo, *The Longest Journey*, p. 141.

17 'Albany History', *The Albany*, http://www.thealbany.org.uk/about/26/ Albany-History, accessed 2 September 2016.

18 George Padmore Institute, 'New Cross Massacre Campaign' in *George Padmore Institute Archive Collection*, http://www.georgepadmore institute.org/archive/collection/new-cross-massacre-campaign, accessed 8 August 2016.

19 Anim-Addo, *The Longest Journey*, p. 136.

20 La Rose et al., *The New Cross Massacre Story*, p. 12.

21 Mike Phillips and Trevor Phillips, *Windrush: The Irresistible Rise of Multi-racial Britain* (London: HarperCollins, 1999), p. 324.

22 Finsbury Park, George Padmore Institute (GPI), GB 2904, NCM 1/2/1/3/7, 'New Cross Fire Statement', n.d.

23 'New Cross Fire Statement'.

24 GPI, GB 2904, NCM 1/2/4/1/1, 'Letter from John La Rose to HOC', 23 February 1981.

25 GPI, GB 2904, NCM1/2/4/1/3, 'Letter from John La Rose to Margaret Thatcher', n.d.

26 Lucia Tambini, 'Loving Hands: The Story of Sibyl Phoenix', 2013, https:// vimeo.com/65037719, accessed 31 August 2016.

27 GPI, GB 2904, NCM 1/2/4/1/3, 'Letter from John La Rose to Margaret Thatcher', n.d.

28 Tambini, 'Loving Hands'.

29 Interview conducted by author with Baroness Howells of St Davids, 26 May 2016.

30 La Rose et al., *The New Cross Massacre Story*, p. 8.

31 Dee Lahiri, 'I Don't Think I Can Die Before I Find Out What Happened to My Son', *Guardian*, 25 February 2002, https://www.theguardian.com/ world/2001/may/15/race.london, accessed 8 August 2016.

32 La Rose et al., *The New Cross Massacre Story*, p. 8.

33 Darcus Howe, 'Why I Still Think the New Cross Fire Was a Massacre', *New Statesman*, 12 February 1999, http://www.newstatesman.com/ why-i-still-think-new-cross-fire-was-massacre, accessed 26 February 2016.

34 GPI, GB 2904, NCM 2/1/1/4/4, 'Racist Letter to Howe', 9 March 1981.

35 Darcus Howe, 'The Night that 13 Black Teenagers Died', *New Statesman*, 28 May 2001, http://www.newstatesman. com/node/153503, accessed 8 August 2016.

36 La Rose et al., *The New Cross Massacre Story*, p. 59.

37 Interview conducted by author with OBV David Michael, 20 January 2016.

38 '1981: Nine Die in New Cross House Fire', BBC News, 18 January 1981, http://news.bbc.co.uk/ onthisday/hi/dates/stories/january/18/ newsid_2530000/2530333.stm, accessed 8 August 2016.

39 Interview conducted by author with Baroness Howells of St Davids, 26 May 2016

40 Phillips and Phillips, *Windrush*, pp. 334–5.

41 Phillips and Phillips, *Windrush*, p. 234.

42 'Death of the Innocents', *SE London Mercury*, 22 January 1981, pp. 1, 12–13.

43 'How the Killer Blaze Swept the House', *SE London Mercury*, 22 January 1981, p. 13.

44 Commander Stockwell cited in 'Hunt for the Killer', *SE London Mercury*, 5 February 1981, p. 6.

45 Chris Foster cited in 'Man in the Middle', *SE London Mercury*, 29 January 1981, p. 14.

46 Anim-Addo, *The Longest Journey*, pp. 136–7.

47 La Rose et al., *The New Cross Massacre Story*, p. 7.

48 GPI, GB 2904, NCM 1/2/1/1, 'Flyer for Fire Fund Benefit Gig at 190 Centre Deptford', 14 February 1981.

49 GPI, GB 2904, NCM 1/2/2/2/2, 'Anonymous Account of the Black People's Day of Action', n.d.

50 Marhita Wearing, 'The Day to Remember', *SE London Mercury*, 5 March 1981, p. 13.

51 'Day of Dignity', *SE London Mercury*, 5 March 1981, p. 1.

52 Anim-Addo, *The Longest Journey*, p. 138.

53 Wearing, 'The Day to Remember', p. 13.

54 GPI, GB 2904, NCM 1/2/1/2/8, 'Suggested Slogans for the BPDA', n.d.

55 GPI, GB 2904, NCM 1/2/2/1/1, 'NCMAC Declaration of New Cross', 2 March 1981.

56 GPI, GB 2904, NCM 3/3/2, 'Brixton Black Women's Group New Cross Fire Statement', n.d.

57 GPI, GB 2904, NCM 1/2/1/3/7, 'New Cross Fire Statement by FRFI', n.d.

58 Linton Kwesi Johnson, *Selected Poems* (London: Penguin Books, 2006), p. 55.

59 Interview conducted by author with Linton Kwesi Johnson, 4 July 2016.

60 Joe Jarret, 'A Lot to Explain', *Grassroots*, March 1981, p. 3.

61 Christopher T. Husbands, *Racial Exclusionism and the City: The Urban Support of the National Front* (Oxford: Routledge, 2007), p. 45.

62 GPI, GB 2904, NCM 3/1/3/3, 'Racist Letter', n.d.

63 Interview conducted by author with Professor Les Back, 13 June 2016.

64 Interview conducted by author with Professor Les Back, 13 June 2016.

65 Interview conducted by author with John Turner, 8 June 2016.

66 GPI, GB 2904, NCM 3/1/3/3, 'Message from the Moonshot', n.d.

67 Interview conducted by author with William (Lez) Henry, 3 June 2016.

68 Phillips and Phillips, *Windrush*, p. 324.

69 Gilroy, *There Ain't No Black in the Union Jack*, p. 129.

70 HM Government, 'The Stephen Lawrence Inquiry Report by Sir William Macpherson', Gov.uk, https://app.refme.com/home#/project/1545250, accessed 4 September 2016.

71 'Unhealed Scars of New Cross Fire', BBC News, 14 May 2001, http://news.bbc.co.uk/1/hi/uk/1329432.stm, accessed 8 August 2016.

72 Heather Bishop, 'New Cross Fire Bursary Allows Students to Achieve Dreams', *Eastlondonlines*, 25 January 2011, http://www.eastlondonlines.co.uk/2011/01/new-cross-fire-bursary-allows-students-to-achieve-dreams/, accessed 29 August 2016.

10 | THE LONG ROAD OF PAN-AFRICAN LIBERATION TO REPARATORY JUSTICE[1]

Esther Stanford-Xosei

Introduction

This chapter is concerned with what I and other UK-based reparations activists (reparationists) refer to as the International Social Movement for Afrikan Reparations (ISMAR).[2] Although this is an international movement, it has a long history in the UK, its antecedents dating back to the eighteenth century. In this chapter I provide insights as an insider scholar-activist researcher of the ISMAR who has been a driving force in shaping some of ideas and approaches being championed by this movement.[3] Notably, this is the first historical study on the presence of an ISMAR in the UK, or indeed of its local, national or international dimensions, albeit focusing on London as a site of novel reparations knowledge production and other forms of activism on reparations.[4] I draw on the ideas and knowledge of selected groups and individuals who have been part of the ISMAR, including the use of movement terms and vocabularies.

In utilising insights gained from my own reparations scholar-activism, and a series of oral history interviews conducted with thirty-five activists who have been involved with organising to achieve reparations, two central claims emerge. Firstly, the ISMAR is a social movement with international dimensions and one whose trajectory goes beyond the confines of the UK. Secondly, the ISMAR is an intergenerational knowledge producer, which continues to contribute innovatively from the African-centred intersectionality perspective of cognitive justice to what we know about Pan-African liberation-focused organising and reparations social movement building in the UK. By this, I refer to the fact that Pan-Africanism, particularly in terms of the activism of women Pan-Africanists who organised in the UK, such as Amy Ashwood Garvey, Claudia Jones, Funmilayo Ransome-Kuti and Constance Cummings-John, has been advanced from perspectives of intersectionality. These highlight not only issues of race but also those of gender and class, and have done so with explorations of indigenous African knowledge contributions.[5]

It would appear that there has been scant examination of the political culture, ideas, writings, activities and organisations that African refugees and exiles from Africa and other regions of the African diaspora are developing here in Britain. There is little recognition of the fact that history is continuing to be made in the present by groups and individual activists who are perhaps not widely known to others outside the ISMAR. In this regard, it is important for researchers with an interest in African history and the African diaspora experience in Britain to take seriously the ethical responsibility to recognise the ontological and epistemological frameworks of knowledge production within the ISMAR. This includes grappling with movement ideas and terminologies, including those conceptualised and theorised in indigenous African languages and cultures from the African-centred perspectives of cognitive justice.[6]

The UK is a vibrant site of successive waves of resurgence of the reparatory justice endeavours of black peoples from various parts of the continent and diaspora of Africa. As such, the UK – and London in particular – is a terrain for male and female activists from communities of African reparatory justice interest seeking to glocally (thinking globally, acting locally) unify their efforts so as to build themselves into a movement of global might, one that is capable of compelling adequate redress for the historical and contemporary injustices of the *Maangamizi*. Maangamizi is a Kiswahili term popularised by Professor Maulana Karenga to describe the genocidal intentionality of African people's enslavement.[7] The Pan-Afrikan Reparations Coalition in Europe (PARCOE) has since extended this term to describe the continuum of what has been referred to by African heritage community activists as the African 'Hellacaust' of chattel, colonial and neo-colonial enslavement. The term was also popularised in a song by UK hip-hop artist Akala called 'Maangamizi', which was penned after attending the first short course on the ISMAR developed by myself in 2012.[8] This is important to note because there is an erroneous perception by many commentators that reparations are sought just for the atrocities of chattel slavery in the past, rather than seeing the quest for reparations as part of a continuum of unbroken struggle for emancipation and restitution in the present. It is also important to bring out more the role of the female intergenerational contributors to the Pan-African advancement of reparatory justice because the activist contributions of women to the ISMAR are often diminished if not ignored altogether.

In my view, this intergenerational focus of Pan-African-oriented reparations organising in Britain is being distorted and sometimes even ignored and denied in recent discourses and scholarship on Pan-Africanism.[9] Unlike in the past, where there was a recognition that Pan-Africanist organising in Britain contributed to the ongoing struggle for Pan-African liberation, there is now a tendency to mistake and misrepresent contemporary African diaspora activism within the UK as simply activism for 'good causes', embracing neoliberal NGO and charitable aid gimmicks, instead of connecting such efforts to a programmatic movement-focused fight for liberation and the attainment of holistic reparatory justice. It appears that many Pan-African activities have mainly become writing about Pan-Africanism of the past and mere talking shops about wishes for the future; something that is always someone else's responsibility to create rather than the responsibility of those pontificating in speech and writing about it. Some commentators tend to focus nowadays on the thinking and actions of state actors in the African Union and CARICOM while ignoring the thinking and actions of non-state actors from grassroots educational organisations, trade unions, peasant farmers' unions, cooperatives, community formations, women's, youth and student organisations, networks and campaigns.[10]

The 'freedom visions' of some of those laying claim to being Pan-African activists have recently become reduced to petty nationalistic schemes, the entrenchment of various national exceptionalisms, neoliberal development projects and business ventures.[11] As such, this type of activity is far removed from the grand intergenerational Pan-African vision of a globally unified African people across the continent of Africa and the diaspora that typifies earlier phases of Pan-African organising. In fact, much contemporary historical thinking and writing about African diaspora activism in Britain negates the continuity of Pan-African liberation struggle and history making in recent times. This chapter therefore seeks to highlight how UK-based reparationists are disrupting this trend in practice.

My central argument and observation is that the core objectives of Pan-Africanism are the attainment and securing of holistic reparatory justice and that Pan-African liberation and nation-building goals have been central to reparations activism in Britain. In effect, the attainment of holistic and multifaceted reparatory justice as a goal has been fundamental to what is known about the Pan-African Movement. The defining features of this include the taking back of Africa, restoring and building it into an unconquerable super-powerful state which is collectively governed by people on the continent and the diaspora. Such a state would have the power and capacity to unite African people globally in protection and defence of their group and geopolitical interests worldwide.

I shall elaborate on the reparations quintessence of Pan-Africanism based on the critical insights from the activism of reparations organisations and the experiences of activist formations in which I have played a leading role for almost two decades. These include PARCOE and the Global Afrikan People's Parliament as well as the Afrikan Emancipation Day Reparations March Committee (the March Committee) and its partner campaign the 'Stop the Maangamizi: We Charge Genocide/Ecocide!' campaign.

Formed in 2001, PARCOE is a UK-based grassroots reparations advocacy alliance working in Europe to amplify the voices of African communities of reparations interest all over the world. Some of PARCOE's contributions to the long road of Pan-African liberation reparatory justice in recent times are highlighted in this chapter, given its vanguard role in advocating and organising towards the attainment of what we refer to as 'Pan-African Reparations for Global Justice'. This simply means that the struggle for the attainment of holistic reparations for Africans and its attendant reshaping of the world order should be waged in such ways and means that do not further entrench inequalities within and between different ethnicities and nationalities nor result in their oppression or further acts of dispossession. PARCOE is a vanguard alliance in that it has a scouting and pioneering role that purposefully shows leadership by example in the development of transformatory ideas about Pan-African reparations and works in partnership with others to implement and evaluate such ideas through the praxis of action learning.

The co-produced perspectives that I articulate in this chapter are a result of the co-produced knowledge of PARCOE scholar-activists, with responsibility for their articulation the mandate given to myself and to fellow co-founder of PARCOE, Kofi Mawuli Klu. It is from the knowledge and experience gained from nearly twenty years of Pan-African internationalist reparatory justice scholar-activism that I would like to share with you some perspectives on struggle that I am involved in waging as a politically engaged reparations scholar-activist. It is necessary to emphasise the fact that, in the PARCOE perspective, African people's struggle for reparatory justice is a long-established worldwide struggle to counter, everywhere, the legacies of genocide and ecocide, as an aspect of the continuing Maangamizi. We relate to the struggle for reparations in a holistic way and spend a significant amount of our time educating people about the goals of reparations, as well as mobilising various sections of the ISMAR and the wider international movement for reparations of other oppressed peoples, which we refer to as the People's Reparations International Movement.[12]

Defining Pan-Africanism

Despite its historicity, there is a common perception and scholarship abounds regarding the notion that Pan-Africanism was formulated in response to European domination and that, in the twentieth century, Pan-Africanism is deemed to have emerged as a distinct political movement initially formed and led by people of African heritage living outside the continent of Africa. According to historians Professor Hakim Adi and Marika Sherwood, there has never been one universally accepted definition of what constitutes Pan-Africanism, since it has taken different forms at different historical moments and in different geographical locations. Their own definition lends itself to describing 'those women and men of African descent whose lives and work have been concerned in some way with the social and political emancipation of African peoples and those of the African Diaspora'.[13]

So, in building on this recognition, I wish to question the assumptions inherent in approaches to defining Pan-Africanism where Pan-African organising starts in the diaspora. I argue instead that Pan-Africanism did not begin outside Africa in her diaspora of Abya Yala (the so-called Americas), with efforts from the nineteenth century onwards by the likes of David Walker, Martin Delany, Marcus Mosiah Garvey, Akosua Boahemma aka Amy Ashwood Garvey, W. E. B. Du Bois, Henry Sylvester Williams, George Padmore and Queen Mother Audley Moore.[14]

It can no longer continue to be convincingly argued that it was only when Africans started being forcibly trafficked en masse as enslaved chattel from the fifteenth century onwards into the diaspora of Europe and the Americas that they began to organise in defence of their own social and political emancipation. As PARCOE scholar-activists argue, the countless abortive and sometimes successful aggression by foreign powers against Africa have very often compelled responses from visionary African political, military and spiritual leaders to unify their communities.

Such responses to foreign aggression against Africa have included the use of armed struggle in order to unify such communities into greater, stronger and therefore more impregnable polities, such polities being capable of independently defending their sovereignty, safeguarding their own geopolitical interests locally, nationally and internationally, and maximising their own self-determined developmental potentialities in the world of their times. The aforementioned is the rationale not only for the conceptualisation in ancient times of unique value systems such as Maat and Ubuntu but also for the building of historically magnificent polities in ancient times, such as the unified Kemet, Nubia, Dahomey, Ethiopia, Congo, Zimbabwe and KwaZulu.

Thus far, histories of Pan-Africanism have tended to privilege definitions and movements for Pan-Africanism outside Africa. Through my action research, I have also been exposed to notions of Pan-Africanism that have come from African grassroots activists in the UK. The following is offered as a definition popularised by PARCOE reparations activist Kofi Mawuli Klu:

> Pan-Africanism is an anti-imperialist decolonisational movement
> rallying together a broad array of all-Afrika-loving forces that
> are interested in link-networking glocally in pursuit of various
> configurations of an independent worldwide politico-ideological,
> cultural and organizational framework of struggle for the total
> liberation, unification and self-determined progression of Africans and
> their kith and kin worldwide.[15]

One of the reasons why I argue that this is a preferable explanation is because it is a more inclusive definition of the various tendencies within Pan-Africanism. For example, very often people refer to Pan-Africanism as an ideology, and some would ascribe a particular ideology to it. Some try to limit Pan-Africanism to the particular aspects and preferences of their choice and not to the general definition that is inclusive of the majority of the tendencies of Pan-Africanist thought and action. However, in my view, the above definition provides a whole framework within which the various tendencies can fit. It also recognises the right of all tendencies to legitimately claim that they are Pan-African.

On the meaning of reparations

Reparations, or repairing the harm done, is an ancient concept that continues to resurface in public discourse due to the existence of the ISMAR, which has continued to make and act on the demands for reparations throughout the ages in addition to increasing academic and media interest and debates on the subject. In a paper presented at the Birmingham Preparatory Reparation Conference organised by the African Reparations Movement UK (ARM UK) on 11 December 1993, Dr Kimani Nehusi asserted that understanding the term reparations:

> demands that this notion be applied to the specific historical experience and the related contemporary condition of Africans[, illustrating that] the meaning of this term transcends repayment for past and continuing wrong, to embrace self-rehabilitation through education, organisation and mobilisation.[16]

This is a reiteration of the concepts with which the likes of Amy Ashwood, Funmilayo Ransome-Kuti, Claudia Jones, Constance Cummings-John and Una Marson did reparatory justice work for the regeneration and unification of African heritage communities in and beyond Britain to galvanise anti-colonial resistance against European imperialism. That is why it is necessary to recognise that reparations activists in the UK have been organising for holistic and transformative reparations as part of the continued Pan-African liberation struggle. This means that, in the cause of advocating and participating in the national and social liberation struggle of African people at home and abroad, such activists have sought to promote the kind of fundamental radical change that will repair African people and their communities. And that they have done so in ways and means that will bring about their global unification, development and prosperity in a new order of society that will compel the entire world to respect their own hard-won freedom, justice and self-determination in all things, thereby embracing the 'conceptual' definition of reparations advanced at the 1993 'First Conference on Reparations for Slavery, Colonisation and Neocolonisation' held in Abuja, Nigeria (the Abuja Conference).

In his paper 'Reparations and A New Global Order: A Comparative Overview', Professor Chinweizu defined reparations in this way:

> Reparation is mostly about making repairs. self-made repairs, on ourselves: mental repairs, psychological repairs, cultural repairs, organisational repairs, social repairs, institutional repairs, technological repairs, economic repairs, political repairs, educational repairs, repairs of every type that we need in order to recreate and sustainable black societies.[17]

Similarly, under international law, 'reparation must, as far as possible, wipe out all the consequences of the illegal act and re-establish the situation which would, in all probability, have existed if that act had not been committed'.[18] In 2005, the United Nations General Assembly adopted the 'Basic Principles and Guidelines on the Right to a Remedy and Reparation for Victims of Violations of International Human Rights and Humanitarian Law', stating that holistic reparations include: restitution, rehabilitation, satisfaction and guarantees of non-repetition. This is known as the operational framework for reparations within the ISMAR. It can thus be concluded that popular conceptions of reparations within the ISMAR should be viewed as an obligation for various parties to make the repairs necessary to redress current harms caused as a result of past and continuing violations of human rights and group rights in such a way that restores the dignity of the affected groups. Articulated as such, reparations have two dimensions: the internal or 'self-repairs', or what affected communities have to do for themselves; and the external – what others outside those communities, including governments and institutions, have an obligation to do to rectify enduring injustice.[19]

Selected landmarks in UK reparations historiography

Given the limitations of space, I am not able to include a comprehensive timeline in this chapter; instead, I point to key aspects in the UK timeline of reparations organising which I think the reader should be aware of. I particularly focus on those landmarks that demonstrate Pan-African organising.

1797: The emergence of the ISMAR can be traced back to include the forming in London of the 'Sons of Africa', which was a late eighteenth-century political group led by African abolitionists who campaigned to end slavery. Its members were educated Africans in London and freed enslaved persons and included Ottobah Cugoano, Olaudah Equiano and other leading members of London's African Heritage Community. The group addressed meetings and organised letter-writing campaigns, published campaigning material and lobbied parliament. They wrote to figures such as Granville Sharp, William Pitt and other members of the abolitionist movement, as well as King George III and the Prince of Wales, the future George IV. The Sons of Africa were closely connected to the Society for the Abolition of the Slave Trade, a non-denominational group founded in 1787, whose

members included Thomas Clarkson. Quobna Ottobah Cugoano –
an enslaved African originally from the Fante village of Ajumako, in
present-day Ghana – used his newly acquired freedom from slavery in
Grenada and subsequent resettlement in London to write and publish,
with the help of his associate Olaudah Equiano, the book *Thoughts and
Sentiments on the Evil and Wicked Traffic of the Slavery and Commerce of
the Human Species.* In this political treatise, Cugoano raised the issue
of 'adequate reparation' and 'restitution for the injuries' enslaved persons received.[20] In the 1791 edition of his book, Cugoano was the
first published African writer in the English language to denounce the
transatlantic traffic in enslaved Africans as a crime against humanity,
declaring that enslaved Africans had not only the moral right but also
the moral duty to resist enslavement. Between this time and the next
landmark I highlight, the reparations struggle can be identified in each
successive generation.

1900: From 23 to 25 July, the First Pan-African Conference took
place in Westminster Hall, London, organised under the leadership
of the Trinidad-born barrister Henry Sylvester Williams to 'protest
stealing of lands in the colonies, racial discrimination and deal with
other issues of interest to Blacks'. This conference drafted a letter to
European rulers, appealing to them to fight racism and grant independence to their colonies.[21] It was the very first event of its kind to
raise the global interests and welfare of African people under the banner of Pan-Africanism. According to W. E. B. Du Bois, it 'put the word
"Pan-African" in the dictionaries for the first time'.[22] The purpose of
this conference was to encourage Pan-African unity by providing a
forum in which Africans and African descendants living in the diaspora
could discuss issues relating to the social, political and economic conditions of African peoples living under colonialism and other forms of
oppression and better work for their emancipation and repairs of harm
that they had suffered from such subjugation. Participants from the
USA included W. E. B. Du Bois, Anna H. Jones, Anna Julia Cooper,
Fannie Barrier Williams and Ella D. Barrier.[23]

According to educator and organiser Dr Ajamu Nangwaya, there
were at least six women among the fifty-one delegates at the conference. In addition to those noted above, these included Mrs Loudin
and Ms Adams from Ireland, and all these women were 'actively
involved in social movements committed to transforming the
oppressed condition of Africans'.[24] The conference led to the establishment of two committees: one demanding reforms to colonialism

in Africa relevant to reparations and another to create a permanent Pan-African association in London.

1928: On 2 September there was the famous speech of Marcus Mosiah Garvey at the Century Theatre, in which, mindful of reparations, he said, among other things, that:

> I am out for human justice, and I am sensible enough to know that so long as the robber retains the loot, the man who has lost his property cannot be at peace with his vicious neighbour or with anyone else whom he suspects. We, 400 million Black people, desire, late though it be, to restore ourselves to the company of nations, with honour, so that we may show the way to the real peace about which these commercial statesmen are talking today, but do not mean, except to the extent of more oil monopolies, more diamond monopolies, more rubber concessions, more disarming of the weaker peoples whose lands are so valuable as to supply them, the monopolists, with the resources and wealth that they need.[25]

1945: With the impetus gained in the aftermath of the first Pan-African Congress from the global organising and mobilisations towards emancipation and repair of the conditions of African people that continued, the Fifth Pan-African Congress was convened in Manchester from 15 to 21 October under the chairpersonship of Amy Ashwood Garvey and W. E. B. Du Bois. Preparatory contributions were made to the Fifth PAC by activists of the West African Students Union (WASU), including Kwame Nkrumah and Constance Cummings-John, with active support from Claudia Jones. It was for such support that Kwame Nkrumah expressed the gratitude of himself and WASU to Claudia Jones in a letter dated 27 October 1942 that was found in the National Archives of Ghana in 2015.[26] The congress declared, among other things, that 'the struggle for political power by colonial and subject peoples is the first step towards, and the necessary prerequisite to, complete social, economic and political emancipation'. This articulation advocated for restitution of the rights of the colonised, which is a vital aspect of reparations.[27]

1993: On 10 May the African Guyanese Labour MP Bernie Grant tabled an early-day motion recognising the Abuja Proclamation arising from the Abuja Conference, which was signed by forty-six Labour MPs, including the current Labour leader, Jeremy Corbyn. The early-day motion called on 'the international community to recognise … the unprecedented moral debt owed to African people' and urged 'all those countries which were enriched by enslavement and colonisation to review the case for reparations, to be paid to Africa and Africans in the Diaspora'. Such a framing reiterated the pursuit of reparations as a Pan-African endeavour.[28]

1993: In response to the Abuja Conference, Bernie Grant MP co-organised, with other members of the ARM executive, the first working conference of the African Reparations Movement (ARM UK) in the City Hall of Birmingham on 11 December 1993. Members of the ARM executive included Dorothy Kuya, Linda Bellos, Sam King and Dr Patrick Wilmott. This endeavour was supported by affiliates of ARM UK such as the Africa Liberation Support Campaign and the Pan-African Grassroots Educational Network. African Liberation Support campaign representation included Carla Antonieta Santana of the All-Africa Students Union in Europe, Lindiwe Tsele, Maria-Teresa Mawete Santana and Affiong Limene Southey. The 'Birmingham Declaration' stated that one of the core goals of the intergenerational fight for reparations is to ensure that 'the African identity is proclaimed, maintained and developed and that Africa is restored to its rightful place in the centre of world politics'. It called upon:

> all people of African origin in the Caribbean, Africa, Europe and the Americas and elsewhere to support the movement for reparations and join forces with a view to forming a strong united front capable of exposing, confronting and overcoming the psychological, economic and cultural harm inflicted upon us by peoples of European origin.[29]

Despite this lofty declaration, ARM was not able to realise its objectives fully or to be an effective vehicle for Pan-African mobilisation. However, it went on to organise events that raised awareness about reparations and to demand from the British authorities the return of stolen African artefacts without any success at the time. ARM ceased its operations in 2000 following the death of Bernie Grant. This was largely due to the fact that ARM was mostly built around the persona of Bernie Grant, with heavy reliance on his stature as a member of the parliamentary institution of the British state. This was confirmed in an oral history interview I conducted with Linda Bellos.[30] Another weakness contributing to its decline was the fact that, in spite of the presence in its front ranks of outstanding female activists such as Dorothy Kuya, Linda Tsele and Maria-Teresa Mawete Santana, including even those with experience as state actors, like Linda Bellos, there was no serious effort made to encourage them to rise up on their own merits to achieve equal prominence with Bernie Grant, in order to develop a gender-balanced collective leadership for ARM. Indeed, intersectionality and other concerns raised by African Liberation Support members for developing ARM were deemed by some of its key players as pushing too far in the direction of the revolutionary kind of Pan-Africanism with which they did not want to be associated.[31]

One of the clearest articulations of reparations being at the heart of Pan-African organising and liberation aspirations was the following excerpt contained in a paper presented at the Birmingham Conference on behalf of the All-Africa Students Union in Europe, where it was stated that the organisation:

> sees reparations from the perspective of African youth as the actual
> conscientisation of the objectives of our whole people's liberation
> struggle under the banner of revolutionary Pan-Africanism.[32]

It further stated that:

> the reparations the youth of Africa are demanding must restore to all
> people of African origin throughout the world full sovereignty, the
> absolute ownership of the whole of our Homeland, including all its
> resources, and the renaissance of Maat and other value of our classical
> civilisation, in order to give us the concrete basis for independently
> achieving our own material and spiritual prosperity.[33]

1998: The Jubilee 2000 Africa Campaign, an autonomous formation within the wider Jubilee 2000 Campaign on cancelling international debt, was launched in London, spearheaded by its international coordinator, Pan-Africanist Kofi Mawuli Klu. Among the most active promoters of this petition and the Pan-African reparatory justice perspective of the Jubilee 2000 Africa Campaign was Malika Ayo Bediako, currently the chair of PARCOE.

It was after the death of Bernie Grant and the operations of ARM ceasing that I came to prominence as a leading reparations activist when I co-founded PARCOE in 2001 and subsequently became involved with organising the African and African Descendants World Conference Against Racism, the official follow-up for African descendants to the 2001 United Nations World Conference Against Racism, Racial Discrimination, Xenophobia and Related Intolerance.

The Barbados Conference took place from 2 to 6 October 2002. An outcome was the formation of the Global Afrikan Congress, including a UK chapter, and the development of the reparations platform of its founding guide, the 'Bridgetown Protocol'.

Notably, the foundational document and other ideas arising from what was envisioned as a global non-governmental organisation that could bring together Africans were coined by activists of the Forum of Africans and African Descendants Against Racism, a forum I convened with Kofi Mawuli Klu, Yoruba Priestess Chief Omilade Oladele, and Muzemba Kukwikila, the Pan-African activist co-founder of the organisation Chimurenga from the Congo. The forum was chaired by Methodist minister Reverend Hewie Andrews and coordinated the UK delegation that participated in the Barbados Conference.[34] It was by far the largest country delegation at the Barbados Conference, consisting of over seventy members. At the conference, it was agreed that reparationists in key centres connected with the enslavement of African people would target European nations for legal action in pursuit of reparations. The UK group that took up the mantle to do so was the Black Quest for Justice Campaign.

2003: On 6 May, ten years after the 5 May 1993 early-day motion in the British Houses of Parliament, the Black Quest for Justice Campaign, in association with PARCOE, initiated its Pan-African legal challenge to British justice. The Black Quest for Justice Campaign was formed in 1995 to bring together groups of African, Asian, indigenous American, Kouri and non-European origin in a quest for 'justice against the hydra-headed evil of racism in fortress Europe'. Its campaign statement identifies as one of its aims 'to harness individual campaigning efforts into a broadening whole and provide unified support rooted in the politics of Black liberation struggle highlighting reparations'.[35] This entailed taking steps of class action in law to secure their right to reparations by calling on the then attorney general, Lord Goldsmith QC, to trigger the power to investigate and prosecute the appropriate persons associated with the 'British Crown, its agencies and corporations' under the 2001 International Criminal Court Act.

The pleadings referred to the basis of the prosecution being that the British Crown continues 'to perpetrate crimes against humanity from the era of chattel enslavement through colonialism to the present era of neo-colonialism against Africa and people of African descent worldwide'. They further stated that the parties were 'suing on behalf of themselves, the global Pan-African Community, Africans, including those of

African descent being Descendants of formerly enslaved, colonised, and neo-colonised African victims of genocidal British Imperialism'. Such a framing articulated the legal case of Africans as a Pan-African case rather than simply arguing that reparations should be for black people in Britain in isolation from the wider case that people of African heritage have been making for centuries.

2006: PARCOE's conceptualisation of 'Pan-African Reparations for Global Justice' was instrumental in the orientation and planning of the Global Pan-African Reparations Conference, held in Accra, Ghana from 22 July to 3 August.[36] It was a landmark conference that sought to build on the Abuja Conference held in 2003. Driven most energetically by Queen Mother Moore disciple Queen Mother Dorothy Benton-Lewis, co-founder of N'COBRA, (the National Coalition of Blacks for Reparations in America), the conference was organised by N'COBRA's International Affairs Commission, of which PARCOE activists were members (including myself and Kofi Mawuli Klu). It drew support from key figures such as Johnny Hansen, the renowned Nkrumahist Pan-African doyen of the Ghanaian left, with participants including Croydon's first black councillor, Gee Bernard. The purpose of the conference was 'to review, assess and improve the worldwide efforts of the Global Pan-African Reparations Movement'.[37] In the press release for the conference issued by N'COBRA, London-based reparations activist Kofi Mawuli Klu stated:

> This conference will be an eye opener in showing African people that we are one family in the Continent and the Diaspora in our fight against a common oppressor. This conference will demonstrate that without true reparations and Pan-African unity in this contemporary world of heightening imperialist globalisation, there is no viable solution to any problems faced by continental and diasporan Africans in all spheres of life at local, national, and international levels.[38]

The rationale for my inclusion of these two international conferences is to demonstrate that African activists in the UK have been involved in Pan-African linkages that transcend the country borders of the UK. This leading role in influencing contemporary global reparations endeavours is a notable aspect of the UK contingent of the ISMAR.

Another key aspect of this Pan-African organising has been championed under the auspices of the Global Afrikan People's Parliament (GAPP), which was formed in London in 2015 as a governing body of 'Afrikan people working in the UK to regenerate their communities towards sovereign peoplehood in quest of national self-determination', citing a key priority as being 'to rally Afrikan people, from diverse backgrounds, into creating ONE Afrikan Heritage Community for National Self-Determination (AHC-NSD)'.[39] GAPP advocates that securing justice by way of reparations for African genocide, enslavement, colonialism and neo-colonialism and their legacies 'requires developing a global African perspective and organising framework'.[40] In its 'Emerging Position on CARICOM Reparations', it stated that an essential self-reparations task Africans have to undertake is to 'regenerate African communities and engage in the task of global African identity-formation, community and nation-building beyond the dictates of Euro-American imperialism'.[41] GAPP also pointed out that:

> If we are to reassert ourselves as the masters of our own destinies, we must organise for reparations on the basis of a strategic global African identity that sets a line of demarcation from our oppressors and the redefined identities they imposed upon us.[42]

This makes sense given that one of the key injuries that have been caused to African people and that has had enduring effects is what is referred to as the injury to self-determined peoplehood and nationhood for African people resulting in 'identity misrecognition'.[43] This is supported by US-based N'COBRA, which has identified five injuries caused as a result of enslavement and its enduring legacies for people of African heritage. These include injuries to peoplehood and nationhood, followed by education, criminal punishment, wealth/poverty and health.[44] There is continuing discussion on these ideas and perspectives within African heritage communities.

This is why a key focus of activism identified by the contemporary generation of Pan-African-minded reparationists in the UK is the need to address what has been referred to as the 'national question' first and foremost. The national question refers to the need for an oppressed people to exercise national self-determination as an aspect of that group's empowerment. The rationale for this is the fact that it was African people's national sovereignty that was violently usurped by the Maangamizi. So, leading UK reparationists are of the view that it is African people's sovereignty that needs to be restituted by way of self-repairs first and foremost. As Pan-Africanist organiser Jendayi Serwah, one of the activists I interviewed for my research, aptly stated:

People of African heritage have had quite a specific experience of empire particularly through the [transatlantic traffic in enslaved Africans] … ours is quite unique in that we were transported to other parts of the world and had our entire civilisations wiped out but our bodies remained … So, in order to seek reparations for these acts I think it is important for us to strive for material, intellectual, cultural and social resources in order to rebuild everything that was taken away from the African people that were enslaved.[45]

This idea of reparations being linked to nationhood and Pan-African nation building is a key feature of UK-based reparations activism. In this regard, PARCOE and GAPP have been foremost in consistently advocating for what they consider to be the reparatory justice substance of Pan-Africanism. Thus, the following political goals of what they refer to as 'applied reparations' have been identified by activists within these groupings:

1   Learn about, recognise and 'Stop the Maangamizi!', including the horrors of enslavement, colonisation, neocolonisation, recolonisation and other imperialist and foreign impositions on Africans at home and aboard, including forced Europeanisation and Arabisation.
2   Counter Afriphobia (anti-African prejudice and discrimination) as a manifestation of white-supremacy racism, eradicate African dehumanisation, and assert the 'African personality'.[46]
3   Restore African sovereignty by redressing with MAATUBU NTUMANDLA (a Pan-African Government of People's Power) the disrepair in African people's power and usher in a fundamental change to the existing world order that would definitively bring about new geopolitical realities such as MAATUBUNTUMAN: the anti-imperialist sovereign Pan-African Union of Communities or polity of African people's power.[47]
4   Effect systemic change globally to ensure the expropriation and redistribution of ill-gotten wealth, resources and income worldwide.
5   Implement new paradigms of development including a new legal, political and international economic order.
6   Institutionalise the African cosmovisions and ethical principles of Maat and Ubuntu in terms of global justice for all.[48]
7   Enforce environmental elements of global justice, including full respect for Mother Earth rights, or in the Akan (West African) formulation what is known as 'Nana Asase Yaa' rights.

As can be gathered, such goals of the ISMAR, as articulated by PARCOE and GAPP, are a far cry from simply reducing reparations to compensation, as is widely promoted in the mass media and in popular discourse on reparations. Increasingly, this envisioning of a post-reparations future for Africa and her people at home and abroad is building on the scholarly and activist works of Pharaoh Narmer, Pharaoh Hatshepsut, Gbeto Nyonufia Hangbe of Dahomey, Ngola Nzinga Mbande of the Nbundu polities of Ndongo and Matamba, Mbuya Nehanda, Aimé Césaire, Frantz Fanon, Kwame Nkrumah, Cheikh Anta Diop and many other Pan-Africanist luminaries, to imagine, plan and work for a future Pan-African state that redresses the structural injustices inherent in maintaining European borders in what is known as Africa.

The future African superstate that UK-based reparations activists envision is actually a Pan-African union of communities rather than a union of countries. This MAATUBUNTUMAN is rooted in the indigenous knowledge systems, values and nation-building practices of Africa and her people. MAATUBUNTUMAN will be founded on the African ethical and moral principles of Maat, which also practises Ubuntu (interconnectedness) in relation to her people, all of humanity and the cosmos.[49] This is a specifically African-centred evolution of reparations envisioning, emanating from London-based reparationists. For PARCOE and GAPP activists, reparations will be completely meaningless without achieving the transnational project of building MAATUBUNTUMAN.[50] A Bristol-based reparationist who is part of GAPP expressed it in this way:

> The day something happens to me and some [entity] representing all of the governance in the Motherland says actually that's one of our citizens, that's a citizen of Afrika, that would be an achievement. Because we would have recognition that wherever we are we have protection and we have a Homeland, and we have the benefits of formally belonging to an [African] nation.[51]

Such an Afrofuturist vision is spectacularly depicted in the blockbuster *Black Panther* superhero movie's portrayal of Wakanda, which, like MAATUBUNTUMAN, represents a futuristic and transformed Africa that has not been colonised. However, unlike Wakanda, which is fictional, the building blocks of the future MAATUBUNTUMAN are being fashioned in the African community's self-repair organising of reparationists and their allied transnational networks within and beyond the UK. This refers to the self-determined efforts that need to be made in building our own power, in such a way that African heritage communities are able to identify and enhance ongoing work towards stopping the contemporary manifestations of the Maangamizi, which are putting the individuals, families and other social groups that make up African heritage communities in a state of disrepair. In addition, it also refers to consciously fashioning reparatory solutions for glocally rebuilding their power base as communities, in such a way that they are transformed in the process.

Organising towards the establishment of MAATUBUNTUMAN of Africans in the diaspora is being mirrored by Africans on the continent, for example in the recent establishment of the Global African Family Reunion International Council (the Council), established by chiefs and other traditional leaders in West Africa, as well as in communities of resistance that are engaged in anti-colonial resistance to the colonial borders instituted after the 1884–85 Berlin Conference. This coming together of activists from Africa and members of her diaspora in Britain is being facilitated through scholarly-activist engagements as part of the newly formed UK-based International Network of Scholars and Activists for Afrikan Reparations.[52]

This work of UK activists with members of the Council is significant in charting the contemporary history making of Afrikan reparationists in Britain because representatives of the Council, in association with Ghana civil society formations such as Vazoba Afrika and Friends Networking Forum, are working jointly with activists from PARCOE and GAPP in the UK to develop a memorandum of understanding to guide the development of familial relations between African nationalities and communities in Africa and locations in the diaspora such as Britain. This partnership is also developing a campaign for the establishment of a Pan-African Reparatory Justice Law of Holistic Rematriation/Repatriation, which in effect enshrines in law the right of voluntary return for people of African heritage.[53] This aspiration of having African citizenship is a reparations demand made by a significant number of Africans in the diaspora who identify with the cause of reparations.

Another example of contemporary Pan-Africanist organising that has reparatory justice at its centre is that of the annual Afrikan Emancipation Day Reparations March (the March). First initiated in 2014 under the auspices of the Rastafari Movement UK, the March assumed new leadership under the auspices of the March Committee, which has organised marches from 2015 onwards. The March Committee is co-chaired by Bristol-based reparationist Jendayi Serwah and Pan-African activist Kwaku Bonsu.

Since 2015, and under the leadership of the March Committee as a cross-organisational and interest group committee, the March has adopted an explicit Pan-Africanist approach to organising. Together with its official campaign partner, the 'Stop the Maangamizi!' campaign, it cites 'attempts to recolonise Afrika' as one of the aspects of the Maangamizi that it is concerned to prevent.[54] The March Committee has stated in various publicity documents that it is 'in pursuit of comprehensive holistic land-based reparations'.[55] It advocates that 'reparations as Afrikans in the Diaspora is umbilically connected to the liberation of our Motherland, Afrika; including restoration of her sovereignty and the self-determination of African people worldwide and the establishment of structures of non-territorial autonomy in the Diaspora'.[56] Hence PARCOE and GAPP's advocacy for political and legal recognition of African people in the diaspora who choose to identify as such in the UK argues for an 'Afrikan Heritage Community for National Self-Determination (AHC-NSD)', entitled to have resources to develop autonomous institutions of education, healthcare and self-governance.[57]

The March has embraced a number of African liberation and reparations struggles, including featuring participants such as representatives of the Economic Freedom Fighters of South Africa, who have been advocating land expropriation in South Africa as a form of reparations; the Ovaherero Genocide Foundation in Namibia, which is seeking reparations and redress from Germany for the Ovaherero and Nama genocide; as well as the 'Free Gbago – Free Afrika' campaign, which is targeting French imperialism in Africa. In fact, the last two years have seen the March headlined by two leading female Ovaherero Genocide reparations activists who flew in from Namibia. They not only provided keynote speeches at the March but were part of the delegations that handed in the 'Stop the Maangamizi!' petition to the office of the UK prime minister at 10 Downing Street. These were Utjuia Esther Muinjangue, chairperson of the Genocide Foundation, and Kambanda Veii, secretary for the 2017 and 2018 Marches.[58]

According to Kofi Mawuli Klu, co-vice chairperson of the 'Stop the Maangamizi!' campaign:

The March visually displays a freedom-fighting unity of African people from all over the world, on the streets of London, rallying together as one defiant family, inside the belly of the beast; that is no longer happening in African protests, in any other parts of the world, including those on the Continent of Afrika. I am an Afrikan born and bred in Ghana and I know what the power of this image meaningfully conveys to Afrikans at home and all other peoples across the world.[59]

The March also serves as a conduit as part of an ongoing parliamentary and extra-parliamentary strategy including a campaign for the establishment of an All-Party Parliamentary Commission of Inquiry for Truth and Reparatory Justice at the levels of the Westminster and European parliaments as well as at the Ubuntukgotla Peoples International Tribunal for Global Justice, an alternative world court *from below*.[60] Hence the delivery of the annual 'Stop the Maangamizi!' petition charging the British state with the crimes of genocide and ecocide against African people worldwide as a key feature of the annual March.[61] The petition, which was co-authored by myself and Kofi Mawuli Klu, demands an end to the state's role in the continuing Maangamizi, of which the organisers cite several NGO reports highlighting British government complicity in the modern-day looting of African mineral and natural resources, as well as calling for African people to 'shut down Maangamizi crime scenes' as a form of civil disobedience.[62]

In conclusion, the key point of emphasis in this chapter is that there is ongoing activism taking place driven by UK-based reparationists that also creatively advances the reparatory justice quintessence of Pan-Africanism. Given the fact that this is contemporary history in the making, it is important for researchers of the African diaspora to give greater academic recognition to such cutting-edge examples of progressive scholar-activist work taking place in the UK. In addition, it is important that spaces are created or strengthened that facilitate dialogue, knowledge sharing and co-production on matters regarding the knowledge being produced in ongoing Pan-African and reparatory justice struggles.

Notes

1   While the standard spelling of African is with a 'c', the spelling of Afrikan with a 'k' is done to respect the spelling that organisations use to describe themselves, or in quotes pertaining to such organisations.

2   https://reparationsscholaractivist. wordpress.com/2015/02/20/what-is-the-ismar/, accessed 20 February 2015.

3 https://reparationsscholaractivist. wordpress.com/2015/02/20/what-is-the-ismar/, accessed 20 February 2015.

4 https://reparationsscholaractivist. wordpress.com/2015/02/20/what-is-the-ismar/, accessed 20 February 2015.

5 http://www.agi.ac.za/sites/ default/files/image_tool/images/429/ feminist_africa_journals/archive/02/ features_-_pan-africanism_transna tional_black_feminism_and_the_limits_ of_culturalist_analyses_in_african_gen der_discourses.pdf, accessed 13 March 2018.

6 https://www.inosaar.llc.ed.ac.uk/ en/principles-participation, accessed 20 September 2017.

7 http://www.ncobraonline.org/ wp-content/uploads/2016/02/Karenga-THE-ETHICS-OF-REPARATIONS.pdf, accessed 20 September 2018.

8 https://www.youtube.com/ watch?v=U9XoMcxAWm8, accessed 16 July 2014.

9 For example in Kehinde Andrews, *Back to Black: Retelling Black Radicalism for the Twenty-First Century* (London: Zed Books, 2018).

10 https://issafrica.org/research/ papers/institutionalising-pan-africanism-transforming-african-union-values-and-principles-into-policy-and-practice, accessed 31 August 2018.

11 Robin D. G. Kelley, *Freedoms Dreams: The Black Radical Imagination* (Boston MA: Beacon Press, 2002).

12 https://reparationss cholaractivist.wordpress.com/2016 /04/27/what-is-the-prim/, accessed 9 September 2016.

13 Hakim Adi and Marika Sherwood, *Pan-African History: Political Figures from Africa and the Diaspora since 1787* (New York: Routledge, 2003), p. 8.

14 The term Abya Yala in the Kuna language means 'land in its full maturity' and refers to the American continent in its totality among increasing numbers of her indigenous people of various nations, nationalities and ethnicities throughout the northern, central and southern parts of the continent.

15 Kofi Klu, 'Definition and Precolonial Trailblazers', unpublished article, December 2017.

16 Kimani Nehusi, 'The Meaning of Reparation', unpublished paper presented at the First UK Preparatory Conference on Reparations, 1993, Bernie Grant Archives, Bishopsgate Institute, London.

17 http://ncobra.org/resources /pdf/Chinweizu-ReparationsandANew GlobalOrder1.pdf, accessed, 5 April 2012.

18 Permanent Court of International Justice, Factory at Chorzów, Judgment No. 13, 13 September 1928.

19 Jeff Spinner-Halev, 'From Historical to Enduring Injustice', *Political Theory* 35/5 (2007), pp. 574–97.

20 Quobna Ottobah Cugoano, *Thoughts and Sentiments on the Evil and Wicked Traffic of Slavery and the Commerce of the Human Species* (London: Penguin, 1999).

21 Tajudeen Abdul Raheem, *Pan-Africanism: Politics, Economy and Social Change in the Twenty-first Century* (London: Pluto Press, 1996), p. 2.

22 Toyin Falola and Kwame Essien (eds), *Pan-Africanism and the Politics of African Citizenship and Identity* (London: Routledge, 2014), p. 87.

23 https://www. telesurtv.net/english/opinion/ Pan-Africanism-Feminism-and-Finding-the-Missing-Women-20160524-0054. html, accessed 16 May 2018.

24 https://www. telesurtv.net/english/opinion/ Pan-Africanism-Feminism-and-Finding-the-Missing-Women-20160524-0054. html, accessed 16 May 2018.

25 Liz Mackie, *The Great Marcus Garvey* (London: Hansib Publications, 2008), p. 140.

26 http://www.the-platform.org.uk/2015/08/30/we-need-to-talk-about-claudia-jones/, accessed 3 July 2018.

27 George Padmore, *Pan-Africanism or Communism* (London: Dennis Dobson, 1956), pp. 170–2.

28 http://www.parliament.uk/business/publications/business-papers/commons/early-day-motions/edm-detail1/?edmnumber=1987&session=1992-93, accessed 9 October 2012.

29 Birmingham Declaration, 1 January 1994.

30 Oral history interview with Linda Bellos, 24 September 2014.

31 Oral history interview with Linda Bellos, 24 September 2014.

32 A. C. Santana, 'Our Struggle for Reparations in African Youth Perspective', draft paper for presentation to the 11 December 1993 Birmingham Working Conference of the African Reparations Movement (ARM UK), Bernie Grant Collection, Bishopsgate Institute, London.

33 Santana, 'Our Struggle for Reparations'.

34 https://www.gacuk.org.uk/the-bridgetown-protocol, accessed 20 September 2018.

35 Black Quest for Justice Campaign leaflet, 1995.

36 http://www.ncobra-intl-affairs.org/Supportletters.html, accessed 18 October 2013.

37 http://www.ncobra-intl-affairs.org/Supportletters.html, accessed 18 October 2013.

38 http://www.ncobra-intl-affairs.org/Supportletters.html, accessed 18 October 2014.

39 https://globalafrikanpeoplesparliament.org/about/, accessed 15 August 2018.

40 https://globalafrikanpeoplesparliament.org/2018/07/15/gap-emerging-position-on-caricom-reparations/, accessed 15 July 2018.

41 https://globalafrikanpeoplesparliament.org/2018/07/15/gap-emerging-position-on-caricom-reparations/, accessed 15 July 2018.

42 https://globalafrikanpeoplesparliament.org/2018/07/15/gap-emerging-position-on-caricom-reparations/, accessed 15 July 2018.

43 John Lie, *Modern Peoplehood* (Harvard: Harvard University Press, 2004), p. 1.

44 http://www.ncobraonline.org/five-injuries-slavery-defined/, accessed 21 November 2016.

45 Oral history interview with Adam Elliott-Cooper, 26 November 2013.

46 http://www.hungerforculture.com/?page_id=1096, accessed 12 January 2018.

47 https://globalafrikanpeoplesparliament.org/, accessed 29 November 2015.

48 Maulana Karenga, *Maat, the Moral Idea in Ancient Egypt: A Study in Classical African Ethics* (London: Routledge, 2004).

49 https://them.polylog.org/3/frm-en.htm, accessed 4 April 2012.

50 https://www.opendemocracy.net/kofi-maluwi-klu-esther-stanford-xosei-and-zena-edwards/climate-justice-through-pan-afrikan-reparator, accessed 3 December 2015.

51 Oral history interview with Jendayi Serwah, 17 April 2015.

52 http://www.inosaar.llc.ed.ac.uk/about, accessed 30 October 2017.

53 https://www.inosaar.llc.ed.ac.uk/sites/default/files/atoms/files/osie-adza-tekpor-vii.pdf, accessed 14 April 2018.

54 http://www.reparationsmarch.org/, accessed 30 June 2017.

55 https://stopthemaangamizi.com/2017/08/05/after-the-reparations-march-what-next/, accessed 5 August 2017.

56 https://stopthemaangamizi.com/2017/08/07/after-4-years-of-marching-what-has-been-achieved/, accessed 7 August 2017.

57 https://www.theguardian.com/commentisfree/2015/sep/30/should-britain-government-reparations-slavery, accessed 30 September 2015.

58 https://stopthemaangamizi.com/2017/06/02/reparations-march-2017-profiling-the-reparatory-justice-change-we-are-organsing-to-bring-about/, accessed 2 June 2017.

59 https://stopthemaangamizi.com/category/the-2016-1st-august-afrikan-emancipation-day-reparations-march/, accessed 1 September 2016.

60 https://stopthemaangamizi.com/2015/10/12/about-the-commission-of-inquiry-appcitarj/, accessed 12 October 2015; https://stopthemaangamizi.com/2016/01/31/the-ubuntukgotla-peoples-international-tribunal-for-global-justice-pitgj/, accessed 31 January 2016.

61 https://stopthemaangamizi.com/petition/, accessed 13 August 2016.

62 https://waronwant.org/resources/new-colonialism-britains-scramble-africas-energy-and-mineral-resources, accessed 13 April 2016.

11 | QUEST FOR A COHESIVE DIASPORA AFRICAN COMMUNITY

Reliving historic experiences by Black Zimbabweans in Britain

Christopher Roy Zembe

Introduction

On arrival in Zimbabwe as an imperial power in the nineteenth century, the British were confronted with a fragmented African society of the Shona- and Ndebele-speaking communities divided by language and defined territories. The term 'Shona' was a collective noun conflating the linguistic, cultural and political attributes of a community of people who inhabited the Zimbabwean plateau and did not identify themselves with that term until the late nineteenth century. In contrast, the Ndebele originated as a small clan in South Africa under the leadership of Mzilikazi, a trusted general under Zulu nation leader Shaka. They occupied the south-western part of the Zimbabwean plateau in 1839 through plunder, pillage and violent raids on their Shona neighbours. Just like the term Shona, Ndebele as a terminology also evolved to be an ethnic and linguistic identifier of the community. The Shona had been the dominant community with an approximate share of the population of 80 per cent, with the Ndebele being the second largest ethnic community at approximately 15 per cent.[1]

The precolonial violent nature of Ndebele settlement in Zimbabwe marked the start of ethnic particularism and consciousness that would evolve and blossom throughout the subsequent phases of Zimbabwe's history. It was therefore inevitable that upon attaining independence on 18 April 1980, the new Zimbabwean government faced insurmountable challenges in uniting a black community that had been polarised by historical ethnic allegiances and tensions. This chapter will therefore unveil a Black Zimbabwean diaspora community in Britain imbued with imported historic memories of communal tensions and prejudices that ultimately had an impact on relations. To facilitate a detailed analysis of the impact of historical experiences on the Black Zimbabwean immigrant community, the chapter's findings were extracted from testimonies of participants complemented by secondary and primary sources. The interview process had to be reflective of the uneven dispersal of the Black Zimbabwean population throughout Britain. This was essential in constructing a comparative discourse on how members of the community were constructing their social interactions between themselves.

This study of Zimbabwean immigrants in Britain is set within the historiographical paradigms that trace the history of African immigrants' settlement in the country. By focusing on Zimbabweans in Britain, the chapter not only offers an alternative perspective on Black British migration history by moving away from the traditional areas of black immigration study, such as eighteenth-century slavery and post-1945 African-Caribbean migration, but also acknowledges an increase in contemporary sub-Saharan Africans in Britain, especially those from its former colonies in Southern Africa. Using the Black Zimbabwean community in Britain as a case study also develops a critical narrative on why relations within a black African diaspora community from the same country should not always be treated as a product of fixed essence, but as a consequence of imported memories of historical processes that can be traced back to the precolonial era.

Zimbabweans in Britain

The Office for National Statistics (ONS) identified Zimbabweans as one of the African Commonwealth countries that have been adopting Britain as their first-choice migration destination, a trend that continued into the new millennium.[2] While the chapter concentrates on contemporary Black Zimbabwean immigrants who arrived in Britain from the 1990s, it is important to note that the trend of immigration had started in the colonial era. The armed liberation struggle for independence had an impact on immigration trends, as a sizeable number of Zimbabweans arrived in Britain to escape the violence. In 1966, the nationalist movement launched an armed liberation struggle for independence that ended with a ceasefire agreed on at the Lancaster House Negotiations in 1979, and that paved the way for a manageable transition to multiparty democracy. A significant number of whites, coloureds and Asians who emigrated as the armed struggle intensified were young men in their mid-teens escaping conscription into the Rhodesian army.[3] Within the African community, there was also a sizeable number of young academically able blacks leaving for Europe and the US to further their education.[4] The Commonwealth Secretariat and British government had created opportunities for academically able Black Zimbabweans to study in Britain as a response to colonial Zimbabwe's discriminatory and restrictive educational policies, which had stifled the educational progression of blacks.

The rapid rise of the Zimbabwean population in Britain is illustrated by the graph below (Figure 11.1). Zimbabwe's special relationship with its colonial master had always been cemented by ties of kinship, economic interdependence, preferential trade arrangements, sport, tourism, education and academic certification.[5]

Since the attainment of independence in 1980, Zimbabwe has experienced three waves of postcolonial emigration: in the 1980s and 1990s and post-2000.[6] The patterns and circumstances of migration varied between racial communities. A majority of whites and to a lesser extent coloureds used the ancestral route, while a majority of blacks used student, work permit and political refugee routes. As for Asians, a significant number utilised family networks that had already been established with other Asians of Indian descent settled in Britain. Despite the varied means used to migrate, socio-economic and political events triggered the postcolonial exodus during the three identified phases of emigration.

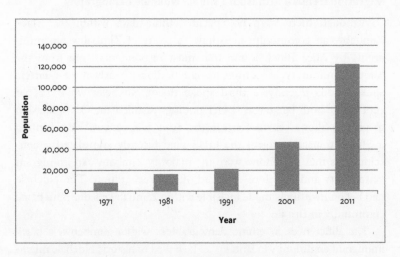

Figure 11.1 Zimbabwean-born population in Britain.

Sources: ONS, 2011; International Organization for Migration, 2006.[7]

For a majority of blacks with no ancestral links with Britain, the distance between the two countries did not deter them from migrating. As a former colonial master that had benefited economically from Zimbabwe's resources, there were perceptions among blacks that Britain 'owed' them.[8] Black Zimbabweans' migration to Britain in both the colonial and postcolonial era could therefore be classified into the following four categories: visitors, students, political asylum seekers and those on work permits. The Black Zimbabwean community was unevenly dispersed across Britain, with cities such as Leicester having one of the largest concentrations of Black Zimbabweans. The 2011 census statistics showed Leicester, with a population of 3,377, as having the largest concentration of Zimbabweans in the East Midlands.[9] The high concentration of Black Zimbabweans in Leicester can be attributed to two main factors. First, De Montfort University unwittingly encouraged chain migration into the city by facilitating the enrolment of Zimbabweans to train as nurses. Secondly, the city was chosen as one of the designated dispersal areas for political asylum seekers following the passing of the Immigration and Asylum Act of 1999. The Act empowered the UK Border Agency to relocate asylum seekers from London and the South-east of England to cities and towns in northern England where accommodation was affordable.[10]

Migration trends and diaspora Shona–Ndebele demography

Although there were no specific ethnic data within the Black Zimbabwean community in Britain, a study of Zimbabwean immigrants by Alice Bloch found that most respondents were from the Shona community. According to her findings, nearly three-quarters spoke Shona fluently; a third spoke fluent Ndebele; while 12 per cent spoke both languages.[11] Her findings justified the ONS decision to print a Shona census form in the 2011 UK census.[12] By printing a Shona translated form, the ONS inadvertently stimulated a consciousness that the Shona were the majority Zimbabwean immigrant community and therefore deserved official recognition. The Ndebele had been unwittingly made invisible within Zimbabwe's diaspora black community in Britain.

The differences in ethnic demographics within Zimbabwe's black immigrant community in Britain can be linked to historic Ndebele migration trends in which South Africa had always been a natural and viable destination for the Ndebele because of ancestral links.[13] In contrast, the

Shona did not have ancestral ties to make South Africa their natural migration destination. In the absence of close historical ties with South Africa, there was consensus among the respondents (both Shona and Ndebele) that those from the Shona were the first to utilise opportunities to migrate to Britain in greater numbers than those from the Ndebele community from the 1990s.

This was evident when a sizeable number of the Shona took advantage of the organised recruitment of Zimbabwean professionals by UK-based employment agencies that needed nurses, engineers, social workers and teachers.[14] JoAnn McGregor explains how the agencies enticed the professionals (especially in the health sector) by holding periodic recruitment drives in Zimbabwe's public venues, such as hotels in Harare, between 1992 and 2002.[15] Taking advantage of the recruitment drive was Sharai, a Zimbabwean trained nurse who migrated at the beginning of 2002 after being issued with a work permit. On arrival in Britain, she undertook an adaptation course at a Leicestershire nursing home so as to be able to work as a qualified nurse. When asked to comment on the ethnic representation of those undertaking the adaptation courses, Sharai admitted that she encountered very few Ndebele nurses.[16]

The British government's initiative to fill vacancies in the health sector also contributed to a surge of Zimbabweans applying for nursing training at British universities. They were encouraged by being able to access non-refundable grants and bursaries. Once again, the Shona were the first to utilise the opportunity in greater numbers. For example, De Montfort University in Leicester provided evidence of the extent to which the Shona were the first to utilise the student-nurse route to migrate to Britain. This was confirmed by Memory, a Shona nursing student at the university from January 2000 to 2003. She could recall only four Ndebele out of over forty Zimbabwean students in her year group.[17]

This visible presence of the Shona at Britain's universities in the early 2000s, mostly studying nursing, resuscitated historically constructed prejudices that the Ndebele had never been as motivated as the Shona in pursuit of higher professional or academic qualifications. The Shona would express the historical arrogance and prejudice towards the Ndebele during the interview process with comments such as *mandex* (a derogatory name used by the Shona when referring to the Ndebele) *haadidi kudzidza* (Ndebele do not want to learn) to explain the low representation of Ndebele immigrants in higher education (especially in nursing). These imported historical communal stereotypes and labelling used by the participants, entrenched in ethnic particularism, were reflective of the failures of the nation-building project after independence.

The failure of the nation-building project within the black community was inextricably linked with the Zimbabwean nationalist movement's liberation struggle for independence, which was 'bankrupt of nation building ideas' as it only succeeded in entrenching a series of ethnic conflicts between the two major nationalist parties – Zimbabwe African National Union (ZANU) and Zimbabwean African People's Union (ZAPU).[18] ZANU and its military wing, Zimbabwe African National Liberation Army (ZANLA), presented themselves as a Shona political party with a Shona-dominated leadership, while ZAPU and its military wing, Zimbabwe People's Revolutionary Army (ZIPRA), drew their main support from the Ndebele.

Without a sustainable unity pact agreement, the two nationalist parties resolved to contest the first democratic elections in 1980 as rivals, thus placing their supporters on a collision course with each other, just as they had been during the liberation struggle. It was therefore not surprising that the 1980 election results that led to the first democratically elected government exposed ethnic polarisation within the nationalist movement when the Shona constituent of 80 per cent of the population voted ZANU PF (Patriotic Front), making it the clear winner with 63 per cent of the votes, while PF ZAPU managed only 24 per cent.[19] The election results had theoretically given Mugabe the mandate to control the entire country, including the two Ndebele Matabeleland Provinces where at most only 10 per cent of the electorate had voted for him.[20]

With Mugabe's ZANU PF government pursuing nation-building policies based on the party's socialist ideological framework of 'absolute power and moral authority within a one-party-state political and ideological framework', PF ZAPU and its Ndebele supporters were always at risk of being accused of derailing any nation-building processes.[21] The vulnerability of the Ndebele became a reality in February 1982 when military weapons were discovered on properties owned by PF ZAPU. Responding to the discovery of the arms cache, PF ZAPU leaders were arrested and detained without trial, and former ZIPRA fighters were side-lined in the newly integrated Zimbabwe

National Army. In protest at what they believed was deliberate persecution and polarisation of the Ndebele, a group of disgruntled former ZIPRA fighters took up arms against the government. Jocelyn Alexander, JoAnn McGregor and Terrence Ranger describe how the dissidents, without a clear political ideology, carried out acts of sabotage on government institutions and infrastructure, and attacked and in some cases murdered civilians and foreign tourists.[22]

Faced with the possibility of the newly independent Zimbabwe disintegrating into political turmoil, Mugabe had to act decisively against the insurgents and their supporters who were identified as Ndebele civilians. He deployed the North Korean-trained Fifth Brigade, an entirely Shona crack unit answerable to Mugabe, along with carefully chosen Ndebele speakers into Matabeleland Province to 'apply a military solution to the dissident problem'.[23] The process of dismantling dissident support included rape, burning food granaries, closing grocery shops in rural areas, forcing people to witness the torture of those accused of supporting the dissidents, detentions without trial, forcing the Ndebele to speak Shona or risk being murdered or tortured, and economic marginalisation of Matabeleland.[24] It is estimated that 20,000 members of the Ndebele community (mostly civilians) were murdered by the security forces between 1985 and 1987.[25]

The attacks carried out by the Fifth Brigade on the Ndebele were known by a Shona word: *Gukurahundi*, translated as 'the rain that washes away chaff from the last harvest before the spring'.[26] To the Ndebele, Ndlovu-Gatsheni describes how this meant that the harvest was the achievement of independence and the Ndebele were the chaff that was to be washed away before the spring rain, which was the establishment of a one-party state in a united Zimbabwe under the control of a Shona government. The postcolonial civil conflict (Gukurahundi) of the 1980s emerged as the most potent factor in erecting imagined social boundaries that would restrict interactions between the Shona and Ndebele communities in Britain.

Gukurahundi legacy on Shona–Ndebele relations in Britain

The government's indiscriminate and disproportionate use of force had psychological effects on the Ndebele that consolidated ethnic particularism, and this was to be reincarnated in Britain. Mabuza, a Leicester-based Ndebele immigrant, revealed the extent of the traumatic experiences members of the Ndebele community went through by pointing out that nearly 'every' Ndebele family in Britain had a family member either killed or tortured by the Zimbabwean Shona security forces.[27] It was therefore an expected response by Ndebele interviewees to unanimously agree that Gukurahundi was a plausible reason justifying disassociation from the Shona diaspora community. This unified response showed the extent to which imported memories of unresolved conflicts had become an emotive and potent force that was crucial in communal particularism and would determine diaspora Shona–Ndebele relations.

Participants' reference to Gukurahundi as a justifiable excuse to instigate separatism trivialised the fact that most of the interviewees could not have personally experienced the atrocities perceived to have been carried out by government security forces. This was because 72 per cent of Ndebele interviewees in 2013 were below forty-five years old, and so they would have been too young to remember or to have personally experienced the events of the conflict. The identification of Gukurahundi as a reason to justify a separatist agenda by these younger respondents therefore revealed the extent to which the events of the conflict had been passed from generation to generation, thus making it an integral part of Ndebele history. The resolve to ensure that Gukurahundi will always be part of Ndebele history has been per-petuated by immigrant Ndebele parents such as Zanele, who admitted that she was part of a group of Ndebele parents in Britain who believed that it was their duty (just as it was for their parents) to tell their chil-dren of the persecution the Ndebele experienced at the hands of the Shona security forces.[28]

The passing of imported memories of Gukurahundi from generation to generation acted as a deterrent in forging cordial relations within the younger generation in Britain. For example, Natalie, a twenty-one-year-old Zimbabwean student of dual Shona–Ndebele heritage at one of Leicester's universities, exposed the generational impact of unresolved ethnic tensions within the young Zimbabwean diaspora community.[29] Natalie's dual ethnic heritage, although not widespread, was not unique or unusual. This was because Zimbabwe had a long tradition of intermarriage between ethnic groups, especially in urban areas where there were greater Shona–Ndebele interactions. However, violent political and social rivalry in both the colonial and postcolonial era fostered a sense of ethnic allegiances that naturally resulted in a decline in intermarriage at the time of emigration.

Having a Ndebele mother and a Shona father made Natalie realise how attitudes of young Zimbabweans on both sides of the ethnic divide were still influenced by historically constructed negative prejudices and stereotypes entrenched in historical events. As someone with dual Shona and Ndebele heritage, she experienced what she referred to as 'banter' with derogatory ethnic undertones based on such events. Her Shona friends would often point out that Zimbabwe 'belongs to us', implying that her Ndebele side of the family were foreigners who migrated from South Africa. Her ability to speak both Shona and Ndebele also courted a backlash from some of her Ndebele friends, who would often rebuke her for speaking Shona, a language they described as sounding disgusting.

Allowing memories of unresolved pre-emigration conflicts to be passed from generation to generation inevitably had a negative impact on diaspora inter-ethnic marriages in Britain. Ralph, an unmarried Ndebele immigrant in his early thirties, admitted that there were a significant number of Ndebele families in Britain who consciously discouraged intermarriage with the Shona, especially when it involved Ndebele women.[30] This discouragement was driven by the need to preserve Ndebele identity, since traditional Zimbabwean marriage practices required the woman to assimilate into her husband's family and adopt Shona cultural and traditional values. This was a situation most diaspora Ndebele families in Britain found difficult to comprehend, especially with the history of violent conflict between the two communities in Zimbabwe. With very little intermarriage between the two ethnic communities, Zanele admitted that it will be a slow process healing the emotional wounds caused by historical conflicts, as long as Ndebele parents like her continue to indoctrinate their children to construct relationships with the Shona through the lenses of Gukurahundi atrocities or ethnic particularism.

Forcing the Ndebele to speak Shona had reinforced a narrative that Gukurahundi was an ethnic conflict in which language was being used as a symbolic gesture to undermine Ndebele identity. It was therefore not surprising that language became a source of diaspora Shona– Ndebele tensions. With the government after independence failing to end the colonial education system of teaching African languages based on geographical ethnic distribution, it meant that Ndebele continued to be taught exclusively in Matabeleland and parts of Midlands Province where there was a visible Ndebele presence, while Shona was taught in the Shona-dominated provinces of Mashonaland, Masvingo, Manicaland and parts of Midlands. As a result, most members of the Shona community had migrated without being able to speak Ndebele. This was evident among the Shona diaspora participants, with only 10 per cent being able to speak Ndebele beyond greeting phrases. Zanele admitted that it was this awareness of the lack of interest to learn or speak Ndebele by most Shona that naturally restricted diaspora interaction. The majority within the Ndebele immigrant community found it difficult to forge intimate interactions with a community that historically had shown no interest in learning their language.

Shona attitudes

However, it would be misleading to conclude that individuals within the Ndebele community were the only ones using memories of unresolved pre-emigration conflicts to fan tribalism within Zimbabwe's diaspora black community in Britain. There were also individuals within the Shona community who were not interested in pursuing a reconciliation agenda with the Ndebele and who trivialised the impact of Gukurahundi. Their biased perceptions and memories of Gukurahundi were constructed by Zimbabwe's state-controlled media propaganda of the 1980s, which blamed Ndebele politicians and civilians for the civil conflict. As a result, most were convinced that the Zimbabwe government's response to the disturbance was the only way to deal with a group of 'Ndebele armed bandits who were using guerrilla tactics' to undermine a democratically elected Shona-led government.[31]

In support of the Zimbabwe government response to the conflict, Leicester-based Shona immigrant David argued that the security forces' response was nothing to do with tribalism, as claimed by some members of the diaspora Ndebele community, and therefore should not influence relations in Britain. Instead, it was an appropriate response to political instability which had been started by a group of Ndebele-dominated 'dissidents' who were using guerrilla tactics to:

> murder the Shona and to disrupt the economy. As a result it would
> have been natural that the security forces would face difficulties
> in distinguishing Ndebele civilians who were mingling with the
> dissidents. The Ndebele should remember that the soldiers fighting the
> dissidents were former guerrilla fighters during the liberation and were
> acquainted with guerrilla tactics of depending on civilians for support.

Therefore, there is no reason why the Shona or the government should feel obliged to apologise to the Ndebele civilians, neither should the Ndebele keep on holding to memories of Gukurahundi to justify their separatist attitude. Gukurahundi is an unfortunate part of our history and should be left as that.[32]

David's perceptions of the conflict were shared by most Shona participants, who made it clear that the Gukurahundi narrative promoted by those within the Ndebele community in Britain was biased as it focused only on Ndebele causalities while ignoring the atrocities committed by the dissidents on Shona communities. Without a consensus on the interpretation of Gukurahundi, interactions between the Shona and Ndebele in Britain were to be engineered by unresolved conflicts of suspicion and mistrust, with no internal or external motivation to end the historic hostilities.

The transformation of ethnic demography and its impact on relations

The formation of the Movement for Democratic Change (MDC) political party in 1999 was a significant development that led to increased Ndebele migration to Britain. The results of the 2000 parliamentary elections, in which the MDC won all except two of the twenty-three parliamentary seats in Ndebele-dominated Bulawayo and Matabeleland Provinces, not only heralded the start of a significant challenge to Mugabe's government by the MDC, but also served to confirm that, just as in the 1980s, Matabeleland Provinces were still anti-Mugabe's government.[33] With memories of Gukurahundi still embedded in the lives of the Ndebele, the political gains by the MDC encouraged them to migrate to Britain as political asylum seekers as they could use their support of the MDC to claim that they would always be vulnerable to persecution by Mugabe's government, just as in the civil conflict of the 1980s.[34]

The increase in the number of Ndebele asylum seekers coincided with implementation of the Immigration and Asylum Act of 1999. As already alluded to earlier, the Act facilitated the dispersal of those seeking political refugee status from London and the South-east of England to cities and towns in northern England.[35] With a criterion of dispersing political asylum seekers to urban areas with cheap housing, Leicester, with relatively inexpensive accommodation in the St Mathew and Highfields areas, was designated a dispersal area for Zimbabwean asylum seekers.[36] Although there might not be statistical verification of Zimbabwean political asylum seekers dispersed to Leicester on arrival, data gathered at the end of May 2004 by the National Asylum Support Service (NASS) identified Zimbabwean asylum seekers as second only to Somalis on the list of asylum seekers needing assistance.[37] The inevitable consequence of the dispersal policy was the rapid ethnic transformation of the Black Zimbabwean immigrant community in cities such as Leicester which were once dominated by the Shona.

As the Ndebele population increased in the city, it did not take long for some members of the Shona community to develop perceptions that the Ndebele were determined to assert their influence. The Ndebele believed that their population was increasing to a level where it would be possible to challenge Shona dominance by initiating a separatist agenda that would not only minimise interactions with the Shona but also curtail their influence in community organisations. With memories of how their minority status had always prejudiced them in assuming leadership roles in organisations where the Shona dominated, it was therefore inevitable that the new arrivals in Leicester aggressively pursued ways of addressing ethnic representation in leadership structures of organisations previously dominated by the Shona.

Mathew, a former secretary of a Leicester-based Zimbabwe support network, experienced Ndebele determination to address what they perceived as unfair Shona overrepresentation in leadership positions. He explained how the election process to choose leaders in his organisation had to adapt to changes in the ethnic demographics.[38] As the membership became more diverse, his position and that of the Shona chairman became untenable, a situation that forced both of them to resign even though they had not completed their tenure in office as stipulated by the constitution. He pointed out that changes were instigated by some Ndebele members in the organisation who demanded an ethnic balance in the leadership structure to reflect what they perceived as the growing superior numerical position of the Ndebele in Leicester.

The influence of ethnic representation in the leadership of Zimbabweans' organisations was also experienced in Derby. Despite the Shona being the majority within Zimbabwe's Derby community, Jacob, who had been living in the city since 2002, admitted a gradual rise of ethnic conflicts within some Shona-run community organisations when the Ndebele realised that their population in the city was increasing. As the Ndebele population increased, Jacob described how some within the community became reluctant to participate in Shona-led community organisations, even when the Shona agreed to incorporate them in the leadership structures.[39] This lack of interest on the part of the Ndebele in Shona-organised activities was described by Jacob as an attitude which not only trivialised the fact that the Shona-led organisations were being 'competently run', but also undermined 'democratically run institutions'.

Happison, a Derby-based Shona community worker who lived in Leicester from 2000 to 2006, also reaffirmed the negative impact on community relations following the rapid increase of the Ndebele population.[40] As someone who used to be involved in organising social activities to unify the community, he recalled moments when consensus on certain issues would be difficult to obtain. Football emerged as one of those platforms on which the diaspora Zimbabwe community would compete for ethnic supremacy and recognition. Disagreements would arise on trivial issues such as assembling football teams for sporting activities, thus resulting in the establishment of teams with an ethnic identity.

Organisations such as Mthwakazi had been capitalising on Ndebele ethnic particularism and the bitterness of Gukurahundi by actively encouraging disengagement from the Shona through political activism with a separatist agenda. Muzondidya and Gatsheni-Ndlovu described Mthwakazi as a 'divisive Ndebele separatist political organisation with an aim of creating "an autonomous Ndebele state called United Mthwakazi Republic" in Matabeleland'.[41] These pressure groups would use internet web forums such as the 1893 Mthwakazi Restoration Movement and uMthwakazi Review to spread their separatist propaganda.[42] According to Ndebele political activist Jabulani, the Mthwakazi organisation had a 'very active Leicester branch' in the 2000s which once invited him to take an active role in organising the commemoration of 'Mzilikazi Day' in Leicester. He declined the invitation on the pretext that celebrating the founder of the Ndebele community would not only consolidate ethnic particularism, but would also promote ethnic animosity without healing the wounds of Gukurahundi.

The impact of homeland-developed ethnic prejudices in determining community relations in cities such as Leicester was not reciprocated in urban areas where there was no significant ethnic transformation to challenge the dominance of the Shona. Using the example of Stevenage, Mathew explained that, during the time he lived in the town between 2004 and 2009, the Shona-dominated community had managed to construct a cohesive and united Zimbabwean black community. He explained how organised community social activities such as sporting events and the establishment of networks to support community members in bereavement were invaluable in uniting the Stevenage Zimbabwean community. As a result, there were no detrimental ethnic conflicts. The minority Ndebele who could also speak fluent Shona were willing participants in Shona-organised events as there was no opportunity or need to promote ethnic differences. Mathew's assertion served to confirm how Shona dominance in urban areas such as Stevenage created pseudo-community relations that offered a false sense of cordial ethnic relations. The Ndebele would have reluctantly accepted the fact that, if they wanted to exclude themselves from the Shona, they would find it difficult to access community support networks dominated by the Shona.

Ethnic identities within the diaspora Christian community in Britain

For a majority of individuals within the Ndebele community in Britain, constructing a united and visible community was seen as the most effective way of dealing with historical memories that the Shona will always use their dominance (as had been the case in Zimbabwe) to impose their will on them. To emphasise this point, Panganayi, a Shona who resides in Reading, gave an example of an incident that occurred at one of the Zimbabwean Days of Fellowship organised by his church.[43] The Days of Fellowship, held at least four times a year, aimed to socialise and fundraise for Zimbabwean projects while holding church services in the way they were conducted back home, especially by singing songs in vernacular languages.

It was the need to recreate a Zimbabwean feel to the services that triggered tensions between the Shona and the Ndebele congregants at one of these meetings in 2005. Panganayi described how the Ndebele took advantage of their increasing numbers to verbally express their displeasure when Shona songs were dominating services. To avoid future disruption of the proceedings, Panganayi pointed out that the organisers of subsequent Days of Fellowship had to ensure that both communities were equally or proportionally represented in all church services, with English being used as the medium of communication when addressing the congregation. Despite the positive response to Ndebele protests, Panganayi was convinced that such protests and subsequent changes would not have occurred in the early 2000s when the Ndebele were significantly in the minority.

The incident in Panganayi's church revealed that the Black Zimbabwean Christian community in Britain was not immune to ethnic identities or tensions that had the potential of hindering Shona–Ndebele cordial relations. Ethnic identities in the churches frequented by Zimbabweans became apparent when the Black Zimbabwean immigrant population started to undergo rapid ethnic transformation with the notable arrival of the Ndebele at the turn of the new millennium. As the ethnic diversity of the Zimbabwean immigrant population increased, there was a spontaneous growth of diaspora congregations whose ethnic demographics were an extension of the churches in Zimbabwe.[44] Just like in Zimbabwe, the diaspora Zimbabwean Home Grown Pentecostal Churches founded by Shona clergy continued to be dominated by members of the Shona community. Examples of these Shona-dominated Home Grown Churches included Family of God, Forward in Faith Mission International, African Apostolic Faith, Apostolic Faith Mission, Johane Masowe Chishanu and Johane Marange.

The diaspora traditional churches' congregations were also not spared Zimbabwe's ethnic identities. While Home Grown Church congregants' ethnic identities reflected the ethnicity of the founding leaders, the traditional churches, such as the Salvation Army, Seventh-Day Adventist, Church of England, Roman Catholic and Methodist churches, could be traced back to the spread of Christianity during the early years of colonial rule. The Ndebele's initial resistance to Christianity, as argued by Zvobgo, could not be ignored when seeking to understand the diverse (diaspora) ethnic representation in the majority of traditional churches.[45]

For example, due to Ndebele resistance to Christianity in the nineteenth century, preceding the Ndebele uprising of 1893, Zvobgo identifies the Seventh-Day Adventist (SDA) church as one of the few churches involved in pioneer missionary activities in Matabeleland. The church consolidated its presence in the region by opening Solusi Mission School in 1894.[46] Although the Ndebele rebellion of 1894 and a severe famine disrupted the evangelistic work, the SDA missionaries were able to organise a church in 1902 – evidence of the church's progress in its evangelistic work. By 1933, an SDA school had been established at Solusi Mission, which over the years expanded into one of the largest church-run private educational institutions in Zimbabwe's Matabeleland region. It is this early presence of the SDA church in Matabeleland that explains why a significant number of the Ndebele, both in Zimbabwe and Britain, are members of the church.

In contrast, Roman Catholic, Wesleyan Methodists, American Methodist Episcopal, Anglicans, Dutch Reformed and Salvation Army churches have always been dominated by the Shona because of their presence in Mashonaland during the early years of colonial rule.[47] As a result, these churches have always had a strong Shona presence, a presence that extended to diaspora congregations. For example, the Roman Catholic church in Britain exhibited the historical dominance of the Shona community in its congregations by holding diaspora 'Mass services' in Shona but rarely in Ndebele.[48] The services were held across the country in urban centres where there was a strong Zimbabwean immigrant population, for example in London, Leicester, Birmingham and Slough. Zivanayi and John, who were both members of the Roman Catholic church, admitted that having Shona 'Mass services' catering for the dominant Shona congregants had naturally excluded or stifled Ndebele participation.

With this historically nurtured sense of collective identity embedded in the Christian community, relations within the Black Zimbabwean immigrant community would continue to be immersed in ethnic particularism. Churches, especially Home Grown ones, failed to be an effective platform for uniting the ethnically polarised Black Zimbabwean diaspora community.

Conclusion

It is undeniable that this chapter's examination of the emerging contemporary Black Zimbabwean immigrant population in Britain has unveiled a community riddled with historically driven ethnic particularism, mistrust and jealousy. By examining the construction of relations within the Black Zimbabwean immigrant population, it has established how the quest for a cohesive Black Zimbabwean immigrant community in Britain has been a fantasy that has been unable to conceal pre-emigration memories of unresolved conflicts. The historical processes that permeated the different phases of Zimbabwe's history formulated ideas of belonging whose outcome was the construction of ethnic attachments and allegiances based on memories of shared historical experiences.

Although the implementation of a 'divide and rule' agenda by the British during the colonial era and subsequent ethnic tensions within the nationalist movement's struggle for independence consolidated ethnic allegiances, it was the postcolonial civil conflict (Gukurahundi) of the 1980s that emerged as the most emotive and potent factor in influencing relations within the African community. The memories of government security forces' brutality in suppressing the conflict within the Ndebele community were not restricted to Zimbabwe but were to extend into Britain.

Contemporary post-independence Zimbabwean black immigrants arrived with identities, prejudices and memories that were devoid of any nation building. As the chapter has demonstrated, the construction of Zimbabwean black diaspora communities in Britain, in which people have migrated without experiencing coherent and inclusive political initiatives, can be understood not only as a contemporary outcome of colonialism, but also as a consequence of tragic failures by post-colonial governments to construct a radical nation-building agenda. With a history of unresolved conflicts within the Black Zimbabwean community in Britain, there is a need to set up a 'truth and recon-ciliation' diaspora initiative to deal with imported ethnic tensions that are inextricably linked with the precolonial arrival of the Ndebele, the nationalist movement and the civil conflict (Gukurahundi).

Notes

1   Statistics cited in Saliwe Kawewe, 'Social Welfare of Indigenous Peoples in Zimbabwe' in John Dixon and Robert Scheurell (eds), *Social Welfare with Indigenous Peoples* (London: Routledge, 1995), p. 280.

2   'Immigration Patterns of Non-UK Born Populations in England and Wales in 2011', ONS, 17 December 2013, http://www.ons.gov.uk/ons/dcp171776_346219.pdf, accessed 29 April 2015.

3   See, for example, Josiah Brownell, 'The Hole in Rhodesia's Bucket: White Emigration and the End of Settler Rule', *Journal of Southern African Studies* 34 (2008), pp. 591–610; Julie Kate Seirlis, 'Undoing the United Front? Coloured Soldiers in Rhodesia, 1939–1980', *African Studies* 63 (2004), pp. 73–93.

4   'How Britain Aids Africans from Rhodesia', *The Times*, 5 October 1974, p. 7; 'Rhodesian Student Influx Is a Challenge to Government', *The Times*, 26 September 1975, p. 4.

5   Robin Cohen, *Frontiers of Identity 1994: The British and the Others* (London: Longman, 1994), p. 17.

6 See, for instance, Alice Bloch, 'Emigration from Zimbabwe: Migrant Perspectives', *Social Policy and Administration* 40 (2006), pp. 67–87; Daniel Tevera and Jonathan Crush, *The New Brain Drain from Zimbabwe* (Cape Town: Idasa, 2003); Josephine Lucy Fisher, *Pioneers, Settlers, Aliens and Exiles: The Decolonisation of White Identity in Zimbabwe* (Canberra: ANU Press, 2010).

7 Statistics sourced 'Immigration Patterns of Non-UK Born Populations in England and Wales in 2011', ONS, 17 December 2013, http://www.ons.gov.uk/ons/rel/census/2011-census-analysis/immigration-patterns-and-characteristics-of-non-uk-born-population-groups-in-england-and-wales/story-on-immigration-patterns-of-non-uk-born-populations-in-england-and-wales-in-2011.html?format=print, accessed 29 April 2015; 'Zimbabwean Mapping Exercise', International Organization for Migration, December 2006, http://unitedkingdom.iom.int/sites/default/files/doc/mapping/IOM_ZIMBABWE_MR.pdf, accessed 29 April 2015.

8 Dominic Pasura, *African Transnational Diasporas: Fractured Communities and Plural Identities of Zimbabweans in Britain* (Basingstoke: Palgrave Macmillan, 2014), p. 43.

9 Statistics from the *Leicester Mercury*, 5 July 2013.

10 See, for example, Patricia Hynes and Rosemary Sales, 'New Communities: Asylum Seekers and Dispersal' in Alice Bloch and John Solomos (eds), *Race and Ethnicity in the 21st Century* (Basingstoke: Palgrave, 2010), p. 39.

11 Alice Bloch, 'Zimbabweans in Britain: Transnational Activities and Capabilities', *Journal of Ethnic and Migration Studies* 34 (2008), pp. 287–305.

12 http://www.ons.gov.uk/ons/guide-method/census/2011/the-2011-census/collecting-the-information/the-national-campaign/written-translation-support-in-the-2011-census.pdf, accessed 2 August 2015.

13 Jonathan Crush and Daniel Tevera, *Zimbabwe's Exodus: Crisis, Migration, Survival* (Pretoria: Institute for Democracy in South Africa, 2010), p. 69.

14 JoAnn McGregor, 'Professional Relocating: Zimbabwean Nurses and Family in Britain', 2006, https://www.reading.ac.uk/web/FILES/geog/GP178.pdf, accessed 4 November 2012.

15 McGregor, 'Professional Relocating'.

16 Interview with Sharai, Leicester, 14 March 2013.

17 Interview with Memory, Leicester, November 2013.

18 Quotation from Sabelo Ndlovu-Gatsheni, 'Dynamics of the Zimbabwean Crisis in the 21st Century', *African Journal on Conflict Resolution* 3 (2003), pp. 99–134.

19 Statistics from Masipula Sithole and John Makumbe, 'Elections in Zimbabwe: The ZANU PF Hegemony and its Incipient Decline', *African Journal of Political Science* 2 (1997), pp. 122–39.

20 Jeffrey Herbst, *State Politics in Zimbabwe* (Harare: University of Zimbabwe Publications, 1990), p. 3.

21 Ndlovu-Gatsheni 'The Post-Colonial State and Matabeleland: Regional Perceptions of Civil–Military Relations, 1980–2002' in Rocky Williams, Gavin Cawthra and Diane Abrahams (eds), *Ourselves to Know: Civil–Military Relations and Defence Transformation in Southern Africa* (Pretoria: Institute of Security Studies, 2003) p. 22.

22 Jocelyn Alexander, JoAnn McGregor and Terence Ranger, *Violence and Memory: One Hundred Years in the Dark Forests of Matabeleland* (Oxford: James Currey, 2000), p. 192.

23 Herbst, *State Politics in Zimbabwe*, p. 169.

24 See, for example, Ndlovu-Gatsheni 'The Post-Colonial State and Matabeleland', p. 25; Ian Phimister, 'The Making and Meanings of the Massacres in Matabeleland', *Development Dialogue* 50 (2008), pp. 197–214.

25 Phimister, 'The Making and Meanings of the Massacres', pp. 197–214.

26 Ndlovu-Gatsheni, 'The Post-Colonial State and Matabeleland', p. 25.

27 Interview with Mabuza, Leicester, 9 June 2013.

28 Interview with Zanele, Leicester, March 2013.

29 Interview with Natalie, High Wycombe, October 2014.

30 Interview with Ralph, Leicester, 13 May 2013.

31 Interview with David, Leicester, January 2013.

32 Interview with David, Leicester, January 2013.

33 Africa Watch, 'Recent Data, Statistics and Indicators: Zimbabwe 2000 Parliamentary Election Results', *African Security Review* 14 (2005), pp. 59–63.

34 Alice Bloch, 'Emigration from Zimbabwe: Migrant Perspectives', *Social Policy and Administration* 40 (2006), pp. 67–87.

35 Patricia Hynes and Rosemary Sales, 'New Communities: Asylum Seekers and Dispersal' in Bloch and Solomos, *Race and Ethnicity in the 21st Century*, p. 39.

36 Information Centre about Asylum and Refugees (ICAR), 'Current Situation',

http://www.icar.org.uk/9971/leicester/current-situation.html, accessed 4 March 2012. ICAR is a Runnymede Trust-based academic research and information organisation.

37 ICAR, 'Current Situation'.

38 Interviews with Mathew, Stevenage and Leicester, February 2013.

39 Interview with Jacob, Derby, January 2013.

40 Interview with Happison, Derby, January 2013.

41 J Muzondidya and S Ndlovu-Gatsheni, '"Echoing Silences": Ethnicity in Post-colonial Zimbabwe, 1980–2007', *African Journal on Conflict Resolution* 7/2 (2007), pp. 275–97.

42 http://1893mrm.org/Mthwakazi-Restoration; http://www.umthwakazireview.com/index-id-inkundla.html.

43 Interview with Panganayi, Reading, March 2013.

44 Dominic Pasura, 'Religious Transnationalism: The Case of Zimbabwean Catholics in Britain', *Journal of Religion in Africa* 42 (2012), pp. 26–53.

45 Chengetai J. M. Zvobgo, *A History of Christian Missions in Zimbabwe 1890–1939* (Gweru: Mambo Press, 1996), p. 67.

46 Sylvia J. Clarke, 'Solusi: From Secondary School to College', *Adventist Heritage* 15/1 (1992), pp. 4–14; Zvobgo, *A History of Christian Missions*, pp. 1–81.

47 Zvobgo, *A History of Christian Missions*, pp. 1–81.

48 Interview with John, Slough, March 2013.

SELECTED BIBLIOGRAPHY

Adi, Hakim, *West Africans in Britain, 1900–1960*. London: Lawrence and Wishart, 1998.

Adi, Hakim and Marika Sherwood, *Pan-African History: Political Figures from Africa and the Diaspora since 1787*. New York: Routledge, 2003.

Andrews, Kehinde, *Resisting Racism: Race, Inequality and the Black Supplementary School Movement*. London: Institute of Education Press, 2013.

Anim-Addo, Joan, *Longest Journey: A History of Black Lewisham*. London: Deptford Forum, 1995.

Asante, Molefi and K. Ama Mazama (eds), *The Encyclopedia of Black Studies*. London: SAGE Publications, 2005.

Bartels, Emily Carroll, 'Too Many Blackamoors: Deportation, Discrimination and Elizabeth I', *Studies in English Literature* 46/2 (Spring 2006), pp. 305–22.

Barthelemy, Anthony Gerard, *Black Face, Maligned Race: The Representation of Blacks in English Drama from Shakespeare to Southerne*. London: Louisiana State University Press, 1987.

Beckles, Hilary, *The First Black Slave Society: Britain's 'Barbarity Time' in Barbados, 1636–1876*. Mona: University of the West Indies Press, 2016.

Bindman, David, Henry Louis Gates and Frank M. Snowden (eds), *The Image of the Black in Western Art*, Volumes I–V. New York: Harvard University Press, 2014.

Bloch, Alice, 'Zimbabweans in Britain: Transnational Activities and Capabilities', *Journal of Ethnic and Migration Studies* 34 (2008), pp. 287–305.

Bourne, Stephen, *Black Poppies: Britain's Black Community and the Great War*. Stroud: History Press, 2014.

Boyce Davies, Carole, *Left of Karl Marx*. Durham NC: Duke University Press, 2008.

Braude, Benjamin, 'The Sons of Noah and the Construction of Ethnic and Geographical Identities in the Medieval and Early Modern Periods', *William and Mary Quarterly* 54/1 (January 1997), pp. 103–42.

Bryan, Beverley, Stella Dadzie and Suzanne Scafe, *The Heart of the Race: Black Women's Lives in Britain*. London: Virago Press, 1985.

Bunce, Robin and Paul Field, *Darcus Howe: A Political Biography*. London: Bloomsbury, 2013.

Bundock, Michael, *The Fortunes of Francis Barber: The True Story of the Jamaican Slave Who Became Samuel Johnson's Heir*. New Haven: Yale University Press, 2015.

Burnard, Trevor, '"A Matron in Rank, A Prostitute in Manners": The Manning Divorce of 1741 and Class, Gender, Race and the Law in Eighteenth-century Jamaica' in Verene Shepherd (ed.), *Working Slavery, Pricing Freedom: Perspectives from the Caribbean, Africa and the African Diaspora*. Oxford: Oxford University Press, 2002.

Chater, Kathleen, *Untold Histories: Black People in England and Wales During the Period of the British Slave Trade, c. 1660–1807*. Manchester: Manchester University Press, 2011.

Coard, Bernard, *How the West Indian Child is Made Educationally Sub-normal in the British School System*. London: New Beacon Books, 1971.

Costello, Ray, *Black Salt: Seafarers of African Descent on British Ships*. Liverpool: Liverpool University Press, 2012.

Costello, Ray, *Black Tommies: British Soldiers of African Descent in the First World War*. Liverpool: Liverpool University Press, 2015.

Cugoano, Quobna Ottobah, *Thoughts and Sentiments on the Evil and Wicked Traffic of Slavery and the Commerce of the Human Species*. London: Penguin, 2007.

Dabydeen, David, John Gilmore and Cecily Jones (eds), *The Oxford Companion to Black British History*. Oxford: Oxford University Press, 2007.

Dresser, Madge, *Slavery Obscured: The Social History of the Slave Trade in an English Provincial Port*. Bristol: Redcliff Press, 2007.

Edwards, Brent Hayes, *The Practice of Diaspora: Literature, Translation, and the Rise of Black Internationalism*. Cambridge MA: Harvard University Press, 2003.

Edwards, Paul and James Walvin, 'Africans in Britain, 1500–1800' in M. Kilson and R. Rotberg (eds), *The African Diaspora: Interpretive Essays*. Cambridge MA: Harvard University Press, 1976.

Egbuna, Obi, *Destroy This Temple: The Voice of Black Power in Britain*. London: MacGibbon & Kee, 1971.

File, Nigel and Chris Power, *Black Settlers in Britain 1555–1958*. London: Heinemann Educational Books, 1981.

Fryer, Peter, *Staying Power: The History of Black People in Britain*. London: Pluto Press, 1989.

Gerzina, Gretchin, *Black London: Life Before Emancipation*. New Brunswick: Rutgers University Press, 1995.

Gilroy, Paul, *There Ain't No Black in the Union Jack: The Cultural Politics of Race and Nation*. London: Routledge, 2002.

Glass, Ruth, *Newcomers: The West Indians in London*. London: Centre for Urban Studies, 1960.

Green, Jeffrey, *Black Edwardians: Black People in Britain, 1901–1914*. London: Routledge, 1998.

Gribble, John and Graham Scott, *We Die Like Brothers: The Sinking of the SS Mendi*. Swindon: Historic England, 2017.

Grundlingh, Albert, 'Mutating Memories and the Making of a Myth: Remembering the SS *Mendi* Disaster, 1917–2007', *South African Historical Journal* 63/1 (2011), pp. 20–37.

Guasco, Michael, "Free from the Tyrannous Spanyard?' Englishmen and Africans in Spain's Atlantic World', *Slavery and Abolition: A Journal of Comparative Studies* 29/1 (2008), pp. 1–22.

Habib, Imtiaz, *Black Lives in the English Archives, 1500–1677: Imprints of the Invisible*. London: Ashgate, 2008.

Hall, Catherine, *Civilising Subjects: Metropole and Colony in the English Imagination, 1830–1867*. London: Polity, 2002.

Hall, Kim, *Things of Darkness: Economies of Race and Gender in Early Modern England*. New York: Cornell University Press, 1996.

Hayes, Katherine Howlett, *Slavery Before Race: Europeans, Africans, and*

Indians at Long Island's Sylvester Manor Plantation, 1651–1884. New York: NYU Press, 2014.

Hiro, Dilip, *Black British, White British: A History of Race Relations in Britain.* London: Paladin, 1992.

Hodges, Graham Russell and Alan Edward Brown (eds), *'Pretends to Be Free': Runaway Slave Advertisements from Colonial and Revolutionary New York and New Jersey.* New York: Garland, 1994.

Hogsbjerg, Christian, *Mariner, Renegade and Castaway: Chris Braithwaite.* London: Redwords, 2013.

Howe, Glenford, *Race, War, and Nationalism: A Social History of West Indians in the First World War.* Jamaica: Ian Randle Publishers, 2002.

James, Leslie, *George Padmore and Decolonization from Below: Pan-Africanism, the Cold War, and the End of Empire.* London: Macmillan, 2014.

Jarrett-Macauley, Delia, *The Life of Una Marson 1905–1965.* Manchester: Manchester University Press, 1998.

Jenkinson, Jacqueline, *Black 1919: Riots, Racism and Resistance in Imperial Britain.* Liverpool: Liverpool University Press, 2009.

Jenkinson, Jacqueline, '"All in the Same Uniform?" The Participation of Black Colonial Residents in the British Armed Forces in the First World War', *Journal of Imperial and Commonwealth History* 40/2 (June 2012), pp. 207–30.

Johnson, David A. and Nicole F. Gilbertson, 'Commemorations of Imperial Sacrifice at Home and Abroad: British Memorials of the Great War', *History Teacher* 43/4 (August 2010), pp. 563–84.

Joshua, Harris et al., *To Ride the Storm: The 1980 Bristol Riot and the State.* London: Heinemann, 1983.

Kaufman, Miranda, *The Black Tudors.* London: Oneworld, 2017.

Killingray, David, 'The Idea of a British Imperial African Army', *Journal of African History* 20/3 (1979), pp. 421–36.

Killingray, David, 'All the King's Men? Blacks in the British Army in the First World War, 1914–1918' in Rainer Lotz and Ian Pegg (eds), *Under the Imperial Carpet: Essays in Black History 1780–1950.* Crawley: Rabbit Press, 1986.

Killingray, David, 'Race and Rank in the British Army in the Twentieth Century', *Ethnic and Racial Studies* 10/3 (1987), pp. 276–90.

Koller, Christian, 'The Recruitment of Colonial Troops in Africa and Asia and their Deployment in Europe during the First World War', *Immigrants and Minorities* 26/1–2 (March–July 2008), pp. 111–33.

Kwesi Johnson, Linton, *Selected Poems.* London: Penguin Books, 2006.

La Rose, John, Linton Kwesi Johnson and Gus John, *The New Cross Massacre Story: Interviews with John La Rose.* London: New Beacon Books, 2011.

Lewis, Arthur, *Labour in the West Indies: The Birth of a Workers' Movement.* London: Victor Gollancz, 1939.

Lowe, Kate and Thomas Earle (eds), *Black Africans in Renaissance Europe.* Cambridge: Cambridge University Press, 2005.

MacKeith, Lucy, *Local Black History: A Beginning in Devon.* London: Archives and Museum of Black Heritage, 2003.

Maguire, Anna, 'Colonial Encounters', *History Today* 65/12 (December 2015).

Matera, Marc, *Black London: The Imperial Metropolis and Decolonization in the Twentieth Century.* Berkeley: University of California Press, 2015.

Myers, Norma, *Reconstructing the Black Past: Blacks in Britain, 1780–1830.* London: Frank Cass, 1996.

Northrup, David, *Africa's Discovery of Europe: 1450–1850*. Oxford: Oxford University Press, 2002.

Olusoga, David, *Black and British*. London: Macmillan, 2016.

Onyeka, 'The Missing Tudors: Black People in Sixteenth-century England', *BBC History Magazine* 13/7 (July 2012), pp. 32–3.

Onyeka, 'What's in a Name?', *History Today* 62/10 (October 2012), pp. 34–9.

Onyeka, *Blackamoores: Africans in Tudor England – Their Presence, Status and Origins*. London: Narrative Eye, 2013.

Onyeka, 'Artisans, Servants, Musicians and Kings: Africans in Tudor England' in Kate Bystrova (ed.), *The Commonwealth Year Book 2010*. Cambridge: Nexus Strategic Partnerships, Commonwealth Secretariat, Commonwealth of Nations, 2015.

Pasura, Dominic, *African Transnational Diasporas: Fractured Communities and Plural Identities of Zimbabweans in Britain*. Basingstoke: Palgrave Macmillan, 2014.

Perry, Kennetta Hammond, *London Is the Place for Me*. New York: Oxford University Press, 2016.

Phillips, Mike and Trevor Phillips, *Windrush: The Irresistible Rise of Multi-racial Britain*. London: HarperCollins, 1999.

Pilkington, Edward, *Beyond the Mother Country: West Indians and the Notting Hill White Riots*. London: I. B. Tauris, 1988.

Polsgrove, Carol, *Ending British Rule in Africa: Writers in a Common Cause*. Manchester: Manchester University Press, 2009.

Ramdin, Ron, *The Making of the Black Working Class in Britain*. London: Gower, 1987.

Romain, Gemma, *Race, Sexuality and Identity in Britain and Jamaica: The Biography of Patrick Nelson 1916–1963*. London: Bloomsbury, 2016.

Schaffer, Gavin (ed.), *Racializing the Soldier*. London: Routledge, 2013.

Scobie, Edward, *Black Britannia: A History of Blacks in Britain*. Chicago: Johnson Publishing Company, 1972.

Searle, Kevin, '"Mixing of the Unmixables": The 1949 Causeway Green "Riots" in Birmingham', *Race and Class* 54/3 (2013), pp. 44–64.

Sherwood, Marika, *Claudia Jones*. London: Lawrence and Wishart, 2000.

Sherwood, Marika, 'Blacks in Elizabethan England', *History Today* 53/10 (2003), pp. 40–2.

Sherwood, Marika, 'Pan-African Conferences, 1900–1953: What Did "Pan-Africanism" Mean?', *Journal of Pan African Studies* 4/10 (January 2012), pp. 106–26.

Shyllon, Folarin, *Black Slaves in Britain*. Oxford: Oxford University Press, 1974.

Shyllon, Folarin, *Black People in Britain, 1555–1833*. Oxford: Oxford University Press, 1977.

Sivanandan, Ambalavaner, *A Different Hunger: Writings on Black Resistance*. London: Pluto, 1982.

Smith, Richard, *Jamaican Volunteers in the First World War: Race, Masculinity, and the Development of National Consciousness*. Manchester: Manchester University Press, 2004.

Strachan, Hew, *The First World War in Africa*. Oxford: Oxford University Press, 2004.

Taylor, Simon, *A Land of Dreams: A Study of Jewish and Afro-Caribbean Migrant Communities in England*. London: Routledge, 1993.

Trew, Winston, *Black for a Cause … Not Just Because: The Case of the 'Oval 4' and the Story of Black Power in*

1970s Britain. Peterborough NH: TaoFish, 2012.

Ungerer, Gustav, *The Mediterranean Apprenticeship of British Slavery*. Madrid: Verbum Editorial, 2008.

Williams, Elizabeth M., *The Politics of Race in Britain and South Africa: Black British Solidarity and the Anti-apartheid Struggle*. London: I. B. Tauris, 2015.

Wilson, Kathleen, *A New Imperial History: Culture, Identity and Modernity in Britain and the Empire, 1660–1840*. Cambridge: Cambridge University Press, 2004.

Winegard, Timothy C., *Indigenous Peoples of the British Dominions and the First World War*. Cambridge: Cambridge University Press, 2012.

Wright, William, *Black History and Black Identity: A Call for a New Historiography*. Westport: Greenwood Publishing Group, 2002.

INDEX

ZED

Zed is a platform for marginalised voices across the globe.

It is the world's largest publishing collective and a world leading example of alternative, non-hierarchical business practice.

It has no CEO, no MD and no bosses and is owned and managed by its workers who are all on equal pay.

It makes its content available in as many languages as possible.

It publishes content critical of oppressive power structures and regimes.

It publishes content that changes its readers' thinking.

It publishes content that other publishers won't and that the establishment finds threatening.

It has been subject to repeated acts of censorship by states and corporations.

It fights all forms of censorship.

It is financially and ideologically independent of any party, corporation, state or individual.

Its books are shared all over the world.

www.zedbooks.net
@ZedBooks